DECEMBER 25, 1990

MERRY CHRISTMAS, RYAN —
WITH LOVE,
Uncle Paul and Auntie

Indians of North America

INDIANS
of NORTH AMERICA

Geoffrey Turner

BLANDFORD PRESS
Poole **Dorset**

First published in the U.K. 1979 by Blandford Press,
Link House, West Street
Poole, Dorset BH15 1LL

Copyright © 1979 Blandford Press Ltd.
Reprinted 1982
Reprinted 1985

British Library Cataloguing in Publication Data
Turner, Geoffrey E S
    Indians of North America – (Blandford colour series)
    1. Indians of North America   2. Eskimos
    I. Title
    970'.004'97   E77

ISBN 0 7137 0843 3 (Hardback)

ISBN 0 7137 1122 1 (Paperback)

Printed in Hong Kong by South China Printing Co.

Contents

Acknowledgements		vi
Preface		vii
1	The Indian Discovers America	1
2	Southeastern Woodlands: Mounds and Monarchs	14
3	Northeastern Woodlands: Wampum and Wild Rice	31
4	The Magnet of the Buffalo Plains	46
5	Southwest I: The Enduring Pueblos	73
6	Southwest II: Villagers and Raiders	98
7	Great Basin: The Living Past	182
8	California: The Brittle Eden	187
9	The Impressionable Plateau	197
10	Northwest Coast: American Gothic	203
11	The Wide Subarctic	218
12	The Resourceful Eskimo	227
13	The Indian Discovers Himself	239
Further Reading		245
Tribal Index		248
General Index		255

Acknowledgements

Illustrations

The colour artwork was specially painted for this book by Pierre Turner, who also prepared most of the line illustrations within the text. Additional line illustrations were drawn by David Dowland.

The author and publisher also gratefully acknowledge the sources of illustrations listed below.

Colour Photographs

Pitt Rivers Museum, University of Oxford: Plates 20, 22, 32, 41, 45, 48, 54, 62, 67
Western American Picture Library: Plates 8, 28, 29, 36, 43, 60
WAPL/Buffalo Bill Historical Centre, Cody, Wyoming: Plate 33
Hon. Jon Petre/Hudson's Bay Company: Plate 21
Royal Ontario Museum: Plates 37, 58
British Museum: Plates 12, 13, 14, 17
Yale University Beinecke Rare Book Library: Plate 34
Tradescant Collection, Ashmolean Museum, Oxford: 15
Dr. Joel Wilbush: Plate 65
National Film Board of Canada (Canada House, London): Plates 68, 69
Picturepoint: Plate 70
Bruce Coleman Ltd/Nicholas Devore: Plate 71
New York Public Library: Plate 30

Black and White Photographs

Anthropological Museum, University of Aberdeen: page 232
Keystone Press Agency Ltd: page 242
Pitt Rivers Museum, University of Oxford: page 37, 43, 215
Western American Picture Library; pages 29, 30, 47, 49, 50, 62, 67, 68, 70, 80, 85, 172, 201, 207, 208, 210, 212
Lowie Museum of Anthropology, University of California: page 188
Smithsonian Institution National Anthropological Archive: page 45, 56, 65, 71, 94, 95, 185, 216
Los Angeles County Museum of Natural History: page 54
Denver Museum of Natural History: page 2
National Film Board of Canada (Canada House, London): page 219
Lars Rengfelt: pages 241, 243
Geoffrey Turner: pages 86, 99, 165, 175, 179, 180

Preface

Trying to press all of aboriginal North America into one small volume is like trying to pour Lake Superior into a duck pond; a great deal has to be evaporated off in the process. Since this is, after all, a picture book, I have paid most attention to the visible and tangible aspects of Indian and Eskimo life, such as clothing and dwellings, food-getting and fighting, dancing and making useful things decorative, and not delved deeply into the intricacies of social structure or the immensely rich and repetitive folklore. Readers interested in pursuing those topics will find extended bibliographies in the more technical of the works listed as Further Reading (page 245).

It would not be feasible nor particularly useful to attempt a complete list of known Indian tribes and subtribes, but the names of all those referred to in the text, illustrations or maps appear in the Tribal Index (page 248), together with a selection of tribes not otherwise mentioned. Each entry in the Tribal Index includes a coded indication of the culture area and major language group to which the tribe belonged, and (except for those in Mexico) its estimated population before disturbance by Europeans. As the list is incomplete, the figures do not add up to the total for pre-Columbian North America. In quoting estimates I have followed those authorities who believe that the aggregate did not greatly exceed one million.

Many tribal names have one or more alternative spellings; I have tended to use the simplest. As an aid to pronunciation an acute accent has been added to the stressed syllable of some of the less familiar names on their first appearance, e.g. Cócopa, Tawákoni. Where French or Spanish forms are in use, the accents are integral parts of the name, e.g. Nez Percé, Cochimí.

No one classification of North American languages has yet been produced that is acceptable in detail to all linguistic specialists, although there is general agreement on most of the major groupings. The scheme followed in the Tribal Index seems to me to represent a fair compromise with current opinion, but some of the relationships must still be regarded as tentative.

The brief summary of present-day conditions given in the final chapter is intended to be as objective and impartial as possible, facts being allowed to speak for themselves. The assessment of what constitutes fact is my own.

Geoffrey Turner
Oxford, 1978

Chapter 1

The Indian Discovers
America

Long, long ago there was only water. No America, no Indians. The world
was empty, and boring. So, Old Man Coyote used mud which the diving
ducks had brought him to make Earth, and more mud to make men.
After a while, at the prompting of the ducks (who were really drakes), he
made women; and they were so successful that he made female ducks as
well.

That is what some Crow Indians say, although not all tribal story-
tellers would agree in detail. The white man, of course, has always
known better. In the 1830s Lord Kingsborough dissipated his whole
fortune in proving that the New World was populated by the Lost Tribes
of Israel, a view later sanctified by the Mormon Church. Other theorists
have traced the American Indian back to Egypt, Wales, Outer Space, the
lost continents of Atlantis and Mu, even to America itself. It is perhaps
ironic that the wholly untenable ideas of Atlantis and Mu hinge on one
feature which is fundamental to the true story of the peopling of
America: the existence of land now submerged. But the real lost
continent lies not beneath the Atlantic or the Pacific, but under the
Bering Strait and Chukchi Sea. Beringia, forming a land bridge a
thousand miles wide between Asia and America, is now accepted as the
route by which Man came to colonize the New World, from Alaska to
Tierra del Fuego. Monkeys were there before him, but no trace of early
hominids has been found anywhere in the Americas to throw doubt on
his status as an immigrant. And the physical characteristics of both the
Indian and the Eskimo point to Asia as the land from which they came.

In the matter of American origins, the question of *whence* is intimately
bound up with the question of *when*? For many years conservative
American scientists maintained not only that Man was an immigrant to
the New World but also that he was an extremely recent one. The
argument was that Alaska and Canada had been locked beneath the ice

1

sheet of the last glacial period until 8,000 years ago or less, and since no human fossils of higher antiquity had been found (or the few that had could be discounted), the Indian must have come in after the final recession of the ice. He could then, it was thought, have walked across the 52 miles of the frozen Bering Strait in winter or crossed it in some primitive watercraft in summer. Foremost among the defenders of this view was Aleš Hrdlička of the U.S. National Museum, whose august and polemical scepticism in the face of any discovery suggesting real antiquity had at least one good effect: it ensured that when apparently significant finds were made by the archaeological opposition the most rigorous scientific controls were applied.

Unlocking the Past

As time went on, Hrdlička himself became more flexible in his views, and in 1926 resistance to the idea of Pleistocene man in America was

Fluted dart point among the ribs of extinct bison, found near Folsom, New Mexico, in 1926. This discovery finally confirmed the co-existence of Man and Pleistocene animals in North America.

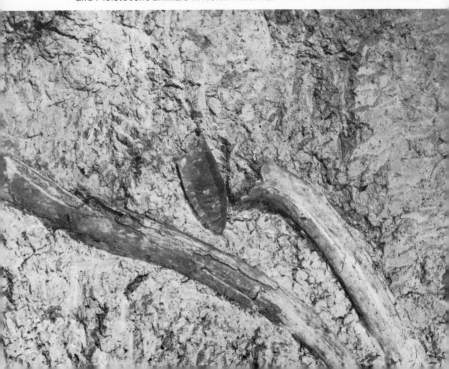

finally breached. Near the town of Folsom in New Mexico, a deposit of buffalo bones, reported years previously by an observant cowhand, was being excavated by the Colorado Museum of Natural History. The bones belonged to an extinct subspecies, now called *Bison antiquus figginsi*, and embedded among them were parts of a flint projectile point, skilfully worked. In the following season, more broken points were found, and then a whole one, in conditions which allowed no doubt that its user had been hunting the beast among whose ribs it lay. Moreover, most of the bison skeletons lacked tail bones, indicating that the hunters had carried away the skins with the tails intact. Leading archaeologists of the day professed themselves convinced, and the hunt was up for further evidence of ancient man. It was soon forthcoming.

The Folsom points were of a distinctive type not hitherto known: leaf-shaped, neatly chipped on both sides, and conspicuously fluted or 'hollow-ground' by the striking off of a long flake from each face. With attention focused on them, more began to be found, and some already in museums to be recognized. On the Lindenmeier horse ranch in northeast Colorado, digging revealed perfect Folsom points in association with extinct camel, deer and bison bones. Near Clovis, New Mexico, another type of fluted point, longer and narrower than the Folsom, was discovered at the site of a kill, and here the quarry had been mammoth.

As more sites were discovered it became clear that the Clovis points were older than the Folsom; at Lindenmeier both types occurred, with the Clovis at the lower level. The usual association of Clovis with mammoth remains, and Folsom with bison, was assumed to confirm this sequence but the actual age in thousands of years could only be estimated. On geological and palaeontological grounds a lapse of from 8,000 to 10,000 years was favoured, but some scientists, still reluctant to concede so early a date to the Indians, argued that the big Pleistocene animals – the megafauna – must have taken longer to become extinct in the New World than they did in the Old. We have as yet no method of testing a piece of worked flint and reading off its age in years (although there is some hope with obsidian).

In 1952, however, a dating technique of inestimable value was unveiled by the American nuclear chemist, Dr W. F. Libby. Called radiocarbon, or carbon 14, dating, the method depends on the fact that a radioactive isotope of carbon is absorbed by all *living* tissue until the moment of death, after which it is discharged at known rates. In physicists' terms it has a half-life of 5,570 years, and becomes inert after ten half-lives. Measurement in the laboratory of the rate of C-14 emanation makes it possible to calculate the time elapsed since the death of the object tested. Portions of bone, wood, charcoal from campfires etc. can be dated to something over 50,000 years, with varying margins of error that can be statistically determined. There are possibilities of undetermined error too, arising from contamination of the specimen between excavation and treatment, or the inadequate size of the sample, but the technique is now generally accepted as a reliable method of arriving at the absolute, as distinct from the relative, age of an object. As stated above, inert material like the flint of implements cannot itself be measured, but the associated organic remains can be. The only basis for argument is whether or not the association is really valid. On the whole, carbon 14 has tended to confirm rather than upset the provisional dates assigned to the early hunters and their successors.

On the evidence available today it seems safe to say that the big-game hunting era lasted for over 5,000 years, beginning about 13,000 B.P. and declining by about 7,000 B.P. (B.P. means Before Present, 'present' being reckoned as A.D. 1950.) At the upper end of the scale it was the way of life that faded out, not the human population itself. But what came before 13,000 B.P.? Here the record is less precise, but the possibilities are tantalizing. Many claims for high antiquity have been put forward which have not withstood critical examination, but there remain evidences that are difficult to refute. From southern Chile we have a C-14 date of around 20,000 B.P. for extinct sloth bones associated with crude stone tools; dates of 23,000 and 22,000 years ago have been accepted for two sites in Mexico; while in the far north, at Old Crow Flats on the Yukon River, a scraper made from a caribou bone has been reliably dated at 27,000 B.P. No doubt much more awaits discovery, not only in the Americas but also in northeast Asia where, logically, it should be possible to trace the types of equipment brought in by the first comers. Some analogies have been suspected between tools recovered from the earliest American sites and those from sites in the trans-Baikal region of Siberia, but much more material is needed for study before firm conclusions can be reached.

At least we are sure that Man was present in America nearly 30,000 years ago, and that by 13,000 B.P. he was actively and successfully preying on the splendid meat supply offered by the great Pleistocene grazing animals. And with that time span in mind, we may glance again at his point of entry.

The Bering Land Bridge

The mean depth of Bering Strait today is 120 feet. Withdraw 150 feet of water from the oceans, lock it up in glaciers and pack ice, and you expose a bridge between Asia and America 200 miles across. Withdraw more water until sea level drops to over 400 feet below present shorelines and the whole continental shelf is exposed. We know that happened repeatedly in the long succession of ice ages and that this allowed an early interchange of Old and New World animals and plants, with American horses and camels munching their way into Asia and passing Eurasiatic elephant, muskox, bison and deer species bound for America. Geophysicists are less unanimous than archaeologists could wish about the precise times of high and low water, but it does seem to be agreed that the continents were joined for a long period up to about 37,000 years ago, and again between 26,000 and 11,000 years ago, with possibly two late and brief interruptions. Man could have arrived dry-footed in either of those two periods. But how far could he have got? The ice which drained the seabed blocked the land of Canada from shore to shore, perhaps for 7,000 years, although Beringia and central Alaska remained ice-free. Some scientists have believed that the palaeo-Indians, as we may now call them, stayed in the north until the ice-fields parted to leave a long clear passage down the eastern flank of the Rocky Mountains. Evidence is now accumulating, however, that they could have had up to 5,000 years to move south into the middle of the continent before the ice-fields merged to bar the way. Certain it is that by the time the Wisconsin glaciation was in its final retreat, some 5,000 years ago, the main American Indian population had long been settled. Only the Aleuts and Eskimos, and possibly the Athapaskan Indians had yet to stake their claims.

The Big Game Hunters

For a clear picture of our palaeo-Indians, we must lean heavily on deduction. As hunters they were notably successful at killing without being killed; among all the piles of bones with which the hunters littered the land there are almost none of their own. Human skeletal remains from the period can be numbered on the fingers. All so far studied are of Recent or Modern Man, wryly classified as *Homo sapiens sapiens*, and could be duplicated from among the wide range of present-day Indian types. His skull tended to be long in relation to its breadth, his upper jaw to project slightly below the nasal region. His colour we guess as sallow to brown, with hair dark and straight. Since he had passed through what has been called the cold-filter of the Far North, he (or she) must have been competent in the making of warm clothing from animal skins. He

5

understood the use of fire. For shelter he may have utilized brushwood or skins, with caves and naturally overhanging rocks where available, although in one site at about the 8,000-year mark a circle of post-holes hints at the beginning of more substantial dwellings.

Stone, bone, antler and wood were the raw materials of his tool kit. In addition to the projectile points already mentioned, chipped flint and chert were used for knives, hide-scrapers, choppers and hammers, and gravers (burins) for woodworking. Bone too could be sharpened for points, and antler hammers were used in flint-knapping.

Weapons were the lance and javelin, the latter propelled by the spear-thrower, which the Aztecs and modern American anthropologists call an *atlatl* and the Australian aborigines a *woomera*. It consists of a short length of wood, sometimes weighted, with a finger grip at one end and a peg at the other against which the butt of the javelin rests as it is swung forward. Some few millenia would elapse before the arrival of bow and arrow.

To tackle up to ten tons of reluctant pachyderm with such armament called for courage and almost certainly some social organization. The fact that kill-sites are often found beside former swamps suggests that the quarry was deliberately driven into mire which hampered escape. An alternative theory is that the game was speared wherever opportunity allowed and then followed until exhausted by loss of blood; but in at least one case it is known that heavy stones were used in finishing it off. Cooperative effort is clearly indicated, but the basis on which bands were formed we do not know. Nor do we know whether the palaeo-Indian had any views on life after death, although there are some indications of occasional cremation. An aesthetic sense there certainly was. Nothing remotely resembling the cave paintings of Western Europe has ever been found in the Americas, but we find incised bone discs which must have been used for personal adornment. More significantly, it has been pointed out that the fluted Folsom blade itself shows a refinement of craftsmanship unnecessary to its function as a weapon. The pride of the swordsmith may have roots very far back in time.

The three mammoths – Imperial, the slightly smaller Columbian, and more rarely the Woolly – and the mastodon were not the only prey of the Big Game Hunters. Outsize bison, of various races now extinct, were taken, and so on occasion were camels, horses, tapirs, antelopes and ground sloths. Of the last mentioned there were several species, ranging in size from the seven-foot *Nothrotherium* to the lordly *Megatherium* at nearly twenty feet; encounters with these may not have been eagerly sought. Rival hunters on the game market were the fearsome sabre-toothed cats *Smilodon*, and the sinisterly named dire-wolf.

For five or six thousand years, then, or three times the length of the Christian era so far, American life continued with no great changes. The Clovis people, whom we must now call Llano, lived on mammoths, while presumably taking smaller game as well since mammoth skin makes a very intractable breech-cloth. The Folsom people, coming a little later but still overlapping with Llano, preferred bison, at first the tall, long-horned species now extinct. But while these were still surviving the modern form, *B. bison*, had made its appearance. The shift from mammoth to bison may have been caused by the retreat of the mammoth into Mexico. Following Folsom, again with overlapping, came the culture we call (confusingly) Plano, characterized by long and rather narrow spear points, beautifully worked but with no fluting. It is to Plano folk that the following episode refers.

Flintwork of the Big Game era, with approximate age in years: (*left to right*) Clovis fluted point, 13,000; Folsom point, 11,000; Eden point and Cody knife, 7,000. Pride of workmanship shines across the millennia in the symmetry and balance of these 'primitive' tools.

The Hunt at Kit Carson

One early summer's day in Colorado, near the spot where 10,000 years or so later the town of Kit Carson would stand, a party of about 150 people stampeded 200 bison southward into the wind and over the rim of a steep-sided arroyo or streambed. Those animals that tried to break away to east or west were turned back by the flanking spearmen. It cannot have been long before the bellowing, heaving mass of animals became still, the greater part crushed and suffocated, the upper layer dispatched by the hunters. Then the butchering began. Those carcases that could be were dragged clear, skinned and cut up in a surprisingly methodical sequence: first the forelegs and the 'blanket of flesh' underlying the hide, then the hump meat, the ribs, pelvic girdle and hind legs, and finally the neck and tongue. At the ribs stage, the workers refreshed themselves with snacks of raw liver and other prized offal. At the end of the operation, with thirteen animals left untouched in the bottom of the arroyo, something like 7,350 lb of meat and hides had been secured. How much was eaten on the spot and how much back-packed away, we cannot tell, although it seems likely that the tough neck meat was destined for drying and subsequent pounding into pemmican.

The site of this particular kill is known today as the Olsen-Chubbuck after its two discoverers. Lest it be thought that the amount of detail is unjustifiable at a distance of so many thousands of years, it may be explained that the game must have been approached – by hunters unmounted – against the wind; the time of year is indicated by the presence of young calves; spear points were found in some outlying skeletons; and the priorities observed in stripping the meat are shown by the order in which the piles of bones were left. The amount of meat is a straightforward calculation; but interpretation of the evidence is helped by the fact that this way of exploiting the bison was carried on virtually unchanged until just over a century ago, for Victorian travellers to describe and sketch.

The Pleistocene Extinctions

The Big Game hunters could never have numbered more than a very few thousand but they spread themselves just about everywhere the game was to be found, on both the American subcontinents. They were witnesses to the Pleistocene Extinctions in the New World, and there is some reason to think they were at least partly to blame for them. The exact reason for the disappearance of the Pleistocene megafauna, and of many smaller animals as well, is not yet known. It probably was a whole complex of factors, high among them being ecological changes connected with the slow drying out of the soggy post-glacial world. But to specialized animals finding it harder to support themselves in changing habitats, relentless and often wasteful hunting by man may well have given the final nudge into oblivion. A modern elephant spends nearly two years in the womb and up to twenty more before breeding, and then produces one calf at a time. That, when the species is under pressure, is a dangerously slow replacement rate. Mammoth and mastodon cannot have been faster at it.

The mammoth seems to have been the first to disappear from North America, 7–8,000 years ago. The mastodon, more of a woodland species, lingered in the eastern half of the country for another thousand years, and just possibly much later still. The tapirs retreated towards the tropics, the musk ox towards the Arctic. The superbison gave way to the smaller, curly-horned species we know today as the buffalo. The sabre-tooths, adapted to slashing the thick hides of the pachyderms, followed them into extinction. Man the predator, having adapted for adaptability, turned to other prey. The sloths may have bowed themselves out, the camels possibly so, but the horses were certainly helped on their way by the hunters. It is tempting to believe that if the early Indian had learned to appreciate 'horseflesh' as distinct from horse meat his descendants might have met the invaders from the Old World on more nearly equal terms. No other domesticable beast was left to liberate his potential in communication, transport, intensive agriculture and conquest. Great states based on advanced skills would in time arise in the Americas, but they would prove fatally vulnerable beside those of Eurasia.

The Indian World Takes Shape

The calendar of human development has no neat divisions of precise days or years. The palaeo-Indian Big Game era did not end on the day the last mammoth died, to be replaced on the following morning by the Archaic stage. One distinctive era is followed by another, but each has its slow beginnings far back in that which preceded it. It is not to be believed that the mammoth and bison hunters ignored all other sorts of food, but only when the bigger game gave out did the former dietary supplements become staples. What we call the Archaic then is the period in which the Indian learned to exploit other food resources to the full – sources which demanded new tools, new rhythms of life, a new stretching of ingenuity. If in some areas and periods it all came down to making the meagre best of a harsh environment, in others the way was opened to a vastly richer and more complex way of living.

Hunters become Gatherers

Plant foods were the key to the change, in the form of seeds and nuts, fruits and roots. Seeds need to be crushed or ground, to be mixed with liquids and cooked in leak-proof containers. And so it is that stone mortars and pestles, and the flat grinding-stone we call the metate, make their appearance in the technological inventory. Among the earliest containers were baskets, large for gathering the wild crop and smaller for cooking the mush. Bone awls and perforators found at ancient sites indicate basket-making. The problem of cooking in an inflammable basket is solved by the principle of our modern immersion heater: stones heated in a fire are dropped into the food and replaced as often as is necessary to bring the mixture to the boil. Fire-cracked stones survive to attest the high antiquity of the method. In the increasingly forested areas of eastern North America, new stone and antler tools are developed for the cutting and shaping of wood: axes, adzes, wedges and chisels. Hooks and spears of bone reflect the growing importance of fish, while on riverbank and seashore alike the discarded shells of molluscs begin to rise into middens of enormous size.

In the arid west there are fewer trees and no shellfish but here as elsewhere the tool kit becomes more specialized and the yearly round divided into seasonal activities dictated by the ripening of this or that wild crop. Human groups begin to live within chosen areas, moving to and from hunting-grounds and gathering-grounds as appropriate. Game is still important (and will remain so through history) but not paramount. Deer are hunted in the east, pronghorn antelope and mountain sheep in the west, buffalo from the Rocky Mountains eastwards almost to the Atlantic shore. But birds and many smaller creatures are laid under tribute too; in the desert lands small reptiles and insect larvae supplement jackrabbit and gopher. Between the Rockies and the Coast Ranges, in what is called the Great Basin, conditions will hardly alter for 10,000 years. Not so in other areas. The rate of change will differ from place to place but innumerable changes there will be, in the notching of a flint, the carving of a spear-thrower weight, the emphasis on this or that form of shelter or foodstuffs. They are far too many to record, and by no means all are yet fully understood. This book is in any case not, primarily at least, about archaeology. But the Indian's own unadulterated culture – way of life – is already in the past. Some of his most noteworthy cultural achievements had faded centuries before the New World was violated by the Old, but to ignore them would be like defining European man in terms of the Dark Ages with no reference to Greece and Rome. Enough has been said to show how deep are the Indian's roots in America, and something of the tradition on which he was to build.

'Recent' History Begins

So at this point we shall let slip several millennia, pausing only to note that the continent of Beringia has long sunk, leaving the 56-mile Bering Strait, and that a new population of whale and seal hunters, of uncertain relationship to the Big Game people, has been spreading all along the Arctic coasts from Alaska to Labrador and Greenland. These Eskimos we shall meet later in the book, as befits late comers. First we shall survey the descendants of the older settlers and see the products of thousands of years of differential growth, in population and intellectual achievement, and of endless division and subdivision. For native America is a land of very few constants. One cannot say that *the* Indians smoked the pipe of peace, traced descent from their mothers, used birchbark canoes, lived in hide tipis, and scalped their enemies. *Some* Indians did all these things, but others smoked cigarettes or chewed tobacco, belonged to the father's family, paddled around in coracles or on bundles of reeds, lived in stone apartment houses, or took whole heads for trophies. Nor can one speak of the Indian language; by the time of Columbus there were some 500 Indian languages north of Mexico, deriving from half a dozen parent stocks whose origins are still obscure.

'North of Mexico' is specified because this is a book about people living north of Mexico. But is that famous Border a natural boundary? In aboriginal times the line would have been utterly indistinguishable; one would have been more conscious of changes in language and life-style in travelling along it from east to west. From north to south across it one would have met only gradations of change. Far enough to the south, of course, and late enough in time, the gradation would have changed into a steep upward slope to the large city states, complex social and religious order, stone temples and towering pyramids, artistic magnificence and paranoid blood-lust which were the climax of Mexican civilization. It was not always so. Man, pushing on his way south to Tierra del Fuego, hunted mammoths in the Valley of Mexico much as he did further north. One got himself entombed under a laval flow at Tepexpán to flutter the archaeological dovecotes; the discovery of actual mammoth remains with dart points at nearby Santa Isabel Iztapán seems now to have made an honest fossil of him. Here too seed-gathering supplemented and in time supplanted game hunting as the major source of food. And it was here in Mexico that a major revolution began.

The Coming of Maize

Somewhere – more likely here and there – the women who gathered wild plant foods began putting part of the crop back into the soil, to grow and increase. The first of all American cultivated plants may have been one of the small pumpkin-like squashes. Beans came early too, and the amaranth (pigweed) with its generous yield of tiny seeds. At roughly the same time, perhaps seven or eight thousand years ago, another plant was starting on its complicated journey to domestication: *Zea mays* – maize or Indian corn. Appearing first as perhaps a natural hybrid, it went through a series of natural and later deliberate crossings and recrossings that increased its cob size and its adaptability to differing climates. In time it became the touchstone of American high cultures and foremost among the New World's gifts of domesticated plants to the Old World. Others in a long list include the potato (*Solanum*), tomato, tobacco, and chocolate. Not one of these was known outside the Americas before A.D. 1492, and the puzzling case of the sweet potato (*Ipomoea*), which was, does nothing to disprove the Indian's claim to have invented his own agriculture, independently of the rest of the world.

Old as is the idea of cultivation, some thousands of years were to elapse before it could dominate the subsistence patterns of Indian groups, but dominate it did in suitable localities. With the crop trinity of maize, beans and squash as a mainstay, the need to be constantly on the move after game and wild foods was gone. Permanent dwellings became practicable, and larger communities, which in turn required more elaborate social organization. There was also the question of ensuring that the mysterious forces which controlled the growth of crops by dispensing rain and warmth in the right proportions should be kept in a favourable humour by suitable observances and sacrifices. More and different tools and utensils were needed, and there was more time to decorate them in art styles which took on the stamp of their locality. By about 1750 B.C., an irreversible cultural breeze had begun to inflate the bubble of Mexican civilization in the southeastern homeland of the Olmecs. The bubble grew and grew, encompassing the Mayas, Toltecs, Zapotecs, Mixtecs, Huastecs, Aztecs, increasing in size and turgid brilliance until it burst on the point of a Spanish rapier. Stray gleams of its brilliance reached far to the north, into the Arizona deserts and the Mississippi forests. So let us now go back and seek them. We shall start in the Southeastern Woodlands.

Chapter 2

Southeastern Woodlands:
Mounds and Monarchs

We left North America in what the archaeologists call the Archaic Stage: the stage marked by a readiness – born of necessity – to experiment with new sources of food and equipment, to become more and more efficient in making use of what the environment had to offer. In the vast area of eastern North America which we call the Woodlands, it had a great deal to offer. There were deer to be trapped or killed with darts (later arrows), smaller game and birds to be snared, fish to be taken on hooks or in weirs, freshwater mussels and seashore clams to be gathered by the million. The vegetable world gave fruits, seeds, nuts and sweet sap for food; fibres for cordage and basketry; bark and wood for housing, watercraft, tools and containers. Hardware was still of stone, shell and antler, but on the south shore of Lake Superior men found a new sort of malleable 'stone' that could be hammered into useful shapes. If with too much hammering it became brittle, its elasticity could be restored by heating in the fire. This of course was native copper, and it became important in the East and Midwest, as we shall see; but the essential distinction between stone and metal was never to be realized north of Mexico. Annealing was discovered, but not true metallurgy.

Existence could never have been particularly easy or secure, but it does seem that the people came to live in balance with nature. Since nature showed different facets from one area to another, so local human groups tended to become differentiated, necessarily in their activities and, more incidentally, in their outlook, customs and modes of speech. In times when food was adequate or plentiful, the people had leisure to think about how to guard against times of scarcity, by keeping on the right side of the animals and plants. Small acknowledgements and appeals grew into ritual obligations, prohibitions and ceremonies. Such observances, if efficacious, might be seen and copied by a neighbouring group. For although such groups – and we may now begin to speak of tribes – kept more or less within certain bounds and developed their own identities, they did not live in complete isolation. One of the surprises of American archaeology is the evidence of widespread trade in material objects from very early times. That Lake Superior copper found its way to the sea coasts; marine shells were carried inland. Eventually, individual traders journeyed vast distances with their wares, but to begin with it is more likely that things were bartered from one tribe to the next. Similarly, ideas spread far out from their source by a sort of cultural bucket-chain.

The effect of this process was that a broadly uniform way of life – in anthropological terms a culture – could be shared by a large number of communities whose languages might be mutually unintelligible and whose contacts might be warlike as often as cooperative. Two such clearly defined cultures begin to show up around 3,000 B.C.: below the Great Lakes the Old Copper people, and in New England and the Canadian Maritimes the Red Paint people. For 1,500 years the Old Copper smiths pounded with their stone hammers on those lumps of metal without leading America out of the Stone Age; and for a similar period the Red Paint people ground up haematite to daub the linings of their graves, and probably the occupants too, with the colour of blood and life. Beautifully worked tools of slate, quartzite, bone and antler, many clearly made for no other purpose, were buried with the corpses. Here we see an early manifestation of that preoccupation with death which for primitive and later peoples alike has conditioned so much of life.

Adena-Hopewell, the Mound Builders

A little to the west of the Red Paint area, from southern Ontario down into Michigan, people began to be buried in glacial kames, the hillocks left behind by the ice sheet, and when there were not enough natural kames to go round artificial mounds were built. This may not have been an original idea. In Ohio, another group of people, from about 2,000 B.C. onwards, had been elaborating their funerary practices, not only borrowing from the north the custom of smearing the dead with red ochre but also burying their clay or log tombs under mounds. These mounds were all artificial, built basketful by basketful; the Glacial Kame folk may just have been trying to keep up with them, on a labour-saving basis.

Burial mounds were not the only earthworks put up by these Ohio people, whom we call Adena from the modern town nearest to one of their principal sites. Great enclosures, circular or angled, up to a hundred yards across, abound in the Adena country. Some surround burial mounds, others not, but all are popularly known today as 'Sacred Circles'. Adena religion is an intriguing query, to which one vast site in Louisiana, anomalously called Poverty Point, provides a clue. Poverty Point, with its six octagonal ramparts one within another, six feet high and over 400 yards across at its widest, does not quite belong in North America; but much of what has been found there does belong in the Olmec homeland of Vera Cruz. Here, obviously, was one of those pulsations from the vigorous growth of Mexican culture, liberated by agriculture, which were to shape the destiny of the Woodlands. As to how it arrived we have as yet no decisive evidence.

The Adena people did not become Mexicans overnight. They adopted and adapted the mounds, they planted pumpkins, sunflowers and other crops, but not to the point of dependence because wild foods were still abundant. They adopted tobacco and smoked it in tubular pipes. They made fairly simple pottery jars and bowls, rounded or pointed at the bottom. Their houses were circular with outward-sloping walls of wattle and high roofs of thatch or matting. They appear to have tattooed

Wattle and thatch house of the Adena period (reconstruction). Part of the front is cut away to show the central fireplace.

themselves, and they wore river pearls and polished gorgets of stone and copper. They wove vegetable fibres. Unlike the Red Paint people, they did not make a point of burying choice grave goods with their dead, nor – unlike them again – did they accord equal attention to all who died. The differing degrees of ostentation lavished on Adena burials show that social inequality had taken root in the Woodlands, where it would persist down to historic times.

By around 200 A.D. (or, for example, halfway through the Roman occupation of Britain) the Adena influence had spent itself, and another distinct but not dissimilar culture was there to replace it. This way of life – for it does not seem to represent any sort of political conquest – we call Hopewell, again from an Ohio site. Originating apparently in Illinois, Hopewell culture washed down over the Adena country and far beyond. As with Adena, the details of everyday life have largely to be inferred: hunting, fishing, gathering wild plant foods, some increase in cultivation with a minimal inclusion of maize. What makes Hopewell truly noteworthy is its intensified ceremonialism, resulting in more and bigger burial mounds and a plastic art that has nowhere been excelled on the North American continent.

The mounds could be up to forty feet high and contain one burial or several, with a suggestion that some of the dead were sacrificed. They were built in two stages, and the sheer size of them indicates the

Bird's-eye view of the Serpent Mound in Ohio. The embankment measures 1,330 ft from jaws to tail, 15–20 ft across, and up to 4 ft in height. It is thought to be the work of the Adena-Hopewell people.

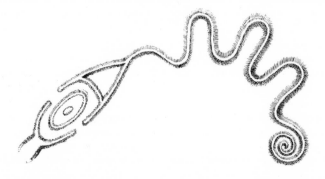

existence of a ruling class, with priestly authority, able to command the work force needed for their construction. One remarkable memorial to their skill and organization survives in the Great Serpent Mound, near the remains of a once populous Hopewell site now dubbed Mound City, in Ohio. The effigy runs sinuously along a natural ridge for a quarter of a mile, its tail tightly coiled, its jaws closing on a small conical mound. Dating from around the beginning of the Christian era, it is not typical of 'pure' Hopewell, but a few centuries later a Hopewell offshoot was to dot a large area to the west with smaller earthen effigies. The illustration shows the outline of the Serpent as seen from the air. It is an intriguing thought that no Indian ever saw it so – unless you credit the writer who asserts that the helmeted figures of Olmec sculpture are not Mexican warriors but visiting spacemen.

Mound Builder Art

Along with and as part of their intense ceremonial and social life the Hopewell people supported a far-flung trade network which brought in raw materials for their artist-craftsmen. Obsidian from the Rockies, Caribbean conch shells, Great Lakes copper, Appalachian mica, Minnesota pipestone, even some Canadian silver, were transformed into tools and ornaments of high aesthetic merit. Sheets of mica were cut into silhouettes of natural and abstract forms, including human heads and bird talons. Copper was beaten into sheets and similarly treated, or was made into axes, awls, fish-hooks and ear-studs. But it was in the modelling of pottery figurines and the carving of stone tobacco pipes that the Hopewell artists excelled all others. The pipes in particular, depicting birds, toads or mammals carved in the round and standing on a rectangular platform, display a fidelity to nature and a delicacy of treatment which give them instant and universal appeal. They also indicate the existence of a class of highly talented specialists such as can flourish only in societies where the quest for food no longer requires the cooperation of every individual.

The tiny figurines show something of what the people looked like, the women wearing belted skirts and wide armlets, their babies nothing at all, and their menfolk with 'G-strings', breast ornaments and partly shaven crowns.

Starting later than Adena, Hopewell spread its influence from New York to the Gulf of Mexico and westward to the Missouri. Yet by 550 A.D. its impetus was spent. As the Dark Ages settled over Europe, so the light of cultural creativity dimmed over the Eastern Woodlands.

However, by 700 A.D., another and stronger pulsation from Mexico made itself felt. The stimulus may have come with Mexican traders, the *pochteca*, bringing ideas as well as goods. One of the new concepts was a different use for mounds – not now for tombs but as bases for temples. A new major culture developed which was to last, even if past its peak, into historic times. Its heartland was on the fertile banks of the Mississippi, and we call it the Mississippian.

The fertility is significant, for here was a way of life based on large-scale maize-growing, and the only farming implement was the flint-bladed hoe. Increased food production made possible increased concentrations of people and so we find real towns, of thatched wattle houses clustered in or near a religious centre of pyramids topped with temples. This is the Mexican pattern, but whereas faraway Teotihuacan faced its mounds and built its temples with stone, Mississippian mounds were wholly earthen and its temples simple one-storey affairs of poles and thatch. As in Mexico the mounds, or pyramids, were rectangular with steeply sloping sides and a stairway (here of earth or logs) leading to the flat top. Height and area varied enormously; periodical rebuilding of the temples was preceded by the addition of a thick new layer to the whole surface of the pyramid. Smaller eminences were built to support the houses of chiefs and nobles, for whom also burial mounds in the Hopewell manner were still provided.

The greatest town – city, rather – of this culture yet discovered lies just outside St Louis, Missouri, and is called Cahokia. At its centre is a huge pyramid covering sixteen acres and reaching a height of 100 feet. Its volume has been estimated at 22,000,000 cubic feet. Other smaller pyramids and platforms are grouped about it on a vast plaza enclosed by an embankment once topped by a palisade. The population of Cahokia at its maximum, around 1200 A.D., has been reckoned at 30,000. Many other populous centres were spread over the South from Florida to Oklahoma.

Mississippian art, if not quite equalling the best of Hopewell, is still impressive. Mica cut-outs and embossed designs on copper sheets are prominent, and there is much incising and even etching of shell. The designs show eagles and vultures, plumed serpents, death's heads, and ceremonially caparisoned warriors and priests leaping and flying – all undeniably Mexican in inspiration. A great part of the symbolism has to do with death. It is the presence of such symbols – a favourite among them is a conventionalized weeping eye – that bespeaks the diffusion of Mississippian ideas across the South and up towards the North. Archaeologists speak of the beliefs involved as the Death Cult, Buzzard

19

The great mound at East St. Louis, Illinois, once the centre of Cahokia, a 12th-century Mississippian city of 30,000 people. This 16-acre mound, reaching 100 ft in height, contains an estimated 22 million cu. ft of earth, all raised by hand.

(i.e. vulture) Cult, or simply the Southern Cult. Effigy pipes are still competently made – a famous one depicts an armoured warrior decapitating a victim – but the best Mississippian art form is its pottery. Bowls, bottles and jars are made in a wide variety of shapes, including those of frogs and birds. Some globular, necked bottles are joined like Siamese twins, and all stand up by themselves on flat bases or legs. Decoration is painted, incised or stamped in geometric and symbolic patterns of unerring accuracy.

Eclipse of the Mound Builders

We said that Cahokia was at its apogee about 1200 A.D. By the time white men reached the Mississippi, its great earthworks were silent and uninhabited. Other cities like Moundville in Alabama and Etowah in Georgia had likewise gone. Overpopulation, adverse seasons, internal dissension or external wars – we do not know the exact reasons for the decline. Suffice it to say that the pattern of rise and fall is characteristic of aboriginal America, if not of all Mankind. But in the case of the Woodlands culture white observers were on hand to record the final plunge, which they themselves precipitated.

We owe the whole of the story so far to the world's most dedicated detective force – the archaeological profession, working away on a myriad tiny clues with spade, brush, sophisticated gadgetry, intuition, and analogy with historic tribes. The file on Early Man is far from complete. Possibly as much remains to be discovered as is known already, and important assumptions could yet be upset by new facts. One outstanding question mark is that which hangs over prehistoric relations between the New World and the Old, but that matter is too speculative to be discussed here. From this point descriptions of the Eastern Woodlands Indians will rest on the records of those who saw them in action.

The Historical Southeast

The unifying theme of Woodlands life is a mixed food economy of hunting and fishing with agriculture important but never dominant; fixed dwellings of poles, thatch or bark, sometimes mud-daubed, occupied by one or more families; simple clothing; watercraft; a tendency towards loose confederations; and warfare for its own sake. The variations are as numerous as the tribes, and they are – or were – very numerous indeed. Ranging in population from a few hundreds to a few thousands, each group had its own language, or at least its dialect, intelligible to a few or none of its neighbours. Four major language families, from two basic phyla, dominate our eastern area. They are the Algonkian/Muskogean and the Siouan/Iroquoian. It must be stated that language and way of life have very little to do with each other, but the groupings are handy for listing; and it is to the heart of the Muskogean country that we shall go first, to the Natchez.

The Natchez

Living in what is now the state of Mississippi, the Natchez were practising the most extreme form of the old Mississippian culture still surviving when visited by the French in the late seventeenth century. Lacking the size and complexity of Cahokia – the Natchez and their neighbours the Taënsa together numbered no more than 5,500 – they still built temple mounds and maintained a rigid social caste system once thought alien to North America.

In appearance the people did not differ greatly from other southern Woodlanders. Basic clothing for men consisted of the 'G-string', almost universal in North America: a strip of buckskin or cloth passed between the legs and hanging at front and back over a belt. For women the equivalent was a knee-length wrap-around skirt. Girls wore a brief netted apron with a long fringe tipped with talons of birds to rattle as they walked. Children wore nothing at all. In cold weather men might add skin leggings, seatless and tied to the belt, and a poncho-like shirt made of two deer skins. Over that they might wrap a robe of buffalo hide with the hair on or of half a dozen beaver skins sewn together with sinew thread. The women used a piece of skin or cloth drawn round the body under one arm and fastened above the opposite shoulder, again with a robe added when necessary. A Southeastern speciality was a robe of turkey or swan feathers tied into a netted fibre base. Both sexes went barefoot except on long journeys, when soft moccasins with a cuff that could be tied up round the lower leg were worn. Women's leggings reached only from the ankle to below the knee.

However, if clothing was simple, personal adornment was elaborate. A contrivance of board and clay pads applied to infants' skulls ensured that they grew up with fashionably pointed heads. The ears of both sexes were pierced and the lobes distended to carry ornaments of shell, stone, copper or feather. Men and women alike wore tattooed designs over most of their bodies, limbs and faces. Young men, however, had to qualify for such decoration by killing an enemy in war, and seasoned fighters used their own bodies as a scoreboard. The tattooing was done by pricking the design into the skin with one or more bone awls or garfish teeth and rubbing charcoal or ochre into the perforations. Less permanent but constantly applied was facial and body painting. 'War paint' has become a cliché, but painting of the person was used just as much in peace as in war, here and throughout the continent. The pigments were mostly mineral, e.g. ochres and clays, mixed with animal fat and applied both overall and in patterns. Personal fancy, ritual rules, or instructions received in dreams governed the colour and distribution of the paints. Protection against insects or the sun was sometimes claimed as a reason for body painting but the ultimate motivation did not differ greatly from that controlling women's makeup in European society. A less common cosmetic activity reported for the Natchez was the blackening of the teeth by daily rubbing with a mixture of tobacco ash and wood ash.

One of the favourite toys of inventive Man throughout the ages has been his own hair. Natchez men shaved it in the manner of a monk's tonsure, leaving a thin braid to hang over the left ear and an islet of a few hairs on top to which feathers could be tied. The head hair was taken off with a cane or shell blade or else singed, but beards were plucked with clamshells or copper tweezers. Both sexes rigorously plucked out eyebrows and all body hair (naturally sparse), as did nearly all Indians in both the Americas.

Shell and stone beads and pendants, strings of freshwater pearls and bracelets of deer ribs polished thin and shaped in boiling water were commonly worn. On festive occasions bird down was put on the head. As mentioned, feathers were tied in the men's hair, but whether the choice was dictated by personal taste or, as in some other areas, by the wearer's achievements, does not seem to have been recorded.

Houses were fifteen feet or more square, with low walls of poles, canes and mud, lined inside and out with woven mats and topped with a high rounded roof thatched with grass. The doorway, two by four feet or less, was the sole opening; smoke from the fire escaped as best it could. The only interior fixtures were the beds, consisting of reed mats on a pole framework supported on four forked posts. The reed mats, up to six feet by four feet in size and decorated with geometrical designs in the course of weaving, were an important feature of everyday life. Reeds were also used for basketry utensils of many shapes and sizes. Softer textiles suitable for clothing were woven from the fibres of mulberry bark and nettle, and sometimes from buffalo or opossum hair.

Natchez pottery seems to have been mostly utilitarian. As everywhere in the New World, it was produced without the aid of the potter's wheel.

Both men and women joined in preparing and tending the maize fields, clearing the land of cane with wooden mattocks and fire, and hoeing the crops with hafted buffalo shoulder-blades. Women pounded the grain in wooden mortars with two-handed pestles and cooked it in a great variety of ways; one French observer reported forty-two recipes for maize dishes. Some wild grains were used too, besides fruits, nuts and fungi.

Fishing and hunting were the men's tasks. Fish were netted or shot with arrows attached to floats. She-bears, the most formidable prey, were traced to lairs in hollow trees and driven out by fire; they could be shot repeatedly while clambering down the trunk. Deer could be stalked by a lone hunter wearing antlers and imitating the movements of his quarry; or up to a hundred men and boys would surround an animal and chase it to exhaustion. Buffalo were taken one at a time by downwind stalking. Meat was boiled, roasted on spits of green wood, or smoked on cane frames set on posts three feet above a slow fire. This cooking- or drying-rack is common to the Antilles and northern South America, where a native name for it is *barbacoa*, which we call 'barbecue'.

Wild turkeys and ducks and domesticated dogs helped out the meat supply. A small breed of dog, raised specifically for the pot, is attributed to some Southern tribes. European poultry reached the Natchez ahead of the French explorers, apparently from a wreck on the Gulf coast, but their eggs were not eaten.

Fire was made by the classic method of twirling one stick in the side of another and igniting tinder at the point of friction. Apart from cooking and warmth, fire was an essential tool for clearing plantation sites and for charring, and so weakening, the bases of trees to be felled. To make their great dugout canoes, the Indians dropped cypress or poplar trees and hollowed them in the same way, lighting fires along the upper side of the log and hacking away the calcined wood until the walls were reduced to an even thickness of around three inches. Damp clay was used to keep the burning within bounds. Such craft might measure forty feet with a three-foot beam, and carry a dozen men.

Life for the average Natchez seems not to have been unduly arduous. Children were never chastised, learning correct behaviour and adult skills by imitation. Girls before marriage enjoyed complete freedom; any accidental child was quietly strangled or adopted by its grandparents, as its mother wished, with no stigma accruing. Within the permitted grades marriage was governed by mutual choice – even though, as we shall see, that choice might carry a suspended death sentence for one of the partners. Divorce was easy for the upper classes, but infidelity as such was rare. For amusements there were guessing games, chunkey – which involved throwing poles after a rolling stone disc and gambling heavily on the results – and a succession of social and religious feasts. Swimming was universally enjoyed, with guards posted to keep the alligators at bay.

Warfare was part of life but confined to the sneak raid. Enemy villages or, for preference, isolated camps were attacked at dawn, the victims clubbed and scalped, and some women and children made captive. If possible at least one warrior too was taken alive. On the war party's return home the women and children suffered no more than enslavement. The warrior, stripped, scalped and spreadeagled on an upright frame, would be studiously tortured by all and sundry, taunting his killers as long as breath stayed in him, which might be three days and nights. Only if a recently widowed girl claimed him as a replacement for her husband could he escape execution. Hernando de Soto's expedition in 1539 found one Juan Ortiz, a shipwrecked sailor, who had been thus plucked from the scaffold by a chief's daughter twelve years previously, anticipating Pocahontas.

The Rule of the Great Sun

With some allowance for minor details, the foregoing may be taken as true of Indian life over the greater part of the southern Woodlands. It is in the realm of social organization that the Natchez more than any other tribe show their heritage from the Hopewell-Mississippian-Mexican past. Here was no sylvan democracy, but an elaborate edifice of social castes ruled over by a hereditary pope-cum-monarch with powers of life and death over his subjects. This ruler-priest, who served the sun, was himself styled the Great Sun, and members of the élite class to which he belonged were known as Suns. Immediately below the Suns were the Nobles and below them the Honoured Men. These three ranks made up the 'peerage'; the rest of the people were commoners, known to their betters as Stinkers. But this class system had a curious built-in mobility. Commoners could marry commoners, but all three grades of the nobility *had* to marry commoners. Descent was reckoned through the female line, so that children of noble mothers and Stinker fathers were born noble. Children of noble fathers and Stinker mothers, however, were born one grade below that of the father, wherefore the Great Sun's heir was his sister's son. The higher a man's rank, the more wives he took from the commoner class. How long the system could have maintained itself is a statistical query that has not been answered.

The Great Sun, although assisted by a privy council, was treated with the deference due to a divine ruler. Eight men carried him about on a litter, that his feet might not touch the earth. If he fell ill children were sacrificed to appease the spirit responsible. When he died his wives, counsellors and servants, anaesthetized with a decoction of tobacco, were ceremonially strangled by their own relatives at the climax of funeral rites and rehearsals lasting several days. Parents who strangled their own infants and laid them to be tramped over by the cortège advanced to a higher rank in the social scale. The Great Sun's house was burned; his bones were eventually placed in the thatched temple. Ritual killing on a lesser scale accompanied the death of lesser nobles, involving at least the strangling of the commoner wife or husband, normally performed by the eldest son.

Apart from drubbing the depleted expedition of de Soto on its retreat down the Mississippi in 1543, the Natchez had no contact with white men until 1682. Thereafter, they were in increasingly close touch with French planters, initially on good terms. Eventually, and inevitably, frictions arose which resulted in killings and counter-killings of mounting savagery. In 1731 a concerted onslaught by the Frenchmen ended with a large number of the Natchez dead or sold into slavery and the remainder scattered as refugees among the Chickasaws, Cherokees and other tribes. A handful of part-Natchez Indians survive in Oklahoma but the language seems to have died out halfway through the present century.

Interesting as the Natchez were as the extreme development of a particular social pattern, they were by no means the most important of Southeastern peoples, in numbers or in power. Natchez ideas were reflected in varying degrees by their neighbours – the Taënsa, Houma, Tunica, Chitimacha and others; as far away as northern Florida the Timucua chiefs were borne on litters. Peninsular Florida was however held by the piratical Calusa, whose linguistic connections have not been determined. Reportedly cannibals, they were in touch by seagoing canoe with the Cuban Arawaks, and it was probably through them that certain Antillean and Amazonian elements like the blowgun and fishing with poison found their way into North America.

Northwards along the Atlantic coastal plain the subsistence pattern shows little basic change, balanced between farming, hunting, fishing and shellfish-gathering. Muskogean, Siouan and Iroquoian peoples are layered with Algonkians, who take over completely from Virginia to Labrador. There are no mounds here, nor sacred fires, but leadership still has features of monarchy. When the English colonists described Powhatan as 'King of Virginia' they were not so wildly out, although 'a king in Virginia' would have been nearer the mark; he did in fact hold sway over thirty tribes or villages, all of them small. His daughter was Pocahontas, *La Belle Sauvage*, who saved one Englishman, John Smith, from execution and married another, John Rolfe, only to die of smallpox at Gravesend in England in 1617. A valuable pictorial record of these coastal tribes as they were in the 1580s has come down to us in the work of John White, now preserved in the British Museum.

The Creeks (Muskogi) and their Neighbours

Across the inland heart of the region lived the most powerful of the Muskogean tribes, the Creeks, Choctaws and Chickasaws, and the Iroquoian Cherokees. The Creeks, who were a loose federation of kindred, and some unrelated, tribes, may serve as a model. Their towns, usually on river-banks (whence the colonists' name, Creek Indians), were designated Red or White. White towns were peace towns, concerned with sanctuary and the maintenance of alliances. Red towns made warfare their business. The towns themselves show echoes of the past in their layout, the houses surrounding a great square bordered with earthen banks to accommodate spectators. This was the arena for a disc game, archery contests, social dancing and the torture of prisoners; here surely in attenuated form is the Mexican ball court. Two buildings normally stood at one end of the enclosure. One, large, circular and clay-walled, served as a sort of community centre. The other consisted of four open-fronted sheds arranged in a hollow square, with tiers of benches for the deliberations of the town council.

For there were no absolute rulers. Each Creek town had its *mico*, whose appointment was normally for life but whose functions were those of a mayor rather than a monarch. He was assisted by a body of lesser officials and advised by a council of respected elders known as Beloved Men. Council met daily, with meticulous ceremony, and its decisions were announced by the 'speaker' or 'crier', an official duplicated in many parts of North America.

The community spirit was encouraged in all things. Each family had its own garden for growing corn, beans and pumpkins but everyone helped in tilling the 'town field'; only at harvests did a family restrict work to the field allotted to itself. All contributed to a common store reserved for visitors, warriors and the destitute.

Obligations to one's community were matched by obligations to one's sib or clan. A clan here means a grouping of people believing themselves so closely descended from a common ancestor that to marry one another would constitute incest. The Algonkian word totem is commonly used to denote the mythical ancestor or tutelary, usually a non-human living organism or a personified natural phenomenon which may or may not be specially revered by clan members. Since marriage within the clan was taboo, parents necessarily represented two different clans; offspring inherited membership of one or the other. Where descent was matrilineal, i.e. reckoned through the mother, the child of, say, an Alligator father and a Fox mother would itself belong to the Foxes and would share in the ceremonial responsibilities, privileges and restrictions proper to that clan. Matrilineal descent was on the whole characteristic of agricultural tribes and patrilineal – in the father's line – of hunting tribes, but the subject is much too complex to be treated at length here. It need only be added that some scholars now prefer the term 'sib' for the basic exogamous unit, reserving 'clan' for a particular development of it.

The highlight of the Creek year was the four-day Green Corn festival or 'Busk' in July or August. All fires were put out and a new fire lit by the senior priests or medicine-men. Old clothing and household goods were burnt and replaced by new. All offenders except murderers were pardoned. Feasts were made of the new season's corn, hitherto taboo, and of deer meat, and the spirits were invoked. Secular diversion was provided by ball games, including the original form of lacrosse, and social dancing. For the men there was much ritual purification with the 'black drink', an infusion of *Ilex vomitoria* and other herbs which promoted instant internal cleanliness besides having some narcotic effect.

Removal

Creek warfare was originally confined to raiding for honours, scalps or vengeance. Choctaws and Cherokees were traditional enemies, with no great execution done. Colonizing Europeans changed that. Spanish reduction of the Florida tribes started a vacuum which the Creeks helped to complete and then to fill. French on the Mississippi and English to the north and east wooed the tribes assiduously in the imperial game. The Cherokees did some fighting for both sides; the Creeks favoured the English but skilfully avoided major hostilities. The colony of Georgia, expanding slowly, had much to offer them, in material goods and in ideas. Traders and planters married into Creek and Cherokee families and their mixed-blood sons played increasingly important roles in tribal affairs. The leading families acquired Negro slaves and lived well. After American independence, relations began to deteriorate. Enforced sales of land gave way to confiscation after open war in 1813–4. By 1817 the more prosperous of the Cherokees were buying land and settling beyond the Mississippi, whither some Chickasaws and Choctaws had already gone. Ten years later the first of the Creeks followed suit. Those who remained were forcibly ejected between 1838 and 1843, in a series of marches often attended by great suffering. In particular the winter migration of the Cherokees in 1838–9 is remembered as the Trail of Tears; one quarter of those taking part were lost, over three hundred of them in a steamboat disaster.

The Creek settlers in Florida, dubbed Seminoles (*Sim-a-no'le*, 'Runaways'), declined to move. Led by the brilliant quarter-Scot, Osceola, they had already fought the United States in the Spanish and

British interest and for seven years from 1835 they fought again in their own – a ruthless struggle in the swamps and jungle which cost the Army 1,500 lives. It ended, inevitably, with the defeat of the Seminoles and the removal of most of them to Indian Territory. A handful secreted themselves in the Everglades. There they live today, in open-sided thatched dwellings graced by the Singer sewing-machines on which they make the highly-coloured patchwork gowns and shirts that have been the tribal uniform since around 1900.

By the time of the Removal the Cherokees were already literate, thanks to the genius of George Geist, or Guess, whose native name was Sequoyah. Son of a German trader and a mixed-blood Cherokee mother, he was brought up as an Indian and is said never to have learned English. After a crippling accident he devoted years to perfecting a Cherokee alphabet or syllabary of eighty-odd characters. It was enthusiastically received and widely studied. Two white printers were engaged and in

Modern Seminole women in Florida stripping corn from the cob for grinding.

Seminoles cooking corn fritters. Note the log mortar and two-handed pestle for grinding the corn.

1828 there appeared the first weekly national newspaper, *The Cherokee Phoenix*. When the reluctant migrants to Indian Territory had pulled themselves together, succoured by their kindred already there, they were ready to adopt written constitutions and set up quasi-independent republics: the Cherokee, Creek, Choctaw, Chickasaw and Seminole Nations, or Five Civilized Tribes. Not until 1907 would they find themselves formally absorbed into the state of Oklahoma.

Chapter 3

Northeastern Woodlands:
Wampum and Wild Rice

The Iroquois

So what about Hiawatha? Longfellow's biography is less than reliable but a Hiawatha there was – in fact a series of them, since the name became a chiefly title among the Mohawks. The first Hiawatha was an influential Onondaga (not, despite Longfellow, an Ojibwa) who collaborated with the Huron-born thinker Deganawida in welding five tribes – the Mohawk, Oneida, Onondaga, Cayuga and Seneca – into the powerful League of the Iroquois. The date is disputed but was probably about 1570. Blood feuds between member tribes were stopped by the establishment of fixed-rate compensation for murders, and a League Council was formed on the lines of the tribal councils. Here was democracy in action. Certain posts of authority might be hereditary within certain families or clans but the actual appointments were decided by the senior women – yes, women – and could be cancelled by them. Fifty chiefs or *sachems* sat as delegates to the League council, which alone (in theory) could sanction or prohibit wars. As with other leagues in history, the extent to which the covenants were honoured varied with the circumstances.

Descent as elsewhere in the East was through the mother, and it was to the wife's home that a husband went to live on marriage. To forestall domestic tensions, however, custom prohibited any communication between a man and his mother-in-law, a taboo widespread among the tribes.

Everyday life was broadly similar to that described for other Woodland peoples, the men hunting deer and fishing and the women raising maize, beans and squash. Housing was different. One of the League's names for itself was The Longhouse, a reflection of the normal Iroquois dwelling. Built of elm bark on a pole foundation, the typical longhouse was from fifty to one hundred feet in length, with a corridor down the middle and a door at each end. Up to twenty families occupied compartments in a single house, sharing cooking fires in the corridor. House life was noisy, smoky, and generally too hot or too cold. The degree of repression necessary to make communal living workable in such an environment has been suggested as a factor in the psychotic cruelty practised by Iroquois women – even more than the men – in the torture of prisoners.

As well as walls and roofs, elm bark provided canoes, utensils and rattles. Birch bark was preferable but rare in Iroquois country, and so was bought with Iroquois corn from Algonkian neighbours to the north. From, or through, the coastal Algonkians too came wampum, the white or purple cylindrical beads laboriously ground from the shells of marine clams or quahogs (*Venus mercenaria*), whelks and periwinkles. Belts of wampum woven on fibre or skin cords signalized and symbolized pacts and treaties, each party retaining a belt with identical designs. Strings of wampum were carried as credentials by tribal ambassadors. They were also used as currency, the purple beads being twice or three times as valuable as the white. Disc-shaped shell beads, perforated with flint drills and rounded by rolling over sandstone when strung, probably came before wampum as it is historically understood. Certainly the

The making of shell beads. Pieces from the column of the shell were held in a wooden clamp and drilled with a stone point (or metal when obtainable).

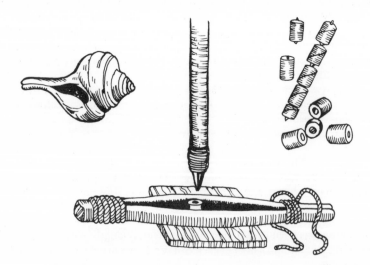

Dutch and English colonists, working with metal tools and grindstones, dominated production from a very early date.

Clothing in the Northeast was virtually all of buckskin, weaving in fibre and wool being confined to bags, belts and garters. Men wore breech-cloths and leggings (in all native North America, only the Eskimos and their Athapaskan neighbours ever taught themselves to put a seat into a pair of trousers). Tailored garments did appear quite early in the historic period, but whether taken from Eskimo or white models is not clear. Moccasins were worn regularly. They were soft-soled, the foot being cut in one piece except, usually, for an insertion or vamp over the instep. An added flap or cuff could be tied up round the ankle. Stitching fine and firm was done with thread made from ravelled and twisted sinew poked through holes made with a bone awl or thorn. Short fringes along seams and edges were characteristic of northern Woodlands clothing.

Porcupine Quills, Moose Hair and Beads

Garments, moccasins, pouches, quivers and cradle bands, especially those intended for 'occasions' – which were numerous – were embroidered with porcupine quills. The quills vary in length and thickness on different parts of the animal, as well as in the proportions of white and dark brown. The white quills could be dyed by boiling or steeping with various vegetal and mineral pigments, giving in particular a warm orange-red, yellows, green, and a rich purplish blue. (Brighter and more varied tints were made available by the white trader.) In use the quill is moistened, flattened either with a bone plate or less cumbrously by holding it between the teeth and drawing the fingernails along it, and then stitched down to the decorated surface with sinew. On drying the quill becomes more or less rigid. Tremendous ingenuity was displayed in the methods of stitching, folding, wrapping and combining quills in tasteful and attractive designs. Aboriginally these were, almost for certain, purely geometrical, in the sense of having no curved lines except the rim of a disc – which does not preclude chunky, schematic human and bird figures. In addition to appliqué (couched) work, quills were woven into bands on a sinew warp held taut on a small wooden bow. The resulting panels could be backed with skin before use or sewn directly on to the pouch or garment, besides being easily transferred from a worn to a new piece.

White hairs from the dewlap, mane and rump of the moose, and from the woodland caribou, were similarly dyed and used in false-embroidery for decorating objects woven from vegetable fibre. In this process the coloured hairs are wound round the weft fibres. Pouches, belts, and particularly the headbands of burden-straps (tumplines) decorated in this way by the Iroquois and kindred Huron survive from the early eighteenth century, and there are grounds for believing that the craft is truly native.

In 1639, French nuns of the Ursuline order opened their first school for Indian girls at the new village of Québec and taught their pupils needlework and embroidery, on French lines. The girls were drawn from many tribes. Floral patterns, more or less conventionalized and re-interpreted, spread inexorably west to the Lakes, across the northern prairies and plains and over the Rockies to the Pacific coast. The Huron and Iroquois women bent their quills into simple flowers and leaves, and couched the more pliable moose hair into figures as delicate and elaborate as anything done in the French silks of the French tradition. The nuns themselves used moose hair when silks from the mother country ran short. It can perhaps never be known whether Indian or white women first substituted hair for silk, but it is reasonably certain that knowledge of the hair's potential was with the Indians from pre-contact days.

When the Dutch bought Manhattan Island from the Wappinger Indians, beads figured largely in the purchase price. To the white men they were a trifle but it is arguable that the Indians were not cheated, in the circumstances of the time. Glass beads, brilliant and permanent in colour, ready-perforated and polished, represented a vast saving in labour and produced the results for which he or she had yearned. Look at the dead-white shell designs on King Powhatan's mantle (Plate 15), or better still, go and see the mantle itself in the Ashmolean Museum at Oxford (England). Compare them with the colourful beadwork illus-trated in this book and try to appreciate the artistic liberation which the bright glass bead brought to the craftswoman, and to her peacock spouse. Granted that some Victorian Indian beadwork went way over the top in its exuberance (something of the same sort is happening to the neo-native costumes of the current Indian revival), but in praising early restraint we risk making a virtue out of what was necessity.

Close behind the bead came European textiles: broadcloth, strouding and calico. Since they had to be paid for, it was a long time before skin clothing disappeared altogether, but by the late eighteenth century most Iroquois women wore long gowns and short leggings, and the men long leggings, seamed up the front, with kilt or breechclout, all of cloth decorated with beads and ribbon appliqué. The warrior's round skin cap became cloth and acquired a silver circlet, with the single plume fixed by a sort of ball-and-socket device on the crown. Later still a bead-encrusted Glengarry bonnet became fashionable.

The Spirit World

Iroquois religion, as was to be expected of farmers, called for regular communal observances in which the Three Sisters – Corn, Beans and Squash – and other spirit beings, were invoked and thanked. Supreme, if not all-powerful, among them was the Master of Life, a Creator whose beneficence was constantly threatened by his own evil brother. At mid-winter a prolonged ceremony of thanksgiving and renewal, preceded by public confessions, involved the whole Iroquois community. Although the initial reaction towards Jesuit missionaries was to grant them martyrdom, there is a suspicion that some Christian ideas had influenced Iroquois theology willy-nilly by the time it was recorded. About 1799, a reformed alcoholic named Handsome Lake launched a puritan movement with a return to the more innocuous of early beliefs, which are still practised today.

One purely aboriginal feature of Iroquois religious life was the belief in a spiritual force, present in all things, which could be accumulated and manipulated – or disastrously lost – by individuals, usually on terms as capricious as those laid on Cinderella by the Fairy Godmother. The Iroquois called this power *orenda*, the Siouans *wakanda*; in English-speaking contexts the term 'medicine' has been much used. Such personal relationship with the spirit world is best developed among the hunting and gathering peoples; it persists alongside the Iroquois communal practices because of the continued importance of hunting in the economy.

Beside the Keeper of the Faith, who regulates the great ceremonies, we find a class of shamans or 'medicine men' whose power, acquired in dreams, enabled them to cure disease by a combination of magical and medical means – which was well for the people, because the forests were plagued by malign spirits with hideous faces and no bodies whose mission was to spread sickness in those who saw them. Victims could be restored to health by members of the False-Face Society who beat the spirits on their own ground by impersonating them with wooden masks. False-Face masks had to be blocked out and cut from the living tree, the detailed carving being completed later. The features were twisted into a sinister leer and painted red or black, with staring eyeballs of shell or tin and a mop of dishevelled hair. A separate society of healers called Husk-

Faces danced with hoes and, digging sticks at harvest and winter festivals, wearing masks of braided corn-husk. Miniature masks of husk were carried as talismans.

Such masks are still used. There is a splendid description in the literature of a False-Face group driving into the village by night, intimidating the evil spirits by banging turtle rattles on the panels of their Ford car.

Trade and War

Early Iroquois warfare followed the usual pattern of raiding for prisoners for the purpose of adoption or sacrificial torture. The favourite weapon was the short wooden club with a heavy ball head. This, the original tomahawk, was later supplemented by the short steel-bladed hatchet of European manufacture. English tomahawks usually had a straight cutting edge; early French ones favoured a pointed blade called a spontoon. The incorporation of a pipe-bowl above the blade was an English invention. These again the Indians had to pay for, like the so-desirable cloth, beads, knives, brass kettles to replace the unimaginative Iroquois pottery, and guns which were more frightening, if hardly more lethal, than bows. The price demanded by the French, Dutch and English traders was beaver skins. All polite Europe wore big felt hats, and the best felt was made from beaver fur.

Wooden ball-headed clubs (the original tomahawk) of the type widely used by the eastern and central Woodlands Indians.

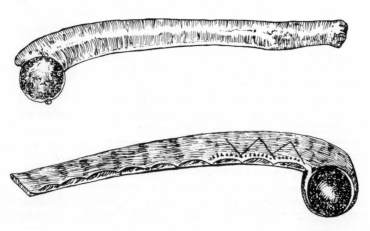

Huron ceremonial 'belts' of purple and white wampum: 1 Treaty belt showing Council Fire *(centre)* and double peace-pipes; 2 Belt associated with no. 1, showing the white Path of Peace; 3 Jesuit Missionary belt with three crosses representing the Trinity and a Lamb, dated before 1649; 4 Four Nations Alliance belt, dated 1710–20.

Trade began at the coast and moved up the St Lawrence River. The Algonkian tribes to the north got the beaver. Sitting squarely between them and the French posts in Quebec were the Huron and their satellites, the Erie, Tobacco and Neutral Nations. By the 1640s the Hurons had grown fat (and a little careless) as middlemen, using corn, tobacco and beans exacted from their dependent tribes to buy western furs which they sold to the traders for manufactured goods. The Iroquois beaver grounds were soon exhausted; not so their hunger for trade goods. Diplomatic efforts to get the furs channelled through them to the Dutch in New Amsterdam (New York) failed. In March 1649 the Seneca and Mohawk fell on a totally unsuspecting Huronia. Badly mauled and worse demoralized, the Hurons burnt their own villages and scattered as refugees to east and west. One group, typically, was absorbed into the Iroquois. In the following December the Tobacco (Tionontati) collapsed under a *blitzkrieg*. Some of the fugitives fled to the Neutrals (Attiwandaronk), who butchered or enslaved them, but in 1650–51 they themselves were crushed and dispersed. In 1654 it was the turn of the Erie. In 1713 the Tuscarora became the Sixth Nation of the League, and the Siouan Tutelo and some Catawba from the south were admitted as 'younger brothers'. Remnants of other seaboard tribes were taken in, difficulties about descent and marriage restrictions being eased by full adoption into clans.

Thus the Iroquois grew in numbers and profited by the use of lands evacuated before their onslaughts, yet their aim to monopolize the fur trade routes was never quite achieved. As the shock-waves of disruption moved westward towards Michigan and Wisconsin, the French traders followed, and the vulnerable Indian fur brigades paddling to Quebec in canoes gave way to stout French boats plying the lakes and rivers. The Iroquois turned on the Susquehanna to their east, and tried vainly to conclude with Ottawa and Illinois. Both France and England sought to use the military power of the enlarged League. Iroquois chiefs were fêted in London, and Queen Anne of England presented communion plate to her Faithful Mohawks. For the most part, the League opted for neutrality, but by so doing may have ensured the British victory. More active help was given to Britain in the War of Independence, at the close of which a large proportion of the Iroquois removed to Canada. Joseph Brant, Thayendenagea, who like his grandfather had visited London, died as a British Army colonel on half-pay at what is now Brantford, Ontario. The Seneca and some other small groups who favoured the United States now possess their own lands in New York and Pennsylvania. The Canadian Iroquois have stoutly maintained their claim to be in direct treaty relations with the British Crown, not subject to Canada, but lobbying at both the League of Nations and the United Nations has failed to gain them recognition.

The Algonkians

We have mentioned in passing the Algonkian tribes of New England. Again we find simple clothing of deerskin, simple pottery vessels, dug-out and bark canoes, and a diet of game, fish, corn, beans, nuts and berries, with maple sugar coming in as we go north. Houses were square of bark, or domed and thatched; villages were sometimes stockaded for defence. Politically there were sixty-odd groups or tribes, mainly small, who united into loose and transient confederacies. Relatively few survived into the eighteenth century. It is said that the Pilgrim Fathers fell first upon their knees and then upon the Indians. It is not quite true, nor yet quite wrong: by the time the Pilgrims landed the Indian population of the seaboard had already been drastically reduced by diseases brought in by European cod fishermen. Indians taught the colonists the use of maize and succoured them through the first hard winter; but a clash was unavoidable. On the one hand stood the white Puritans with their God-given mission to increase the fruitfulness of the land, keep the sabbath, root out witchcraft and press the savage into their

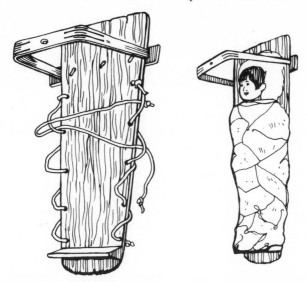

Wooden cradle or 'papoose board' to which infants were laced, swaddled in skins and padded with moss. Amulets dangling from the bow might include the child's navel cord in a beaded pouch.

own mould. On the other, the near-naked heathens, counting time by seasons rather than by the hour, openly committed to polygamy, and summoning spirits to their aid by dancing and incantations. Smallpox solved much of the dilemma, but open strife began with the Pequot War in 1637 and continued sporadically, backed up by a bounty on Indian scalps. Today, many tribal names are recognized only as place-names: Manhattan, Massachusetts, Nantucket. The Mohicans (Mahican or Mohegan) are remembered from Fenimore Cooper's novel, even though history has not strictly speaking seen the Last of them yet. Some tribes, as we have seen, faded into the Iroquois; remnants escaped to the West. Only in Maine and the Maritime Provinces did such groups as the Penobscot, Passamaquoddy, Malisit and Micmac, collectively known as the Abnaki or Wabenaki, preserve a reasonably dignified identity. Remnant communities scattered down the coast are all of greatly mixed Indian, white and negro inheritance but are once more taking pride in their Indian element. The Wampanoag of Mashpee on Cape Cod, who have their own museum and cultural centre, are an honourable example of the new spirit.

The Wild Rice People

Let us look westward now to the Great Lakes proper and the Mississippi headwaters. We are still in the Woodlands, but nearing their edge. The way of life does not change greatly. Houses are domed, conical or rectangular and covered with bark or reed mats according to locality or season (some tribes use all three types). Men shave most of their heads, and keep the cold off them with otter skin turbans. Women wear long slips made of two deerskins with shoulder-straps and detachable sleeves. Bags and belts, garters and packstraps are woven of vegetable fibres or buffalo wool. In the southerly part of the area, rich soils give ample crops of maize, beans and squash. In the north, where maize becomes reluctant to grow, an important new food comes in: wild rice (*Zizania aquatica*). Growing abundantly in the numberless shallow lakes and streams, rice supports a relatively dense human population with none of the backbreaking labour of the Old World paddy fields. When mature, in late summer, the plants stand anywhere between two and

Conical lodge covered with bark, used in addition to the domed wigwam by the Ojibwa and other tribes of the central and northern Woodlands.

twelve feet above the water; poling a canoe through them, the Indian women have simply to bend the stalks inboard and beat out the grain. Brought to land, the rice is poured into a deerskin-lined hole in the ground, six inches deep and two feet across, and there flailed with curved sticks to loosen the husks. Winnowing is done by pouring it from a bark tray in a breeze. Rice is eaten in a great variety of soups and broths, as a vegetable with fish or meat (bear, deer or dog), boiled on its own or mixed with maple sugar, or parched. The name of one important tribe, the Menomini, means 'Rice People'.

Other tribes of this central area include the Ojibwa (whom the Americans call Chippewa), the Ottawa, Potowatomi, Mascouten, Sauk and Fox, Miami, and Illinois, all of Algonkian speech, with the Siouan-speaking Winnebago and Eastern Dakota. Some are there still; others survive, if at all, as tiny groups of mixed individuals in Oklahoma. Some may be descendants of the people who built the effigy mounds. Before disturbance, they raided and traded far and wide (Ottawa means Traders).

Pipes

Their commodities were copper and the rest, but particularly pipestone. This mineral, christened catlinite after George Catlin, the nineteenth-century painter of Indians, was mined in open workings over a limited area. The largest quarry, in Minnesota, was neutral ground for the tribes. Grey or an attractive red in colour, the stone is easily worked when first won, hardening with exposure. It was made into tobacco pipes, sometimes straight like a cigar-holder but more commonly elbowed. In the latter case the slightly flared bowl was usually set an inch or two back from the end of the stem. At least in later times the bowl might be inlaid with lead or other soft metal or embellished with carved figures – never again, however, with anything approaching the artistic merit of the Hopewell-Mississippian pipes.

Always the pipe was fitted with a supplementary wooden stem, painted, carved, or beautifully patterned with closely wrapped porcupine quill, or, finest of all, with the unbarbed guard-hair of the western porcupine. Feathers and beads might hang from the stems of ceremonial pipes, for the pipes, and sometimes the stems alone, were highly important in religious and secular ceremony. The smoke of tobacco, or tobacco and willow bark ('kinikinik') was, like incense, pleasing to the spirits and so became a vehicle of prayer. In particular contexts the pipe replaced the wampum of the East; agreements were

41

sealed by passing the pipe for all to smoke. Emissaries carried pipes as diplomatic passports, and to smoke the pipe of peace was no mere figure of speech. But war leaders also carried them, to ensure supernatural support.

The resemblance of the stem to a (musical) reed pipe prompted the French to dub it *chalumeau*, whence 'calumet'. The English equivalent, not taken up, would have been 'shawm'.

Guardian Spirits

Religion hereabouts is cast in the individualistic mould of the hunter-gatherers, with some rather uncomprehending efforts to adapt to the more formal system of the farmers. There is a Great Spirit – Longfellow's Gitche Manitou – who is titular head of a somewhat unruly host of lesser spirits both good and evil. Thunderbird, bringer of rain, and the Winds are good. Horned Serpent and Underwater Panther are bad. Nanabozho the Hare is the great teacher of men, but is capricious. Virtually every living thing is conceived of as having its spiritual counterpart which has power, if properly approached, to help earthbound humans. So we find boys and sometimes girls being sent into the woods to fast and pray for a vision. Success comes with a dream in which a spirit, usually in animal form, promises support and protection. In return the dreamer may be bidden to abstain from certain foods or be placed under some other apparently arbitrary restraint. He may receive a special song, or the right to paint face or body in a special way. After the vision, a 'medicine' bag or bundle is likely to be prepared, containing objects symbolic of the spirit helper, such as a tooth, claw or feather, paint, arrowheads, or other bric-à-brac of the dream state. The bag will be devoutly preserved, and opened only when the guardian spirit is to be invoked or honoured. Later we shall see clans, societies or whole tribes dependent on the power of such sacred talismans.

The Medicine Men

To cope with malevolent spirits was the function of the medicine-man or shaman, whose origins like the name stretch far back into Siberia. Shamans cultivated the spirit world more diligently than ordinary mortals, made much use of trances, and learned to diagnose and cure disease, find lost property, and foretell the future. They were also great conjurers, impressing their audiences with apparent immunity to burning coals and boiling liquids. Although medicine men, and women,

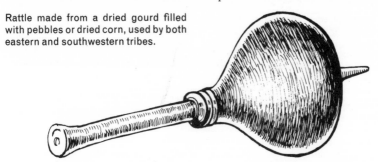

Rattle made from a dried gourd filled with pebbles or dried corn, used by both eastern and southwestern tribes.

were well versed in proven herbal remedies, much of their practice was psychosomatic. Often one shaman diagnosed a condition, leaving the cure to another. This was often effected by sucking some foreign body such as a pebble from the patient's body, with the singing of curing songs accompanied by drum or rattle.

Possibly in answer to Iroquois or even Christian ceremonialism, there arose the Midéwiwin or Grand Medicine Society of the Upper Lakes tribes. Eligibility depended on the appropriate dream, and on paying a stiff entrance fee for each of the four grades to which a member might progress. Once a year (at least) the Society would meet, in a low, mat-covered lodge up to seventy feet long. There they would perform rites, originally secret, of healing, conjuring, and instruction. Members' equipment included a bag made from a whole otter skin containing a seashell

Otter-skin medicine bag of the Ojibwa Grand Medicine Society or Midéwiwin. The paws and tail are adorned with quillwork and tin cones. Such bags held amulets, body paint, and the sacred seashells which Society members 'shot' into initiates to imbue them with healing power. Bags were often buried with their owners.

symbolizing the shell which guided the tribes westward from the Atlantic shore. As part of the performance in the Medicine Lodge, members would shoot one another dead by merely pointing the bag. After a while, the victims would stir, vomit up the shell, and return to life. A notable by-product of these ceremonies were the birchbark scrolls inscribed with pictographic figures used as memory-aids – the nearest approach to writing in native North America.

Europeans Move In

Historically it is difficult to map all these peoples for a given date. We have seen how the creation of a market for beaver pelts precipitated bloody struggles for control of the riverways leading to the French posts, with the Iroquois destroying some tribes and jabbing at others. The turmoil brought an influx of refugees to the Lakes country, some passing through, some allying themselvs with the residents. Fur traders, and soon a few colonists, arrived in the late 1600s. Many married or mated with Indian women, spreading the dilution of Indian blood which must have begun when the first shipwrecked mariner was washed ashore to be adopted. Nevertheless, these Indians took part on both sides in the struggle between French and English up to 1759. After the French withdrawal they got on reasonably well with the victors, the British Crown having declared all land west of the Alleganies to be Indian. The Ottawa chief Pontiac, who had sought to unite the tribes to drive all white men into the sea, could not hold his forces together and made peace in 1763. It was not to last very long. American independence opened the floodgates to settlers and a murderous period of raids and counter-raids began. A Shawnee prophet named Tenskwatawa arose to preach a return to old Indian ways. His brother Tecumseh, a man of exceptional capability, revived the goal of an intertribal grand alliance. While he was away down the Mississippi, negotiating with the Creeks, the warriors thus far assembled were scattered in a premature battle at Tippecanoe in Indiana. Tecumseh retired to Ontario and there, a brigadier-general in the British army, he died fighting the Americans at the battle of the Thames in 1813. As the white tide rose, some Mid-western Indians retreated towards Texas; part of the Kickapoo, and their Negro slaves with them, kept right on into Chihuahua. Others stayed, all but engulfed, on shrinking reservations. At Tana, Iowa, a remnant Fox band lives on lands of its own purchasing.

Star-that-Travels, also called Bacon Rind, an Osage, born in 1863. Note the tattooed shoulders and partly shaven head (a scalplock is hidden by the otterskin headband). Living on the edge of the plains, the Osage retained some Woodlands characteristics.

Chapter 4

The Magnet of the Buffalo Plains

Before the Horse

The high plains stretch for 2,000 miles from Alberta to Texas, dry, windy, broken only by a few islands of low, pine-dotted hills and rivers that are sometimes trickles and sometimes torrents. On the west they are walled by the Rockies. From the east they rise up from the green prairies where the Woodlands phase out. We left them in the possession of the Big Game hunters, with no more big game to hunt. Exactly what became of the earliest Plains people we do not know, but cave finds indicate that they held out for a very long time. They may be incorporated in some of the latter-day Plains tribes; but the Plains Indians as we commonly think of them are very much a latter-day phenomenon.

Year-round, the plains were an uninviting environment for a near-naked pedestrian, especially if he already had shelter and a steady food supply at his back in the woods. Yet they held a barely resistible temptation: sixty million, perhaps a hundred million, buffalo.

Smaller than his Pleistocene predecessor, *Bison bison* could still stand six feet high at the shoulder, and offered the twin advantages of high protein yield and low intelligence. Scary rather than wary, it could be stampeded *en masse* over a cliff or into a pound, or would stand unconcerned while its fellows were picked off by a disguised stalker. Like the European bison it dwelt in forests, but only on the open grasslands did it attain vast numbers – suggesting a build-up over thousands of years with no serious human predation. Animal predators culled the herds, but the biggest single check on population was probably the high drowning rate at river crossings. For the buffalo were great travellers, the major herds swinging widely in seasonal migrations which imposed a truly nomadic life on human beings wholly dependent on them. Some such there were, possibly not many; nor is it certain that the plains have been continuously inhabited since Big Game times.

For those who·followed the buffalo exclusively, the rewards were

Wichita women thatching a 'grass-house', the typical dwelling of the semi-agricultural Caddoan tribes of the southern Plains.

adequate but the cost in effort very high. Most people in aboriginal days preferred to be part-time buffalo hunters, making periodic sorties from permanent villages on the western edge of the Woodlands or the tall-grass prairies. Others ventured up the Missouri and its tributaries, carrying maize cultivation far out into the plains along the more sheltered river bottomlands. Hopewell-inspired peoples were there for some centuries around the beginning of the Christian era, withdrawing possibly because of climatic changes. In the south, tribes speaking Caddoan languages, old neighbours of the Natchez, pushed into eastern Texas, raising their great beehive houses of thatch among their scattered cornfields. Other Caddoans moved north to the Upper Republican River and built large rectangular houses of poles and brushwood covered with packed earth. Later the square houses would become circular, while retaining a square foundation. From the upper Woodlands, Algonkian and Siouan peoples edged or were nudged westward. Maize, squash and beans were still their mainstay, but once or twice a year everyone fit to travel moved out to the buffalo range. Men were the hunters, women and dogs the transport. For shelter a small skin tent was carried, its light poles dragged by the dogs. Buffalo robes for wearing were best taken around February, the best meat in autumn when the beasts were fat from a summer's grazing.

It will be clear by now that the aboriginal population of America was anything but static. If we take a roll-call of tribes along the eastern periphery of the plains at about A.D. 1600 we shall need to start near Lake Winnipeg, with the Cree hunters and fishermen and their close congeners the Ojibwa. Then, from Minnesota southward and more or less in order, we shall meet the Sioux or Dakota (wild rice and a little maize), the Ponca, Pawnee, Omaha, Iowa, Oto, Missouri, Kansa or Kaw, Osage and Quapaw, and finally the related Wichita and Caddo. All these farm at least some of the time. Between them and the coast live the Tonkawa, Atakapa and Karankawa. The Tonkawa and Atakapa eat a lot of buffalo, the Karankawa a lot of fish, and all three of them, by reliable report, ate a lot of other tribesmen. It was indeed their reputation for cannibalism which helped to spark off the massacre of half the surviving Tonkawa by other Indians in 1862.

Once again there are agricultural outliers, in earthlodge villages strung out along the high west bank of the Missouri: first the Caddoan Arikara (Ree), then the Siouan Mandan, and where the river bends west the Hidatsa or Minitari, also Siouan.

What of the plains proper? Northwestwards to the foothills of the Rockies roam the Blackfoot, planting nothing except ceremonial tobacco and fighting the Shoshoni in formal infantry battles from behind big shields. Wandering out of the mountains come the Comanche and Kiowa, perhaps preceded by the various Apache groups from the Athapaskan north. The total human population is perhaps 136,000.

The Coming of the Medicine Dog

In 1540–42 the plains resounded to a noise that had been absent for several thousand years: the thunder of horses' hooves. The horses belonged to the expedition of Francisco Vázquez de Coronado, and it is unlikely that any of them strayed. When in 1603 Spanish colonization began in earnest along the Rio Grande, Indians were forbidden the use of horses, but neither horses nor Indians are utterly docile. Horses escaped, Indians raided. By about 1640 the southern Apache were mounted and soon afterwards the Kiowa were trading horses to the Wichita and Pawnee. Beyond the mountains the Ute shuttled horses north via the Shoshoni to the sagebrush plains of Oregon and Washington, to the Nez

Percé and to the Cayuse, whose name became a synonym for 'pony'. The Comanche, pushed out into the plains about 1700, proceeded to build a reputation as the world's finest light cavalry.

From the south and from the west the equine tide rippled forward. The Mandan and Arikara villages became trading centres through which horses passed to the Sioux and others east of the Missouri. In fact trade boomed, and by the end of the eighteenth century annual intertribal fairs were being held. European goods were the catalyst but the initiative was Indian. On the one hand were horses, and the surplus meat and hides that mounted hunting could provide; on the other, coming through Indian middlemen and alongside the local corn and beans, were cloth, metal goods and particularly guns. Bargaining was helped by the intertribal sign language, whose gestures, being based on actions and shapes, not sounds, enabled speakers of utterly unrelated tongues to converse fluently.

The mounting of the tribes took at least 150 years to complete, but its

Plains Indian dog-travois, a survival from pre-horse days, photographed in the 1870s.

The Plains Indian horse-travois, adapted from the original version drawn by dogs.

effects were profound. Those sixty million buffalo were suddenly transformed from tantalizingly arduous into excitingly easy targets. A herd could now be surrounded and milled into a galloping circle and the choice young cows shot at close range from the saddle. The women, riding with packhorses and horse-travois, could carry off loads of meat and hides vastly in excess of the pack-dog's fifty-pound limit. Wheresoever the buffalo chose to wander, there could man follow – as long as he kept peace with his neighbours, which of course he didn't.

Much as the white men a century later surged west to farm, Indians surged west to escape from farming. Arapaho and Cheyenne, Crow and Teton (Western Sioux or Dakota) abandoned earthlodges and diggingsticks to become full-time hunters. In the north, the Assiniboin ('Stoneys' in Canada) and part of the Ojibwa and Cree forsook the forest margins. The Blackfoot hunters – Blackfoot, Blood and Piegan with their followers the Atsina (Gros Ventres) and Sarsi – grew in power and numbers, humbling their Shoshoni tormentors. Kutenai, Flathead, Nez

Percé and other Plateau tribes regularly rode through the passes to hunt the buffalo. From the back of a horse the plains were seen in a shining new light. Nine tribes at least cut their woodland tethers completely and became exultant nomads.

There should have been food for all and room for all, with an average density of one person to every nine square miles to encourage peaceful coexistence. But that does not seem to be in the nature of the human race. Horses were the key to the new life; possession of many became a matter of prestige, the ability to steal them from other tribes a matter of honour – and a matter for retaliation, for casual killings demanding revenge. There were other causes for rivalry: access to the choicest hunting grounds, and particularly access to white men's trade goods. As early as 1738, the Sieur de la Vérendrye had wintered with the Mandan, and with each decade the trade frontier advanced. The fur companies wanted beaver but were prepared to pay in cloth, metal, powder and liquor for the meat and hides needed to keep their own trappers in the field. Trade channels were often complicated; it was not unknown for a load of beaver pelts to be stolen from one party of white men to be sold to another, and slaves were a useful standby. Considerable numbers of female captives were sold to French Canada before 1759 and later the southern plantations offered a lucrative market. The commerce did not make for intertribal amity; such was the mercurial nature of the Indian that one day's enemies could be next day's allies. And when fashion prescribes the hair of a slain foe as a desirable fringe for leggings, who needs amity?

Life in the Typical Tribes

Of the many tribes who adopted the horse to chase the buffalo, nine have been regarded as most typical of the new Plains culture. They are the Blackfoot, Atsina, Assiniboin, Teton Dakota, Crow, Arapaho, Cheyenne, Kiowa and Comanche. The order is roughly north-south, but tribal locations were none too stable. In the 1870s the Teton were impassioned in claiming the Black Hills as their sacred and immemorial hunting ground, whereas less than a century had, in fact, passed since the first Teton (the Oglalas) set foot there and dispossessed the Kiowa. Furthermore, distance meant little to the Plains Indian, once mounted. Blackfoot from Montana are known to have raided as far south as the Mexican state of Durango.

The basic features of the new Plains culture were full exploitation of the horse and buffalo, whole-time use of the skin tent – the tipi – , the institution of a men's society with disciplinary functions, and the annual sundance. Negative traits were the failure to plant any food crop and the virtual abandonment of pottery. Within this framework there were of course differences between the 'typical' tribes, of language, social patterns, outlook, costume details and artistic preferences. The picture of Plains life which follows must be seen as a composite.

The Plains baby was born in the family tipi, the mother on knees and elbows and grasping two stakes set by her bed. Women relatives would be present but not the father or any other male, except possibly a healer whose dream-power enabled him to assist delivery. His treatment might include singing, incense of sweet-grass (*Hierochloe*), or rubbing the patient with such obstetric specifics as a chewed root or a horned toad. An aunt fed the baby for the first four days, but two days after the birth the mother would pierce the baby's ears with a heated awl and insert greased twigs in the holes. Thereafter the baby spent long hours in a moss-packed buckskin bag laced to a cradle-board from which dangled its navel cord in a quilled or beaded pouch. When it was still a few days old a distinguished warrior might be invited to name it, for a fee payable in horses. The names given, even to girls, were normally cryptic allusions to a past feat in war, and might have belonged to persons now dead. They could be changed several times through life. Flattering female names of the 'Laughing Water' variety were apt to be pet names used alongside the formally given name. The final name-change might take place after death since it was not thought proper, nor very safe, to pronounce the name of the recently deceased.

Childhood was carefree. Chastisement was rare, and a single punishment of water up the nose usually sufficed to cure an infant of wailing, which could alert an enemy. Small boys with small bows made life hell for birds and rabbits. After a buffalo hunt they would seek out lost calves and kill them, giving the hides to the girls to cure. Archery contests were ever popular, and in winter the game of snow-snake, which meant sliding long polished darts as far as possible along a frozen pitch. High spirits were worked off by gangs of boys pelting one another with birds' eggs or mud, or going around from tipi to tipi demanding food to buy off mischief.

The young wore little or nothing, but clothing when they attained it resembled that of their elders. The basic garment for men was the G-string already described; to be caught without it was a cause of acute shame to most Plains males. Next in importance were moccasins, a characteristic Plains type of which had a separate hard sole of rawhide. Soft-soled, one-piece moccasins were also worn. Leggings for men reached the upper thigh as in the Woodlands. Unlike the broad straight tubes of cloth which replaced them, earlier skin leggings were tailored to fit snugly to the leg and those for dress occasions bore horizontal painted stripes and panels of quill- or beadwork along the seam, together with fringes of human or horse hair or thong, wrapped at the base with quill or pericardial tissue. Some had additional skin flaps, short-fringed or perforated, splaying out over the wearer's foot.

An essential item of clothing was the buffalo robe, a whole hide soft-tanned with the hair on, which could be worn with statuesque dignity or huddled into for plain comfort.

Equestrianism probably changed the fashion in men's shirts. In the 1830s many were still wearing a garment reaching to the knees and consisting of two elk (wapiti) or deer skins. Added cape-like sleeves were sometimes but not always seamed along the forearm and wrist. Tailoring became more obvious toward the north where the influence of the tundra-dwellers permeated. The later and more specifically Plains shirt reached only to the hips, in effect forming a sleeved poncho. A pair of bighorn sheep skins made ideal material in size and shape. This garment was sometimes copied in cloth but the more usual substitute for buckskin was the white man's buttoned shirt, civilian or military, worn with the tails outside the belt.

Women wore the short leggings gartered below the knee. The basic dress, like the men's long shirt, consisted of two deer or elk skins sewn together, the animals' legs forming the sleeves. Details of cut varied from tribe to tribe. In the south leggings and a skirt were considered sufficient, with a buffalo robe to cover the shoulders when needed. Best dresses were adorned with pendants of beads, trade thimbles or dentalium shells, and the cape sleeves and yoke covered with quillwork or beads (which latter made them extremely heavy). The most prized decoration comprised rows of elk teeth, sometimes simulated in bone. Long dresses of coloured cloth were similarly decorated later on.

Headgear was generally absent. Men in the north sometimes wore fur toques in winter, and an otterskin hat somewhat like a hussar's shako was popular on the eastern fringe. Eyeshades of rawhide were known. On the high plains men wore their hair long – sometimes artificially lengthened with glued-on tresses. Male hair fashions ranged from the completely unconfined to elaborate arrangements of braids, fringes, sidelocks and cockades. Women's hair, whether braided or worn loose, was generally parted in the middle and the parting line reddened with ochre or vermillion. Feathers worn in the hair – by men only – were usually significant, their number, position, colour and decoration

This Wichita girl, photographed at Fort Sill, Indian Territory, in about 1870, speaks more clearly for the realities of Plains Indian womanhood than the be-feathered 'princesses' of modern Indian parades.

indicating the wearer's achievements and qualifications. Other objects tied in the hair might be charms and even tallies of successful seductions. Plains men shared with their easterly kin a liking for the roach, a crest of dyed deer hair or turkey beard, sometimes spread out by a carved bone strip, running from crown to nape. Originally secured by a lock of hair pulled through it, in these modern short-haired days it has to be tied on with a string under the chin.

Warbonnets

No beaded headbands? Well, hardly any. Eagle-feather bonnets? Yes, but only for distinguished men. The right to wear what has now become the uniform of any 'real' Indian had to be earned by bravery in war and raid, whence the term 'warbonnet'. The foundation of the bonnet is a skullcap of deer or buffalo skin to which the black-tipped tail feathers of the immature golden eagle are attached by loops at the base, with a thong joining them halfway up to keep them properly aligned. A brow-band decorated with quill, beads or even talons runs from ear to ear where it supports pendant ribbons or ermine strips. Downy feathers may be bound to the base of the plumes, and tufts of dyed horsehair glued to the tips. At the back there may be a long trailer of skin or cloth bearing one or more lines of feathers. A thong under the chin keeps the bonnet from becoming the plaything of the high plains wind.

This form of bonnet is thought to have originated among the Teton, and to belong largely to the horse age. In the early nineteenth century, Plains headgear was much more varied in both form and choice of feathers. Caps of skin might have buffalo horns attached, often with an erect crest of eagle plumes reaching to the heels. The Blackfoot favoured a stiff circlet of plumes springing erect from a wide headband. One horned bonnet collected from the Blackfoot is covered with wing, body and down feathers of the eagle and has a wide trailer of scarlet cloth bearing transverse rows of short feathers and brass bells.

The true warbonnet not only recorded valour; it also gave magical protection to the wearer, at the price of some taboo. The Cheyenne chief Roman Nose had a bonnet whose supernatural efficacy depended on his not eating any food touched by metal. While beleaguering Forsyth's troops at Beecher's Island in 1868 he learned that he had been served with meat taken from the fire with an iron fork. Knowing he was to die, he charged repeatedly into the soldiers' volleys until cut down.

In some tribes a man had to trap his own eagles and release them unharmed except for a plucked tail. The Hidatsa method was to hide in a shallow pit beneath a screen of brushwood with a bait of dead meat on top. When the noble bird, betrayed by its plebeian taste for carrion, stooped to the lure it was grasped from below. In view of the size and power of the golden eagle's beak and talons, and predictable reluctance to part with its steering gear, the days of fasting and purification imposed on the trapper may well have been good for nerves as well as external lesions. Not all tribes were averse to killing eagles, but even so, trapping was less frustrating than archery with an aerobatic target.

The Vision Quest

Here too young men sought spirit helpers by means of the vision quest. Stripped and perhaps painted with white clay, the youth would wail and pray for days on end in a lonely place. He might have to lop off a

Teton Dakota (Sioux) sweat-lodge with cover raised, Rosebud Reservation, South Dakota, 1898. Steam was produced by sprinkling water on heated stones passed in from outside. Sweating as a means of ritual purification was wellnigh universal in North America.

finger joint or sacrifice other pieces of his own flesh before the spirits vouchsafed a significant dream. Further vigils might be undertaken throughout life, although revelatory dreams might occur spontaneously. The consistent patterning of such dreams need surprise no one unduly, given the cultural conditioning of the dreamers and the capacity of the human memory to turn dream images into recognizable forms.

Girls did not seek visions. At puberty they were spared the long seclusion suffered by girls in some other less mobile areas. Their days were spent in learning by doing the tasks of the older women, although as Plains affluence increased there was some tendency to pamper them before marriage. Women's work included dressing hides and making them into tipi covers, clothing, moccasins and containers; making sewing-thread from the long back sinews of deer and buffalo; cooking the meat killed by the menfolk, or drying and pounding it with wild cherries into pemmican; berry-picking and root-digging in season; and decorating best clothes, pouches, saddles, cradles – in fact almost anything made of skin or rawhide – with quillwork, beads or paint. Paint was used particularly on rawhide parfleches, the long, flat envelopes in which pemmican was sealed, and on the inside/skin-side of buffalo robes. Designs were geometrical or abstract; the narrative strip paintings of battle exploits were done by the warriors themselves.

Skin-dressing

Skins to be dressed were pegged to the ground or laced on a frame and all traces of flesh removed with a stone scraper. An adze-like tool of horn with a flint blade was then used to reduce the hide to an even thickness. For rawhide the work stopped there. For 'buckskin' the hide was thoroughly rubbed with a mixture of brains, liver, ashes, fat and sometimes soapweed before being soaked in water. Pulling, stretching and further friction were needed before the skin became fully pliable. Dehairing was done in the same way as fleshing, or else with a sort of spokeshave with the hide placed over a log.

From eleven to twenty buffalo cow skins went into a tipi cover. For such a major task women cooperated under the direction of a skilled lodge-maker, and were afterwards feasted by the owner. Tipi poles, for which excursions were made to the pine-clad hills, were cut by the men, but the erection of the tipi was wife's work. Three or four poles, according to tribe, were lashed together a few feet from the tips and raised as a foundation. Other poles were propped against them and the cover hoisted on the last pole, to be pulled round and secured down the front with wooden pegs. Two ear-like flaps, each supported by a free pole at its outer corner, could be manipulated to control draught and the smoke from the fire within. Pegs or stones held down the lower edges of the cover, and the floor might be slightly excavated to leave a bench, and padded with grass. Decorated skin curtains were hung from the poles inside to insulate the lower level. Beds of robes were ranged round the wall, and back-rests made of willow rods bound mat-like and supported by a tripod. The place of honour was at the back of the tipi facing the doorway, and a strict etiquette governed seating arrangements and the manner of entering.

Marriage

There was considerable variation among Plains tribes as to the availability of marriage partners. Both matrilineal and patrilineal clans existed but the rule against marriage within the clan was not always enforced, and the system may have been in process of breaking down. Courting was at least outwardly discreet. Young men would seize a chance to talk with girls fetching water or berry-picking, and would serenade the chosen with simple wooden flutes. Gossip was to be avoided, but after dark both sexes were known to scratch on the tipi wall nearest the loved one's bed. Elopements were not rare, but the 'best' form of marriage involved the giving of horses to the bride's parents, often reciprocated with a substantial dowry. Divorce was a simple matter of one party throwing the other out, but a high proportion of marriages remained stable. Polygamy was general, and increased sharply in the horse era: the more successful a hunter, the more wives he needed to process his kill for the traders. Instances of one man having thirty wives have been recorded from the Blackfoot. Ideally, a man married his first wife's sisters as they matured.

Chastity was everywhere esteemed, but the Cheyenne women's success in maintaining it was a source of wonderment to other tribes. While a man was expected to indulge his fancy, and wife-stealing and even wife-lending were institutionalized, adultery was traditionally punished by cutting off the erring wife's nose.

There were some men, not only on the plains, who felt unequal to the muscular role of warrior. For such there was no intermediate road: they adopted women's clothing and performed women's tasks, and even had certain ceremonial responsibilities assigned to them. They are usually known by the term *berdache*, and they caused the missionaries no end of soul-searching.

Warfare

Training for war began at an early age but a youth on his first war party was seldom more than camp cook and handyman. The prime motives for war were personal glory, the capture of horses, and revenge. Slaughter could be indiscriminate on a vengeance raid but all-out extermination was seldom envisaged. Horses were needed for the prestige accruing from the ability to distribute large numbers of them to the less fortunate. But the highest prestige of all came from the accumulation of war honours, to be publicly recited at feasts. Such honours were quite specifically graded on something akin to a points system. Tribes differed as usual but in all cases the criterion was deliberate courting and cheating of death. Thus to touch an enemy with the bare hand or the butt of a weapon – to 'strike a coup' – was more honourable than merely to kill him, which could be done at long range. (The merit of touching a dead enemy is less obvious.) Capturing a gun, being wounded, taking a scalp, and stealing a picketed horse undetected were other exploits leading to public regard and in some cases qualifying for political leadership.

War parties were commonly initiated by an individual, with or without the backing of a dream. If he had none of his own he invited the possessor of a pipe of known spirit power to lead the expedition. With the sanction of the elders the party would set out, with a woman, a boy or a berdache for fatigue duties. War regalia were carried in rawhide cases. Horse stealers usually departed on foot in expectation of riding home; extra moccasins were always taken, together with rations of pemmican. Arms included the vicious Plains warclub, with its egg-shaped stone head held fast to a flexible stem by shrunk rawhide. Surprise was always the aim: to get away with the horses before the loss was discovered, or if scalps were needed, to catch some isolated traveller or lodge unawares. Real fighting might come with pursuit or a miscalculation of the enemy's numbers. Some tribes had permanent breastworks of stones or logs on debated ground to which warriors could retreat if pressed. Casualties were to be avoided, except by world-weary 'Crazy Dogs' who had announced their intention to die, and even they could be rescued without disgrace. Prisoners stood a chance of adoption, although unceremonious torture might be prompted by anger. Corpses were mutilated if time allowed. Warriors returning from a successful raid donned their finery and painted themselves before making a formal entry into the village, to the eulogies of their womenfolk. It was the women who danced the scalps.

An important feature of Plains life was membership of a men's society. Depending on tribe, the society might be simply a voluntary club or one of a graded series embracing all males between certain ages. After, say, four years each age group would buy out the songs, privileges and responsibilities of the next older group who in turn would take over from their seniors, the group at the top retiring altogether. While the maintenance of public order, especially on communal hunts and migrations, was generally entrusted to one such society, others had privileges bordering on the disorderly such as stealing the wives of rival clubs; the husband who took his wife back again was ridiculed and disgraced. Each society had its own etiquette, insignia and obligations, sometimes extending to suicidal bravery in war.

Sacred Bundles

The concept of the medicine bundle, the pack of venerated symbols of supernatural power, extended up to tribal level. The Cheyenne had their four Sacred Arrows, periodically exposed to every male – but not one female – in the tribe in a complex four-day ceremony. In other tribes there were bundles with special powers that were privately owned and passed from owner to heir, or acquired by purchase. Custody or ownership of these bundles was not to be lightly entered upon, involving as it did the learning of endless songs and ritual minutiae.

Political organization was loose. The unit we have called a tribe normally included all the people speaking a common language, ranging in population from a very few hundreds to a very few thousands. Tribes with closely related dialects might be affiliated in larger groupings: for instance the Blackfoot Confederacy, comprising Blackfoot proper (Siksika), Blood (Kaina), and Piegan. Likewise the western division of the Sioux – the Teton (*Titõwã*, 'Plains-dwellers'), embracing the Oglala, Hunkpapa, Blackfeet (Sihasapa), Brulé, Sans Arcs, Miniconjou and Two Kettles. The word Dakota (locally Lakota) means 'allies'.

Problems of game supply and pasture for horses made it impracticable for large groups to camp together for long, and for much of the year tribes lived subdivided into bands. A band might consist of a few related families or of unrelated followers of a particular leader. The most formal tribal government was that of the Cheyenne, with a council of forty-four representing ten bands. It was usual to separate the functions of war chiefs and peace chiefs. The structure was democratic – sometimes in practice nearing the anarchic – but, inevitably, strong personalities arose from time to time capable of dominating affairs over a very long span. This tendency was strengthened in the emergency conditions of resistance to the white man.

Summer Buffalo Hunt and Sundance

The season for tribal assemblies was summer, with the great communal buffalo hunt and the sun dance. From about June to September the bands, each in its allotted place, camped in one great circle. It was the time for horse racing, gambling on dice and hidden-counter games, feasting, boasting, courting and visiting. The hunt, as has been said, was closely supervised by the police societies; any premature disturbance of the herds was likely to be punished by destruction of the offender's tipi or worse. Summer skins were good for tipis and the young beasts were prime for meat. But there was no part of the buffalo that was not put to use. An authority on the Blackfoot has listed eighty-eight non-food commodities extracted from the animal, from shields to sledges, water-buckets to glue. The great annual hunt may have had its origin in an earlier communal antelope (pronghorn) drive. It has to be said that the ingenuity displayed in exploiting the buffalo was not matched by foresight. Sheer plenty bred improvidence and as early as the 1830s George Catlin was predicting the extermination of the vast herds.

When the berries were ripe the sundance preparations were coming to fruition. This great ceremony of renewal and prayer for blessing, possibly Teton in origin, spread to many other tribes in the nineteenth century. Although sponsored by one individual (usually vowed during a crisis) its staging required the cooperation of men's and women's societies and practitioners with special knowledge of rituals too complex to be detailed here. The focal point was a sacred tree trunk, 'captured' like an enemy and erected at the centre of a circular skeleton lodge of poles and greenery. To the top of the tree a doll was tied, or a rawhide figure sometimes explicitly phallic. In most cases, there were rituals with a sacred bundle. The full ceremony lasted eight days, during which the worshippers gazed towards the sun. A few young men fulfilled vows by doing more. Painted and wreathed, they suffered themselves to be tied to the sacred pole by ropes ending in wooden skewers thrust through the flesh of the chest. Blowing eagle-bone whistles and jerking backwards against the skewers they danced until the flesh gave way – and wore the scars with pride as an assurance of divine blessing honourably won. This feature as much as the affirmation of tribal solidarity led to suppression of the sundance in reservation days but it has since been revived in a modified form. In recent years even the self-

Canadian Blackfoot sun-dancer fulfilling a vow. Gazing constantly at the sun he will jerk against the thongs until the skewers tear out of his chest. Self-torture in this manner was a regular but minor feature of the great annual Sun Dance.

torture has become permissible.

Purification essential to this and other ceremonies was achieved in the low, domed sweat-lodge. Heated stones or clay balls were passed inside and water sprinkled over them. The steam bath was customarily associated with prayer, but like smoking it could be enjoyed simply for relaxation.

Death

The brief flowering of the 'typical' Plains culture was a heyday for the young. Old age was respected and grandparents were important in a child's upbringing, but physical immobility in a highly mobile society was a grave impediment. Young men were constantly told that it was better to die in battle than to wither. Victims of the realities of nomad life, the infirm could without reproach be left beside the trail, or quickly killed by a son. Otherwise death was an occasion for ostentatious grief, widows cropping hair and finger joints and gashing limbs. In the absence of trees it was usual to bind the corpse to a high scaffold beyond the reach of coyotes. A horse and perhaps a dog might be killed at the grave. Funerary operations were prompt, for the souls of the dead were known to seek company for the final journey.

The Village Tribes

The Plains way of life was infectious and might, undisturbed, have lured more tribes out of the mountains and plateaus of the west. The drift to nomadism from the Woodlands may have stopped spontaneously. The Mandan, Hidatsa and Arikara in their earthlodges on the Missouri had the best of both worlds, until smallpox reduced them to a tenacious handful.

The Mandan had been sedentary plainsmen for several centuries. The sundance did not attract them; they had their own annual ceremony, the *okipa*, centred also on a sacred tree trunk. This one however stood permanently in a wood-walled enclosure in the village. The self-torture of young men here involved hanging from the rafters of the lodge by skewers through the chest and shoulders, sometimes with buffalo skulls depending from the flesh for added weight. Phallic symbolism and a period of licence for the increase of the tribe were incorporated in the ceremonial pattern.

Much romantic attention has been lavished on the Mandan because of their supposed Welsh ancestry and their supposed extinction. The

Welsh fantasy has to do with a thirteenth century Prince Madoc who is unknown to history, but has nevertheless been credited with begetting a succession of Indian tribes from the Tuscarora beside the Atlantic to the Modoc (of course!) in California. As for the Mandan, they had some Welsh-like words, and coracles, and some were fair-skinned. But linguists have failed to trace any Celtic element in their Siouan tongue, for all that John Evans from Wales wintered among them in 1796–7; and the circular boat of hide on a withy frame turns up in South America and the Orient as well as in the Principality of Wales and on the Missouri. Nor are fair skins surprising, given the visits of fur traders from the 1770s onward and the Mandan belief in the transmission of power – which the bringers of guns clearly possessed – by sexual intercourse, with one's wife as the intermediary.

From a possible 9,000, the Mandan population shrank tragically under repeated blows from smallpox. After the 1837 epidemic, twenty-three males were left. Reduced to sitting targets for the Tetons, they fought back, adopting men into the tribe to rebuild numbers. United in 1865 in a single village with the Hidatsa and Arikara, they preserved their autonomy. The *okipa* continued to be celebrated up to 1888, and the language was still spoken twenty years ago or even later. It is none the less true that not one *full-blood* Mandan remains.

The Morning Star Sacrifice

Exotic origins are not attributed to the Skidi band of the Pawnee down-river in Nebraska, descended locally from the Morning Star and his bride the Evening Star. Yet details of their most spectacular rite are unequivocally Mexican, possibly learned from itinerant Aztec traders about the time of Columbus. Periodically, a Skidi warparty would raid an enemy camp and there seize a maiden of thirteen or fourteen. For months the girl lived in her captor's lodge, kindly treated and given (ostensibly) no inkling of her destiny. One spring morning she was led out, stripped, the left half of her body painted red for day and the other black for night, and tied by wrists and ankles to an upright frame. As the Morning Star rose, one priest lightly touched her in armpit and groin with a burning torch, another drove an arrow through her heart, and a third drew blood with a flint knife. Then every male old enough to pull a bow was urged to shoot into the body. Thereafter the people went home to dance and sing and beget, and the ravaged corpse was left face down in a lonely place to fertilize the earth.

In 1816, the girl was plucked from the very scaffold by Pita-risaru

Petalésharo (Pita-risaru, Man Chief), leader of the Asking-for-Meat band of
the Skidi Pawnee, photographed in 1858. He is believed to be the Man Chief
who in 1817 rescued the Comanche girl from the Sacrifice to the Morning
Star.

(Petalesharo, 'Man Chief'), son of the principal chief of the Skidi. His deed was much acclaimed in the USA, but sacrifices are known to have continued until 1837 at least.

The Road to the Little Bighorn and Beyond

Built up on hunting and warfare, the Plains culture fought and lost a thirty-year running battle to survive. The Indian wars are fully and variously recorded and can only be summarized here. The story begins in the south with the determination of the Texas Republic to rid itself of Comanche, Kiowa and Lipan marauders; Texas would become one of the United States before that aim was achieved. Further north the solution proposed was to set aside generous areas as permanent Indian hunting grounds, with right of passage only for white men migrating to Oregon and California. The policy led to a succession of optimistic and untenable treaties, signed on the one hand by Indians incapable of taking in the small print and on the other by officials incapable of comprehending the limitations of chiefly authority. The decisive factor was really the advance of European technology. Railroads and telegraphs, wind-pumps, wire and mechanical reapers exploded the myth of the Great American Desert, just when landless immigrants were pouring across the Atlantic in their millions. There was constant pressure on government to reduce the size of reservations, not only from small settlers and large investors but also from the Quakers who directed Indian administration for a decade under President Grant's Peace Policy. The white man acted within his culture no less than did the Indian, and clash was unavoidable. Local outrages by both sides led to retaliation and the Army had the job of restoring peace by curbing the Indian side. It is popular today to cast the US Cavalry as the villain of the piece – which does scant justice to the thousands of miles tramped over burning or icy plains by the US Infantry. And while the commanders had a lethal job to do, it is on record that many of them respected the Indians more than they did the Washington officials. As for casualties, an analysis of what is known indicates that between 1789 and 1898 the Army killed 4,000 Indians for the loss of 7,000 soldiers and civilians. These figures do not take account of the toll of disease and malnutrition.

As European pressure mounted, the Indians continued to resist in uncoordinated efforts, which confused the issues and sometimes led to bands being attacked and slaughtered for raids they had not committed. Some Indian leaders of stature emerged. Red Cloud of the Oglala secured the withdrawal from army posts built on treaty land, but later lost influence by bowing to the inevitability of change. The enigmatic Crazy Horse, also an Oglala, proved his military genius at the Little Bighorn and elsewhere. Sitting Bull, a Hunkpapa, was a warrior in his own right but also a dreamer and politician. He it was whose prestige and determination rallied the largest assembly of Plains Indians ever to come together. This took place in the summer of 1876 beside the river which Indians call the Greasy Grass, and white men the Little Bighorn.

All the Teton divisions were there, with Cheyenne and Arapaho allies.

Red Cloud (1822–1909), a war leader and statesman of the Oglala Dakota. He secured the abandonment of Army posts and a proposed road to the Montana goldfields, but kept peace after the Fort Laramie Treaty of 1868.

Their purpose was to hold a sundance and hunt buffalo, and to show contempt for a government order to withdraw within reservation boundaries or be treated as hostile. A massive military operation was set up to discipline them, under General Terry. The main column advanced up the Missouri and Yellowstone rivers by steamboat, to join forces with General Crook and Lieutenant-Colonel Custer in a converging movement. Crook ran into Crazy Horse on the Rosebud River and was fought to a standstill. Custer foreshortened his march and came upon the great village two days ahead of the main force. Ignoring the omens read by his Crow and Arikara scouts, he split his command into four parts and attacked. In the interval between lunchtime and tea on that Sunday afternoon of June 25 the matter was concluded. By evensong the flanking and support troops, less 57 dead, were penned helplessly on the river bluffs, while beyond their sight the squaws were stripping the 208

Sitting Bull (1831–90), a chief of the Hunkpapa band of the Teton Dakota and spiritual leader of the Indian forces who destroyed Custer's column on the Little Bighorn River in 1876.

corpses of Custer's own detachment and using their skinning knives to sign them with the tribal autographs.

Next day the hung-over camp broke up and bands drifted away, some to hunt, some to skirmish, some to surrender. Crazy Horse was to die next year, bayoneted in an army guardroom. Sitting Bull with several thousand followers moved slowly to Manitoba and placed himself in the care of the Great Mother (Queen Victoria) and Superintendent Walsh of the North-West Mounted Police. Five years later he brought up the rear of a straggle back to the USA, toured the States with Buffalo Bill Cody's Wild West, and settled to an apparently quiet reservation life.

In 1877–78, the Cheyenne under Dull Knife and Little Wolf fought their way north in a tragic bid to escape from an unhealthy reservation in Indian Territory. In the fall of 1877, the Nez Percé under Joseph broke into the plains from Idaho at the end of their brilliant struggle to reach Canada, only to be frustrated thirty miles from sanctuary. In the cities, leather manufacturers found a way of dealing with the heavy hide of the buffalo bull, hitherto unsaleable. The white hunters moved in, and by 1875 the southern herd was gone, and by 1884 the northern. The Indian was on government rations: stringy range cattle driven to the agencies to be 'hunted' in a wry mockery of the old way. A little horse raiding still went on but there would be no more battles. Indian agents, politically appointed, were a mixed lot, the idealists hardly less troublesome to the Indians than the profiteers. Boredom was a worse enemy than semi-starvation to the demobilized warriors. Until a will-o'-the-wisp glimmered in the west.

Ghost Dance

Around 1870, a Paiute Indian named Tävibo prophesied a Second Coming in which the Indians would inherit an Indian earth. In the 1880s the same basic revelation was granted during an eclipse to Wóvoka, who may have been Tävibo's son. The new prophet was a hard-working, married ranch hand known also by his employer's name, Jack Wilson; later he dropped his Paiute name Wovoka, 'Cutter', in favour of his grandfather's more sonorous Kwohitsauq, 'Big Rumbling Belly'. The redemption he taught was open to all believers who danced in the sedate manner prescribed in his vision. The doctrine spread both west and east, with varying success. The Plains Indians, avid now for a messiah, raised train fares for several delegations to Nevada. On their way back to Dakota Territory something happened to the once conciliatory doctrine. Christ, rejected by the white men, would now sweep them all away. The

Arapaho Ghost Dance shirt with sacred turtle and other symbols. The
Dakota version of the 'ghost shirt' was believed to make the wearer
invulnerable, an idea possibly derived from the 'endowment robe' of the
Mormons.

buffalo and the dead would return to eternal life in an Indian elysium.
Men and women must dance, shuffling hand in hand in a great circle
until the favoured collapsed in trance, to receive visions of their own. No
matter if the military objected; shirts of buckskin or flour-sacking,
painted with dreamed designs, would make the wearers invulnerable.
The sceptical and the far-sighted stayed at home. The hopeful and the
desperate, including some ten per cent of the Teton, danced.

White farmers and townsmen of the New West panicked and called
for troops. The Government bumbled. Buffalo Bill Cody left his circus to
get in on the act. The inscrutable Sitting Bull quietly encouraged what

was now known as the Ghost Dance. In December 1890, Indian Police were sent to arrest him. Taunted by his own people for apparent surrender he made a defiant gesture and was shot by Lieutenant Bull Head and Sergeant Red Tomahawk. Six police and eight 'hostiles' died in the ensuing melée.

In response to civilian outcry about a general uprising, 3,000 troops were deployed about the Sioux agencies, and an equal number of Indians fled to the Bad Lands to dance. Experienced agents and officers counselled patience until the cold weather should bring them back. The much feared Hump brought his people in and enlisted as a scout. Then occurred one of those ghastly accidents of war which can be made to rumble across the generations.

Wounded Knee

Big Foot's band of Miniconjou, 300 or so strong, took fright and set out to join those who had in fact already left the Bad Lands. Intercepted by a detachment of the 7th Cavalry and 1st Artillery they camped overnight near the post office on Wounded Knee Creek. The aged Big Foot, dying of pneumonia, was given an army tent with a stove and attended by the surgeon. On the morning of December 29, the troops were paraded to disarm the 106 warriors. The medicine man, Yellow Bird, reminded them that their ghost shirts were bullet-proof. A shot was fired, and in the holocaust which followed, over 200 Indians, half of them women and children, and 31 soldiers died. Others died later of wounds. All that can be said is that few of the cavalrymen and gunners could have been in action before, as for a decade there had been no war on the northern plains.

Nor was there now. After one or two inconsequential skirmishes the

Arapaho Ghost-dancers, about 1893.

Sioux War was officially closed on January 16, 1891. The Ghost Dance itself was not so easily killed off. An Arapaho medicine man, confusingly named Sitting Bull, carried it south to the reservations in Indian Territory, now Oklahoma, where, its apocalyptic promise gradually blunted, it survived as a social dance. A new road to spiritual release took over.

Peyote

Peyote (*Lophophora williamsii*) is a small cactus growing along the Mexican border whose flower heads contain several alkaloids, including mescaline. Chewed, they induce nausea followed by feelings of wellbeing and sometimes psychedelic visions. The cult centred on peyote includes no dancing and no belligerence. It blends Indian and Christian elements and quite early secured incorporation in the USA as The Native American Church, despite orthodox opposition. Its moral code is strict and its all-night services unspectacular, with minutely ritualized singing and drumming, prayer and contemplation. Within this century the cult has spread to Canada. It has also given rise to a limited but interesting native industry for the production of ritual feather fans, beaded containers for the peyote buttons (flower heads) and leaders' wands, besides non-sacred jewellery worn by members of the cult for mutual recognition and solidarity.

Chapter 5

Southwest I : The Enduring Pueblos

The Emergence, in Myth and Reality

No ducks dived into primordial waters for mud to make the Zuñis' Earth. These Indians were themselves down, deep down, in the nethermost of the four worlds which make up the Universe, jostling one another in utter darkness. Sun Father, as agent for He/She, the great blue dome that is over us all, sent his two Divine Sons to lead the Zuñis into the light. First using for a ladder a trunk of ponderosa pine cut in the North, they ascended to the Third World; then, by a ladder of Douglas spruce from the West, to the Second World, by an aspen log from the South to the First World, and finally, by a silver spruce from the East, out into this, the World of Daylight. But before the people could enjoy full liberty a cosmetic adjustment had to be performed on them by the Divine Sons with their flint scalpels: the bobbing of their tails, the trimming of their ears (so long that a man could use one for a bed and the other for a coverlet), and the freeing of their webbed toes and fingers. Webbed feet would indeed have been superfluous, for the site of the Zuñis' Emergence, muddy as it is said to have been round the edges, lay in the middle of the arid Southwest.

We have been there before in this book, watching the extermination of mammoth and superbison and man's acceptance of the need to experiment with other food sources. We called this stage the Archaic, and followed its course through the Woodlands. Now we are back once more in time, to follow the aspect of the Archaic known as the Desert Tradition. The Zuñis have long forgotten it, for their own story of their origins brings in the Corn Maidens almost in the first act. Archaeologists must be more prosaic, but their findings are not without drama.

A paradox of Southwestern culture history is that here, in what would seem to be the least fertile area of the continent below the subarctic, arose the only *purely* crop-dependent civilization in northern America.

The Southwest as we shall review it extends from the southern fringes of Utah and Colorado by way of Arizona and New Mexico to an ill-defined fade-out far below the Mexican border. In the north the land lies high – 5,000 feet and more – and is studded with flat-topped, steep-sided mesas, sometimes carved by erosion into fantastic rock cathedrals like those of Monument Valley, beloved of western movie-makers. On the northwestern side the Colorado River flows between the mile-high walls of the Grand Canyon. Other smaller but still spectacular canyons like Chaco and de Chelly guard relics of the People they have sheltered in the past. Annual rainfall here is less than 20 inches, and usually violent. Daily temperatures may range from 0° to 90° Fahrenheit. Conifers grow where they can. The mean altitude declines to around 1,000 feet in southern Arizona, where the Salt and Gila Rivers offer compensation for an annual rainfall of four inches or less and cactus becomes more prominent than pine.

Between the plateau country and the desert, but a little east of centre, is a region of tortuous minor mountain ranges. The sierra christened in honour of an eighteenth century Spanish governor lent its inelegant name, Mogollón – 'sponger' – to one of the three basic Southwestern cultures. The others are the Hohokam and the Anasazi.

Which of these three patterns of living was the first to emerge is the subject of a debate in which we need not join. For three or four thousand years the Southwesterners lived in accordance with the Desert Tradition, gathering seeds and roots and cactus fruits and snaring small game, and dwelling in caves and brush shelters, with basketry as their major plastic craft and art. Regional differences imposed themselves slowly; the distinctive pattern of the Mogollon region becomes recognizable at about 200 B.C. and continues to develop for a dozen centuries. The evidence is widespread, but much of the story can be traced from the record of a single cave, Tularosa in New Mexico. Maize of a rather primitive sort appears to have been cultivated – by no means as a staple – by 2000 B.C., with beans and squash reinforcing the trend towards horticulture a thousand years later. The source of the innovations, possibly indirect, was Mexico, and from there too, about 200 B.C., came pottery.

Pottery, which is virtually indestructible, is the real key to the understanding of Southwestern developments, specializations, and intercommunications. Even fragmentary potsherds can be referred to particular sources on the strength of form, colour, painted or other decoration, and the kinds of clay and tempering medium used. The index of types and variants already classified is vast.

Mogollon

The earliest Mogollon ware was reddish brown: jars and bowls built up from coils of clay, smoothed inside and out and finished with a 'slip' or wash of fine clay before firing. It is from the introduction of pottery that archaeologists begin to date the Mogollon culture as an independent entity. No less important is permanent housing.

The idea of a semi-subterranean dwelling with a log and earth superstructure was not exclusive to the Southwest; we have already met with it along the Missouri. The Mogollon version could be rounded or (more often) roughly squared and sunk three or four feet into the ground, with a long, narrow ramp on the east side for entry. Heavy logs set upright in the pit supported rafters. Smaller logs forming the walls were either set in the pit floor or leant inward from ground level outside it. Brushwood or mats, with an outer layer of earth, completed the building. Sizes varied and arrangement within the village seems to have been random. Villages themselves were small and usually built on defensible ridges. Certain outsize houses suggest communal meeting places, and foreshadow the intricate ceremonialism that goes with the growing of Mother Corn.

The Mogollones walked in wicker sandals, wore kilts or aprons of fibre, probably superseded by cotton cloth, and kept out the cold with blankets of fur strips or netted feathers. Beads and pendants of shell, stone and bone completed the toilet. They planted with the simple wooden digging-stick, and hunted with the bow and arrows as well as the spear-thrower. They played reed flutes, gambled with wooden dice, and smoked tobacco in stone and clay pipes until the ubiquitous Southwestern reed cigarette came in. In basketry as in pottery they widened and refined their skills as time went on. Here as elsewhere the culture did not stand still. And here as elsewhere the environment played its part: living in a relatively well wooded and watered hill country stocked with game and wild food plants, the Mogollones never, as long as they retained their identity, committed themselves wholly to farming. Not so the Hohokam.

Hohokam

Following the Gila River down from its sources in the Mogollon Mountains we come out on the flat, low desert floor of southern Arizona. Here, perhaps a century before the emergence of the Mogollon culture, began the Hohokam. It might be more accurate to say 'arrived', for there are grounds for believing that the Hohokam people – 'Those who have gone' in the modern Pima tongue – may have come in from Mexico, bringing their culture as a going concern. They did not differ greatly from the Mogollones in appearance, dress, or initially in housing. In language they were widely different, but what really set the Hohokam apart was their total commitment to agriculture. This commitment was made expedient by the paucity of wild foods and possible by the Hohokam mastery of irrigation. Tapping the Gila and its tributaries they watered their cornfields through a network of ditches and canals as much as ten miles in length. Without surveying equipment, they managed their levels by the beautifully simple device of letting the water in as they dug: too far down the legs and the channel was too shallow, too high up the body and it was too deep. Everywhere the flow depended on gravity; no pumping gear was known.

The Hohokam increased and flourished, and a settlement pattern new to the Southwest emerged, with some towns and numerous smaller villages. The inference is that a town and its satellites made up a political unit dominated by a single chief. The trend was apparent among the Mississippians but its homeland was Mexico, and there is much evidence that the Hohokam maintained an active Mexican connection. Ball courts appear – great rectangular arenas for the playing of a formalized contest that can perhaps be best likened to basketball. In classical Mexico the 'basket' was a stone ring set high on a wall for the passage of a rubber ball. Balls of rubber – an alien substance in Arizona – have been found in Hohokam sites. Then again we find platform mounds. At ten feet high or less they are no whit as imposing as their Mexican counterparts but undeniably similar in conception. Mexico too must have supplied the macaws which the Hohokam kept as pets, far north of their normal breeding range, and whose brilliant feathers were an important element in the sacred paraphernalia. Whether like others of the parrot tribe these birds learned to take the sacred names in vain we shall never know.

Art and craft burgeoned in a wide variety of stone and bone figurines (wherein the Hohokam artist was happier with animal forms than with human), beads and pendants, and stone palettes resembling small picture-frames with carved rims. Small discs set with pyrites served as mirrors of a sort (remember that 'primitive' man never saw his own face clearly save in still water). Shells were decorated by scratching the design through a coating of wax and etching out the exposed lines with the acid juice of the giant cactus. Cotton was woven on a horizontal loom held taut by a belt round the weaver's hips. But the truest artistic achievement of the Hohokam was in pottery. Characteristic was a form of jar shaped almost like a crinoline, as was also the practice of covering bowls and pots with close ranks of identical painted figures, human or animal.

Anasazi into Pueblo

The third ingredient in the Southwestern mixture originates in the north, where Utah and Colorado, Arizona and New Mexico come together in the high mesa and canyon country known as The Four Corners. We call the culture by its Navajo name of Anasazi, 'The Old Ones'. Under way a little before A.D. 1, the Anasazi grew like the rest out of the Desert Tradition. In many respects it resembled the Mogollon, to which in fact it owed much although the corn it raised was of a different variety. The earliest of the Anasazi peoples are or used to be known as Basket Makers. What distinguished them from the Desert people was the growing of some maize and squash, and, for a couple of centuries, a unique house type. This was a rounded and probably domed structure of logs laid horizontally and chinked with mud. That gave way to the pithouse of other regions; but some time after 750 A.D. the Basket Makers took up pottery (without abandoning baskets) and, more important, began to build above ground, and with stone. They had become Pueblo Indians.

The basic Pueblo house was a rough, rectangular room, built from available stones laid up in adobe (mud) mortar or wholly of sun-dried adobe bricks. Pine-log rafters supported the flat roof of brushwood and puddled adobe. Doorways were small, and some light was admitted through window-panes of translucent selenite. Originally, it is thought, one room served one family. But what the Pueblos had discovered was that modern planner's joy, the accommodation unit. Square rooms with strong walls could be clumped together to house kin groups or clan groups. Better still, one room could be put on top of another, and another on top of that, stepped back in terraces so that one house's front yard was the roof of the house below. The inner rooms of course were dark, but suitable for storage of crops to carry the people through from one season to the next. Since the ground floor rooms might be vulnerable, it was prudent to omit the door and enter them by ladder through a hatchway in the roof.

Now the pit-house, as a dwelling, was obsolete, but as a social and religious centre it survived and was developed. Usually circular, partly or wholly underground, flat-roofed with a hatchway entry, it would serve as a clubroom for members of this or that fraternity or priesthood, or as a closed chamber for the celebration of restricted rituals. The old pit-house ramp or vestibule became a ventilation shaft; and in the floor, in addition to the fire-pit, there would be a hole representing *sipapu*, the opening through which Man emerged into this upper world. Such chambers are now known by the Hopi word *kiva*, although the Spanish term *estufa* (hot-room or stove) will be found in the older literature.

Pueblo in Spanish means a small town, and was aptly used for the Anasazi end-product. Nourished by the generous crop yields ensured by regular summer rains, Anasazi/Pueblo waxed in population, achievement and influence. In fact all three cultures fertilized one another to some extent, and seemed destined to converge. Mogollon and Hohokam pottery styles went north; Anasazi building methods went south. By about 1050 A.D. the Anasazi heartland had many settlements large enough to rival the Hohokam centre we now call Snaketown. One such was Pueblo Bonito, in Chaco Canyon: 'Handsome Town' indeed, consisting of a huge arc of dwellings up to five storeys high. The extremities of the arc were joined by a straight wall to form a **D**, enclosing two plazas and several kivas. Pueblo Bonito had 800 rooms. It

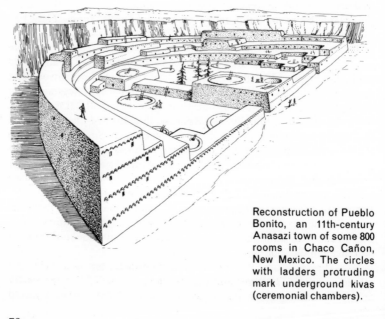

Reconstruction of Pueblo Bonito, an 11th-century Anasazi town of some 800 rooms in Chaco Cañon, New Mexico. The circles with ladders protruding mark underground kivas (ceremonial chambers).

was not unique; ruins of a dozen such towns dot the area. The presence of smaller villages grouped round them suggests the development of tiny states such as had occurred earlier among the Hohokam. But here in the north these tendencies did not survive long enough to produce empires of the Mexican pattern. Anasazi culture rose and spread by grace of a long cycle of favourable growing seasons and the absence of collisions with other human groups. There were vicissitudes, such as Hohokam had been the first to suffer, but at, say, 1000 A.D. the Southwest was supporting a swelling and creative population of farmers, potters, weavers and builders. Sub-cultures reached west towards California (the Patayan) and northwest in Utah (the Fremont). In the centre the Salado and Sinagua variants flourished, the latter particularly after enrichment of the soil following the eruption in the third quarter of the eleventh century of what is now Sunset Crater. Anasazi/Pueblo itself spread eastward into Texas. And then the weather began to change.

There were perhaps too many farmers. Pueblo Bonito presented blank walls to the outside world; entrance was by ladder only. But who was the enemy? Nomadic tribes there certainly were, but probably more parasitic than menacing. It seems likely that pueblo was set against pueblo in rivalry for the shrinking resources of the land. Whatever the threat, the people were driven quite literally up the wall. The great apartment blocks on the canyon floor were abandoned, to be replaced by honeycombs of stone cells high in the cliff faces above them. Wide ledges and shallow cave mouths, once used as shelters by primitive Desert Folk, now became town sites for the Cliff Dwellers. At the classic location of Mesa Verde in southern Colorado the movement was downward as the population left the open top of the plateau to nest like swallows under the eaves.

The cliff-dwelling phase lasted for two or three hundred years, but the contraction of the Anasazi world was not stemmed. By about 1350 A.D. the cliffs were deserted again and the population drained out of the canyons. Some concentrated in the valley of the upper Rio Grande in New Mexico and neighbouring west Texas, some in a small area of mesas in north central Arizona, and some between the two – and there they are today. We shall speak no more of Anasazi, but of Pueblo Indians. Mogollon disappears from the story, leaving only Zuñi Pueblo as its putative descendant. The Hohokam picture is less clear: the chiefdoms certainly collapsed, under pressures which may have included predation by Californian tribes, but the Pima farmers who still live in the area and their Pápago kinsmen in Sonora are generally believed to carry on an attenuated version of Hohokam culture.

Coronado and After

Historical Pueblo Indians have seats in their trousers, wear woollen blankets and silver jewellery, own sheep and donkeys, grow peaches and peppers and live, many of them, in villages named after Spanish saints. Obviously there is a European element in contemporary Pueblo culture. To assess its impact we had best run through 'recent' history.

Word of the Pueblos – hearsay at that – first reached the outside in 1536, borne by Álvar Núñez Cabeza de Vaca and his three companions. Sole survivors of the disastrous Narváez expedition to Florida, they had spent eight years wandering overland to Mexico. They had heard, they said, of seven great cities in a province called Cíbola, waiting to reward the conquistador with a harvest of gold and the missionary with a harvest of souls. A French-born Franciscan, Marcos de Niza (Nice), who had watched the looting of Peru and garrotting of the Inca Atahuallpa, was sent north to reconnoitre. His guide was Esteban, a Barbary negro

A Zuñi Pueblo ceremony in the 1880s. Music is supplied by the singers, left centre, and drummer, far right.

who had been with Cabeza de Vaca. On a day in May, 1539, Esteban, sent ahead with a considerable harem accumulated along the way, entered the Zuñi pueblo of Háwikuh. His importunings did not please the Zuñis who, according to a tradition of their own, dispatched him into outer darkness with one almighty kick, presumably from a rooftop. His widows fled back to the waiting friar and he, after a distant glimpse of the pueblo, forced-marched himself home to Mexico City and confirmed the optimistic reports.

Next year Francisco Vázquez de Coronado led a major expedition north. First contact, briefly hostile, was made at Háwikuh. Then, while detachments ranged east and west from the buffalo plains to the Grand Canyon, the main army marched to the Río Grande pueblos, there to be imprisoned by snow through the winter of 1540–41. When the inevitable flare-up came 200 Indians were condemned to burn at the stake; half of them died by the sword, resisting. The Pueblos tried another tactic and sent Coronado off to seek the glittering kingdom of Gran Quivira. Months later, somewhere in the grassy wastes of Nebraska, Coronado strangled his guide and gave up. In 1542 the expedition departed, treasureless, leaving behind some friars marked for early martyrdom and a lively Indian distaste for the Hairy-Mouths.

The Pueblo Revolt

Serious occupation began sixty years later with the arrival of Juan de Oñate, bringing colonists of Spanish, Mexican Indian and mixed blood. The Pueblos' lands were respected but not their consciences. The Franciscans built churches in most of the pueblos and imposed harsh punishments for non-attendance, and harsher still for any manifestations of native religion. The Pueblos, who already had a full and absorbing ritual calendar, were prepared to add catholic forms but not to drop their own. Floggings and burnings failed to cow them; at dawn on August 10, 1680, most of the Pueblos and some of the mixed-blood colonists set about the slaughter of their oppressors. Over 400 Spaniards were killed, including most of the missionaries. The 2,000-odd survivors mustered in Santa Fe and fought off besiegers, inflicting almost as many casualties as they had themselves suffered, until allowed to flee south to El Paso. The Indians systematically stripped out all signs of Christianity and for twelve years New Mexico knew no white man. Diego de Vargas achieved a piecemeal reconquest in 1692–94 and the colonists returned. So did the Church, but with less appetite, or capacity, for repression. In return for greater tolerance, the Rio Grande Pueblos adopted a process of 'compartmentalization' which allowed them to operate at least the externals of Christian practice alongside their own sacred observances. There arose too some interchange of population, with Pueblo servants, as well as individuals or families who rejected Pueblo social discipline, being absorbed into the colonial community and some colonists marrying into the Pueblos. Both groups had a continual leavening of 'wild' Indians – Apache, Navajo, and southern Plains – traded in as slaves, usually by the Comanches. In 1776 the going rate for a strong girl of 12–20 years was two horses and a cape; less for a lad. Eventually whole villages were established for ex-captives, who were termed Jenízaros ('Janizaries' in Anglo-Turkish).

Among the remote Hopi in the west the pueblo of Awátobi alone came back to the Christian fold, and was totally destroyed by its neighbours. Spanish influence has remained minimal among the Hopi, one of whose pueblos, Hano, was built by Rio Grande refugees from the reconquest and still speaks its alien language, Tewa.

As Spain's imperial impetus declined New Mexico became more and more a political and social backwater, a condition not greatly affected by the change of sovereignty to Mexico in 1821 and to the USA in 1846. In fact the Pueblo world was left pretty much to itself until the latter part of the nineteenth century when the anthropologists and the artists began to move in, and the Government to fret about education. Secure on lands sealed to them first by the Spanish crown, feeding themselves on their own crops, and fighting only as auxiliary troops against the raiding nomads, the Pueblos had no pressing need of white interference. They have had it, of course, but have none the less retained their identity more successfully than almost any other Indian group in North America.

Integrity might be a better word than identity, for the Pueblo Indians, although conforming to one general pattern, are not identical. The description which follows is something of a composite. It stresses the traditional aspect but much of it remains true at the present day.

The Modern Pueblos

The Pueblos speak six mutually unintelligible languages: Hopi, Zuñi, Keres, and the Tanoan group of Tiwa, Tewa and Towa. Each pueblo is a self-contained unit, which elsewhere would be called a tribe; culturally they divide into western and eastern groups. Over all they number around 35,000 souls, more than three times the total for 1900, half as many as the Spaniards found in 1600, and a mere fraction of the presumed population in the Golden Age of the twelfth century.

Southwest I: The Enduring Pueblos

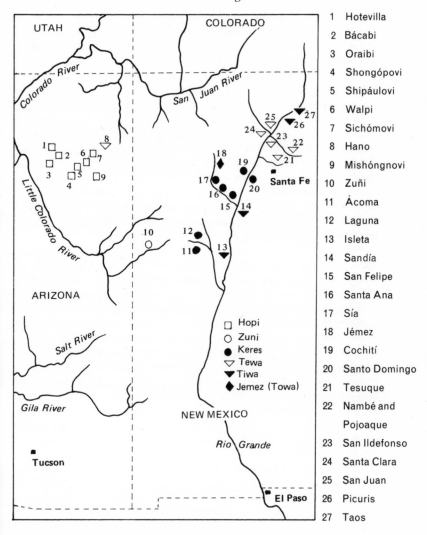

1   Hotevilla
2   Bácabi
3   Oraibi
4   Shongópovi
5   Shipáulovi
6   Walpi
7   Sichómovi
8   Hano
9   Mishóngnovi
10 Zuñi
11 Ácoma
12 Laguna
13 Isleta
14 Sandía
15 San Felipe
16 Santa Ana
17 Sía
18 Jémez
19 Cochití
20 Santo Domingo
21 Tesuque
22 Nambé and
    Pojoaque
23 San Ildefonso
24 Santa Clara
25 San Juan
26 Picuris
27 Taos

The present-day pueblos. Bacabi and Hotevilla date from 1906–7; some other recent outposts are not shown.

The western pueblos comprise the Hopi and the Zuñi. The Hopi, earlier known as Moqui (Moki*), live in nine pueblos built on three lobes of a mesa in northern Arizona. One of them is the Tewa village of Hano mentioned above, which now differs only in speech. Two overspill settlements lie on the desert floor below and a third (Moenkopi) forty miles to the west. Zuñi – 'Cíbola' – is now concentrated into a single large and rambling pueblo on a low hill, just inside the New Mexican border.

The eastern pueblos dot the Rio Grande valley for a distance of 130 miles. Taos and Picurís in the north, and Sandía and Isleta in the south, speak Tiwa. Between them are the Tewa-speaking Pojoaque, Tesuque, Nambé, San Ildefonso, Santa Clara, San Juan; the single Towa pueblo of Jémez; and the Keresan block comprising Santa Ana, San Felipe, Santo Domingo, Cochití and Sía. Between east and west, culturally as well as geographically, stand Ácoma, high on its mesa-top, and Laguna. Both speak Keres. Several pueblos have outstations for seasonal use, where a few families may stay all year.

Western pueblos are built of stone, sometimes faced with adobe mud. Some two- and three-storey houses survive, but with enemy raids no longer a peril ground-floor doors have tended to replace the old ladder and hatchway access. Ceremonial kivas are rectangular and may be subterranean or merely inner ground-floor rooms.

Along the Rio Grande adobe (unbaked) bricks, refaced annually with adobe plaster, are the building material. The north block at Taos rises to five storeys but single-storey houses are commoner nowadays. Characteristic are the projecting log beams (*vigas*) from which hang festoons of corn-cobs and chili peppers drying in the sun. Chimneys are made of old cooking pots with the bottoms burnt out, fitted one above another and mortared with adobe. Large domed ovens, smoothly plastered and closed with a stone slab, are much in evidence outside the houses, where they sometimes double as dog kennels. (An American origin has been suggested for them, but identical ovens can be seen round the western Mediterranean.) A golden eagle, kept for its sacred feathers, may languish in or on a crude cage.

Living-rooms are usually whitened with gypsum, and have a low built-in bench round the walls. Interior doors from room to room make a secure warren in case of siege. An essential furnishing is the set of grinding stones. The grinding surface is a sandstone slab, called a *metate*,

---

*Beware the Smoki Indians, who dress up and dance each summer at Prescott, Arizona. They are local white businessmen but photographs of them have deceived at least one unwary editor.

Taos Pueblo, New Mexico: Klauuma, the five-storey north block. Groundfloor doors are almost the only visible modern feature, although domed ovens (in the right foreground) may be a Spanish introduction.

set at an angle in a shallow bin. The womenfolk kneel behind the raised end of the metate and grind the maize with a stone muller (*mano*) propelled with both hands. The fineness of the meal depends on the roughness of the stone used; metates for three different grades are normally set side by side. Other amenities will be a low stool or two, a suspended pole to hang things on, and wall niches for cupboards. The earthen or flagged floor serves as table and bed.

The people tend to be shortish (5 ft. 4 in.) and stocky, the natural roundness of their heads accentuated by pressure of the cradle-board in infancy. Sedentary life allows plumpness in the ladies. Mildness of expression is assiduously cultivated – an ideal which we will hear more about later. Basic oboriginal clothing for men was a cotton kilt or a G-string. Both are still worn for ritual or chasing rabbits, but the everyday

Dancers resting at Jémez Pueblo, in 1903. They hold gourd rattles and evergreen foliage and wear a grey fox-skin at the back of the kilt.

dress in most of the Pueblo area consists of a cotton shirt worn outside cotton trousers and girt with a bright yarn sash or a leather belt set with oval silver *conchas*. The trousers are wide and short, slit below the knee on the outer side. Footwear is a hard-soled moccasin with a soft brown upper fastened at the ankle with a silver button. Gaiters of soft brown skin are frequently wrapped round the calves and gartered below the knee. Hair may be bobbed all round but is more often grown long at the back and tied into a club while side-locks are cut level with the mouth. It may be fringed – 'banged' – over the brow. Silver, turquoise and shell jewellery complete the costume, but for extra warmth or dignity a wool blanket is worn, either Pueblo-made in sober stripes, or one more strikingly patterned of Navajo weave.

Feathers, fringes and face-paint are not for the workaday Pueblo male. Plains Indian styles have however influenced Taos and to some extent other northeastern pueblos. Men of Taos wear the heavy flannel breechcloth and leggings with beaded panels, and part the hair into two wrapped braids. Fringed buckskin is very occasionally seen hereabouts. Instead of a buffalo robe men of the Summer People – one of the two ceremonial divisions to which everyone in Taos belongs – swathe themselves in a white cotton sheet, and men of the Winter People in a red one.

The standard Pueblo woman's dress is the rectangular *manta* of black or dark brown woollen cloth, blue-bordered and sometimes with a red or yellow cord above the lower hem. It is wrapped round the body under the left arm and fastened on the right shoulder (only the dead, they say, reverse that order). The skirt, formerly just overlapped on the right side, is now stitched up; it is held tightly in at the waist by a red, green and black patterned sash. And that, with or without a short shoulder blanket, completes the essential costume in the western pueblos. Along the Rio Grande, where Spanish ideas of propriety have been more pervasive, a blouse and slip are worn under the manta, with an apron before and a shawl behind, and if attainable a silk shawl over the head in the manner of the Mexican peasant's *rebozo*.

While western women may go barefoot, Rio Grande female foot-fashions can turn up anywhere. The moccasin itself is white with a hard black sole; worn with it is a long strip of white buckskin wound round and round the lower leg like an outsize puttee – the fatter the more prestigious. Some Tewa and Taos women wear a voluminous white boot. Not for Pueblo males the stimulant of a pretty ankle.

Hair styles allow for the long bob, long back hair with short side-locks, fringes or centre partings. Zuñi and Hopi women have their own distinctive mode. Maidens build the hair up over each ear in an eight-inch whorl, sometimes on a foundation of woven cornhusk, symbolizing the open, virgin blossom of the squash (some say a butterfly). After marriage the hair lies forward over the shoulders in two thick rolls representing the closed, pollinated blossom. Much shampooing, ritual and secular, is done by both sexes, using suds from pounded yucca root (*amole*). Couples groom each other with double-ended besoms of spear-grass; the short bristles do for the hair, the long for the floors.

Toddlers, once unswaddled from their basketry cradle-boards, wear nothing.

Social Life

Family life in the western pueblos centres on the maternal kin. Every individual is born into a clan – the mother's – and marriage to a fellow clan member is treated as incest. Women own, maintain (and help to build) the houses, and own but do not till the fields. Bridegrooms move in with their wives, and can be moved out again with little ceremony. It is indeed the husband who goes home to mother, not only in times of friction but regularly to fulfil the religious obligations of his own clan. Maternal uncles take an active part in a child's upbringing, although the father/child bond is always strong; and grandparents loom large and affectionately in a child's relationships.

In the east descent is – offically – of no great significance and the father has a full say in family affairs. Clans weaken and disappear, but their place is taken by non-hereditary associations which fulfil many of the functions of clans. Here too some pueblos, like Taos, are divided into moieties, 'halves', each playing a dominant role in village affairs for six months at a time. Moiety membership may be inherited, chosen or assigned.

Marriage is usually by choice and not elaborately celebrated, but the groom is expected to weave his bride's trousseau. Strict monogamy, rare among Indians, is the rule for both 'pagans' and catholics.

Pueblo social and ceremonial organization is forbiddingly complex. Religion permeates every aspect of life and demands constant attention

Semi-subterranean kiva at San Ildefonso Pueblo. The projecting ladder indicates the traditional entrance through the roof.

to observances large and small, whether it be the dropping of a pinch of sacred corn pollen, the directing of tobacco smoke to the four quarters plus zenith and nadir, or participation in group prayers, retreats, songs and dances. The Immortals thus addressed are those who bring rain, which means fertility, together with success in hunting and curing, and harmony in all things. In Pueblo belief there are a host of them, all with particular powers, and their benign intervention in earthly affairs is assured by the punctual and word-perfect recital of prayers and symbolic acts pleasing to them. There is nothing here of the loud humility and self-mutilation by which the Plains Indians seek to move the gods to pity, no quest for personal spirit power. The Pueblo approach is devout but mechanistic: what you pray for you pay for, and disaster may result from failure to act in strict accordance with the prescribed formulae. And so that intricate hierarchy of the supernaturals is matched by an intricate network of human groups charged with serving them. Family lineages, clans and moieties, and voluntary subdivisions crisscrossing them, have their own ritual duties, privileges and restrictions. Their officiants constitute priesthoods, and in general it is they who control the pueblos. Each pueblo, be it noted, is a self-contained religious as well as political unit; there is no pontiff of an all-Pueblo native church.

Kachinas

The supernaturals best known to everyone are the *Kachinas*, whose ranks are swelled by the spirits of the dead. They are pictured as having human bodies but brilliantly surrealistic heads, and the children know them because they are given wooden dolls carved in their image. The knowledge is important, because some time between the ages of five and nine all boys, and some girls, will be painfully inducted into the kachina cult. Painfully because while the lad stands naked on a sand-painting in the kiva, his hands held in the air by a ceremonial 'father', a 'scare-kachina' will flog him soundly with a yucca-fibre whip to inculcate respect. By the time he is 14 the boy will have had a second flogging and been formally inducted into his ceremonial father's kiva group. He will also have learned that the whipping was administered by a human being impersonating a kachina, as he himself may now aspire to do.

Each cult group has its own kachina masks, which cover the head completely. They are highly elaborate and represent specific beings, and between ceremonies are cared for and fed with sacred cornmeal by the womenfolk of the group. When the masks are paraded the wearers are not so much masquerading as lending their bodies to the spirit personalities, and the consequences of even accidental misbehaviour may be dire. Three times or so a year the kachinas dance through the pueblo 'to make the people happy' and reaffirm the promise of ample rain.

The greatest masks of all are seen in Zuñi at the winter solstice, when the Shálako, six messengers of the gods ten or twelve feet tall, make a solemn visitation, promising good harvests, inspecting new houses, and impressing the young.

In the eastern pueblos there are fewer masks, and the emphasis on rain is perhaps less urgent where river water is available. The ceremonial calender is none the less full. At Santo Domingo and elsewhere men and women perform together in the Green Corn Dance. The men wear embroidered kilts with fox skins hanging over their rumps, and carry gourd rattles. The women dress in the simple manta without the Spanish underwear, and upright on the head they have a thin wood panel (*tablita*) fretworked and painted with cloud and rain symbols and tipped with downy feathers for cloudlets. Music is supplied by an orchestra of drummers and singers.

The attitude of performers and onlookers at these public dances is basically one of pious decorum; most of them come as the climax of days of private physical and spiritual preparation in the kiva. Yet in east and west alike they are often counterpointed by outrageous buffoonery. In the west the Mudheads, *Kóyemshi*, painted pink with bulbous infantile masks, and in the east the slightly more sinister *Kóshare*, Delight Makers, painted from head to toe in black and white rings, their hair tied with cornhusk into two erect horns, run the gamut of irreverence from lighthearted fun to the grossest obscenity. Licensed inversion of the rules of good behaviour is wellnigh worldwide – English morris dancers are belaboured by their Fool – but its development in extreme form here may be taken as an indicator of, and safety-valve for, the tensions which build up under the Pueblo insistence on self-discipline and the quelling of individuality. At the same time the Pueblo clowns are themselves priests who can use their ribaldry to humiliate anyone they think out of line.

The Snake Dance and Others

Some items of Pueblo ritual depend on clever stagecraft, such as stick-swallowing, the instant growth of plants, and possibly the handling of live coals. Others are less easily explained. The apparent unconcern with

Left Sacred clown, *kóshare*, of the Keresan pueblos. He is painted all over in black and white and wears cornhusk 'horns'. The Koshare are concerned with human fertility as well as providing comic diversion.

Right Women's costume for the San Ildefonso Buffalo Dance, showing the white cotton dress with heavy wool embroidery and the wrapped buckskin leggings.

which Hopi snake dancers handle deadly reptiles is a case in point.

The Snake Dance, a late-summer ceremony designed as always to ensure rain, is put on by the Hopi Snake and Antelope fraternities every other year, alternating with the Flute Dance. The full proceedings last nine days, most of them taken up with private rites in the Snake and Antelope kivas. To begin with, live snakes are gathered from the four directions and brought into the Snake kiva. Any snakes will do; it is a zoological accident that sixty per cent or more will be rattlesnakes, which there outnumber the harmless bull and whip snakes. In the kiva they are ceremonially washed, and kept for some of the time in pots and the rest on the open floor, herded by two men armed with 'snake-whips' consisting of two eagle feathers on a short wooden handle. Stroked along the snake's back these feathers distract it from coiling; uncoiled it cannot strike.

On the eighth day the dancers conduct a sort of dummy-run in the plaza, without the snakes, and on the morning of the ninth day there is ceremonial footracing below the mesa. Towards sunset comes the consummation. First the Antelope and then the Snake priests and novices emerge and circle the plaza four times. They wear decorated cotton kilts and sashes, with fox skins pendant from the waist. Bodies and limbs are painted in white or blue; the Snake men have black faces and white chins. Hair is loose below a topknot of bright feathers or a wreath of greenery. At the right knee is a turtle-shell rattle hung with deer hooves. A leader sprinkles holy water as he goes, and another man may be whirling a bullroarer to create the sound of storm. Some of the dancers are mere boys.

To one side of the plaza stands a leafy booth of cottonwood, the *kisi*, and before it a board on the ground represents Sipapu, the entrance to the spirit world. Each Snake priest now dances forward, stamps hard on the Sipapu to alert the gods, and crouches before the kisi. He rises with a snake, very much alive, gripped by the middle between his teeth. Immediately an Antelope priest falls into step alongside, left arm round the Snake priest's shoulders and right hand wielding the feathered whip to engage the reptile's attention. If the dancer chances to draw a very small snake he may take two, and if a big one – and a rattler or a bull snake can top five feet – he supports neck and tail with his hands. One early observer reports that the Snake priests pack their teeth with white clay to avoid injuring the snake.

In step the pairs of priests dance their snake two-thirds of the way round the plaza, showered with sacred meal by a bevy of maidens as they pass. Then with a jerk of the head the snake is thrown to the ground and the dancers jog on to the kisi for another. Before it can scatter the onlookers the dropped snake is pounced on by a Snake-catcher, often a novice, who quickly accumulates a squirming fistful.

When the last of maybe a hundred snakes has been danced the catchers toss them all into one writhing heap inside a ring of cornmeal, and more meal is sprinkled over them. Then each dancer thrusts a hand into the mass, grasps as many as he can hold, and races down to the valley floor to set them free with earnest prayers. Their sojourn in the pueblo at an end, the snakes will glide home to extol the deserving piety of their Hopi hosts and brothers. Those who have honoured them climb back up the mesa and purify themselves with strong emetics. At night there is feasting.

Why no fatalities occur is something of a puzzle. Although the handlers are extremely adept in catching the snakes, they appear to carry them with considerable nonchalance. Some certainly are bitten; ill effects, if any, are concealed. Infusions of herbs (several have been named) are swallowed by the dancers but whether they represent sound pharmacology or sympathetic magic cannot just now be said. In a recent television film a 'converted' snake dancer claimed to know 'what they do to the snakes' but did not disclose it.

Snake cults may well have existed along the Rio Grande but been scotched by the missionaries together with the masked rituals. The eastern Pueblos are all Roman catholics, baptized in church and given (until recently) Spanish names. They attend mass and celebrate the village saint's day. They attend mass wearing jackets and pants and go home to change into kilts and body paint for a rain/fertility/corn dance. The Pueblo mind sees no anomaly: there is room for Tata (Papa) Dios alongside Sun Father and Spider Woman, and the saints reinforce the kachinas. A small comedy of long ago illustrates the point.

In the 1840s the pueblo of Laguna fell upon bad times while its neighbour Ácoma prospered, protected as it seemed by the venerable portrait of St. Joseph hanging in the mission church. Would Ácoma lend San José for a month to intercede for suffering Laguna? Ácoma would, and so influential was the saint that Laguna declined to give him up. The Acomeños threatened war, but were persuaded by the mission father to draw lots. Ácoma won, the *santo* was restored, and the same night an armed party from Laguna kidnapped it back. Eventually Ácoma's claim was upheld by the Territorial supreme court and a triumphant delegation set out for Laguna to collect the picture. Halfway they found it, leaning against a trailside cactus, and no one ever doubted the saint's miracle-working impatience to be home.

On the other side of the coin, while some spectacles are staged by modern pueblos for tourists to photograph at a suitable fee, most kiva rites remain secret and it is many years since cameras were allowed at such sacred festivals as the Snake and Green Corn dances. Nor are the conservatives keen to impart their beliefs to outsiders. There is an old joke about an Indian saying to his companion, 'Here comes another anthropologist – what'll we tell him?' Pueblo priests are known to have amused themselves, with a mild profit, at the expense of research. It

93

Rarely-photographed healing ritual for a sick boy (back to camera) in a kiva at Sia Pueblo, about 1880.

should be added that two contemporary anthropologists, eminent in their fields, are Tewa Indians: Dr. E. P. Dozier and Dr. Alfonso Ortiz.

Crafts, Arts and Chores

Thanks to Spain the Pueblos have long grown wheat, apples, peaches and melons, and their main flesh food is mutton. But it is still maize that is sacred. They plant it a foot below the parched surface, in hillocks six feet apart, and take expert advantage of the brief flash-floods and run-off from the mesas. Some of the river pueblos use irrigation ditches that are faint echoes of Hohokam, with a code of water-sharing that harks back more probably to Valencia. Everywhere they sow with prayer and stud the fields with *pahos*, the short sticks tipped with a downy feather that embody prayers as do Christian candles, but last much longer. The grain comes in several varieties and six colours, each with its own symbolism, and the gift for the newborn is a perfect cob.

For culinary use corn is roasted whole in underground ovens and eaten from the cob, popped, parched in hot sand, boiled, or dried and ground on the metate and served in a wide range of cakes, dumplings, stews and gruels. A speciality is *piki*, the wafer-thin unleavened bread baked on a stone griddle (best greased, the Hopi say, with donkey fat) and rolled into cylinders. Everyday piki is made from blue meal, the colour stabilized with sage ashes or lime water, but for festive occasions a white meal is used and the batter dyed red with flower petals.

In the desert air the drying of foodstuffs is no problem and it is Pueblo practice to store at least a year's supply against crop failures. Tillage and herding sheep are men's work.

So, more surprisingly, are weaving and embroidery, carried on usually in the kivas. Wool blankets are normally striped, but a black and

The governor of San Felipe Pueblo demonstrating the use of the pump-drill for perforating shell and turquoise beads, about 1880. The narrow-striped blanket is typical of Pueblo weaving.

white tartan is also produced. Weaving in cotton is as we know a prehistoric craft here, and the techniques employed are varied and ingenious. The so-called embroidery weave resembling brocade, which is used for dance-sashes, seems to be a late but unique local development. Other than stripes textile designs are limited to a fairly narrow range of geometrical frets and terraces, and the inverted bowls which represent clouds with vertical lines of rain issuing from them. The simplicity of the motifs enhances their aesthetic impact.

Pottery and basketry are the women's artistic outlet. The long and honourable history of Southwestern ceramics has already been noticed, but the nineteenth century saw a sad decline. Two Tewa ladies, Nampeyó of Hano and María Martínez of San Ildefonso, independently led a vigorous revival. Pueblo pottery still is made without the wheel. The clay, tempered with grit, is rolled into long 'sausages' which are coiled up into the required shape and smoothed inside and out with a piece of gourd. For decorated ware a slip or wash of fine kaolin is applied and the outside polished with a smooth (and treasured) pebble. Firing is done in a pyre of cow or sheep dung, which burns more evenly than wood. The Hopi use local soft coal. When cool the pots are painted with vegetable or mineral pigments brushed on with the chewed tip of a yucca leaf, in designs ranging from the geometrical to more or less conventionalized life forms; there are many local styles. The most usual colour schemes are black, or black and red on cream; bases may be solid brick-red or orange. Prolonged firing with the smoke sealed in gives the shining all-over black finish typical of Santa Clara and San Juan wares.

Basketry is restricted to certain Hopi pueblos, and except for wicker creels for farm use is a women's craft. The chief products are the flattish circular trays with figures of butterflies, whirlwinds or dancing gods which are used for sacred cornmeal. In Oraibi they are made in fine wickerwork, but those from Third Mesa are built up in a continuous coil of yucca leaf tightly wound on a core of grass. Some plaited mats and sieves are made as well. Hopi trays, like Hopi textiles, are in wide demand in other pueblos where the crafts have lapsed.

The Pueblos had no metal of their own and seem to have depended on the colonists for such iron tools as they later adopted. About 1850 however they learned to make silver jewellery and to set it with the turquoise which they had always valued. The craft is better known from the Navajo and will be discussed later, but the Zuñi silversmiths in particular have developed a style of great interest. One form exclusive to the Pueblos is the double-armed cross – the cross of Lorraine – prescribed by the friars.

The System and the Individual

We have seen that the Pueblo Indians cherish cooperative harmony and disallow individualism. Although warfare was recognized and there were war captains – even women's societies for the care of enemy scalps (delicately referred to as 'the sacred bark') – its largely defensive nature did not violate that ideal. The Spanish introduced a system of village governors with a personal responsibility foreign to Pueblo thought; it is recorded that one governor accepted office only after spending three days strapped astride a log by his council. The governors are useful for dealing with white officialdom and so have been compartmentalized into a separate, parallel world complementary to 'real' life. Effective power rests as it always has done with the priesthoods. Every individual will belong willy-nilly to several ceremonial groups and live with a multiplicity of duties and a network of loyalties. Some personalities conform more easily than others. Those who resent the pressures have two alternatives: to move out of the Pueblo world or to channel aggression through witchcraft.

Witchcraft has a long history among the Pueblos and although the priests no longer liquidate witches, the fear of them – and even more the fear of being branded as one – are still potent forces. Factionalism too has grown with the return of men from service in the armed forces. At the same time the conservatives are reinforced by those who have found only disillusion in the competitive outside world. Whatever the blemishes behind the façade of serenity, the bedrock of Pueblo culture has proved notably resistant to erosion.

Chapter 6

Southwest II: Villagers and Raiders

South of the Pueblos lies a vast area inhabited by tribes speaking Piman and, to westward, Yuman languages. Culturally they are all grouped in the Greater Southwest, but individual anthropologists tend to draw their own boundaries.

The Pimans

The Pima proper live, and apparently always have done, on the middle reaches of the Gila River and its tributaries, where rainfall is 4–5 inches a year but the heavy silt brought down by the river affords one corn harvest in June and another in October. This of course is the irrigated Hohokam region, and it is widely believed that the Pimans are the Hohokam people, with the ancient drive towards sophistication gone out of them. Perhaps they had no great need of it; certain it is that at almost all levels the Pimas live more simply than the Pueblos. That was already so when the Jesuit missionaries came among them in the seventeenth century. The modern Pimas incorporate the Sobaipuri, a western division driven inwards by the Apaches, and the Maricopa, a Yuman-speaking tribe likewise tacked on in self-defence. Associated with them are the more numerous Pápago, who lived further from the rivers and so beyond the reach of irrigation. Because they were more remote the Papago were slower to change, and much of our knowledge of earlier conditions comes from them.

The people themselves were tall, dark-skinned and broad-faced. Clothing was a cotton breechcloth for men and a kilt of shredded bark for women, supplemented when necessary by a cotton or rabbit-fur blanket. Deerskin moccasins were worn on journeys but otherwise footgear was the rawhide sandal, a Mexican trait here seen at its northern limit. Men grew their hair long, piecing it out if need be with tresses from their wives or their horses. It was twisted into skeins, cut short across the brow, and for convenience wound round the head in a turban-like pile secured by a woven band. Women cut the fringe and let the rest hang free, sometimes dotting it with white paint. Overnight plastering with mud and gum, good for lice and lustre, preceded the weekly washing in amole suds.

Both sexes painted face and often body, mostly in black or red, and used cactus thorns and charcoal to tattoo cheeks and chin. Newborn babes were painted with ochre mixed with mother's milk. Shell beads were much worn, and warriors favoured a skewer through the nose. Unlike the Pueblos these Indians have adopted the white man's clothes without evolving any transitional styles of their own.

The Pimans lived sedentary lives in permanent villages, but had no large communal house-blocks. Dwellings recall the earthlodge in framework but are much smaller – 15–16 feet in diameter – and without smokehole or porch. The walls are of vertical willow poles or cactus ribs; only the roof has a thick insulating coat of earth. A large part of the time is spent in the nearby *ramada*, a shelter built like the house with a rectangular log frame and dirt roof but with no walls, or only one for a windbreak. Square storage huts were also built. Men did all the building. On the death of an occupant the house was burnt, with the result that village alignment soon became irregular.

Traditional Pima homes. The domed house, built of arrow-weed, cactus ribs and mesquite, plastered with adobe mud, is the older of the two types.

The Pimas made some use of the old irrigation canals near the villages in growing their corn, kidney beans and squash (and later large quantities of wheat). The Papagos, less favoured by their location, had scattered and often distant fields, to which they moved out to camp at planting and harvest times. Both tribes retained a considerable dependence on wild plant foods, sharpened by periodical crop failures. The most important wild resource for the Pimas was the bean-like seed of the mesquite tree (*Prosopis* species), while the Papago relied on the edible hearts of the mescal (*Agave americana*) which grows in the hills and is edible after 24 hours' cooking in a pit-oven but all the better for several days of it. The list of plants utilized is long but particular mention must be made of the giant cactus, saguaro, whose fig-like fruit was consumed fresh or dried, as syrup, or as an intoxicant. Wooden tongs were used in gathering the fruits of various *Opuntia* cactuses.

The Pimas took some fish from the rivers, unlike the Pueblos to whom all fish were taboo, and hunted some game although to do so was to risk slaughter by the Apaches. The Papagos had no open water to fish in but ventured further into the sierras after game. Pumas, badgers, beavers and gophers were eaten as well as deer, pronghorn 'antelopes', peccaries and rabbits, but no snakes, dogs or birds of prey. Ritual observances were necessary for success in hunting. Meat was generally broiled, sometimes boiled. Corn recipes resembled those of the Pueblos. Both metates and mortars were used to mill grain, seeds, beans and dried fruits.

In addition to food plants both cotton (*Gossypium* sp.) and tobacco (*Nicotiana attenuata* and others) were cultivated. The cotton was woven by the men on a horizontal loom, the tobacco smoked in cigarettes of hollow reed or tubular stone pipes picked up in Hohokam ruins. Smoking was a religious act.

Social and Ritual Life

Descent was reckoned through the father. Clans and moieties existed but did not affect the choice of a marriage partner. Each village had a chief known as the Keeper of the Smoke (the sacred tobacco smoke) who chose four assistants from among his own kin; one of them would succeed him on death. His main responsibility was the proper conduct of ceremonies.

The most important Papago festival took place in summer after the saguaro harvest. Juice boiled from the fruit was mixed with water and allowed to stand for two days and a night in the council house. On each of the two nights the men circled hand in hand, singing a holy song of

Southern limit
of ice cap

1   North America in the late Wisconsin glacial period, showing the Bering land bridge
from Siberia and the assumed immigration route. While Beringia was exposed, ice
covered the northern half of the continent except for part of northern Alaska and,
for some time, a corridor east of the Rocky Mountains along which the migration
route passed.

2 Pleistocene beasts hunted by the Palaeo-Indians: (from left to right), long-horned bison, mastodon, camelops, ground sloth, horse, mammoth. All are thought to have become extinct in North America by 5,000 B.C.

3 (Opposite) Palaeo-Indian hunter with spear-thrower (*atlatl*), which acts as an extension of the forearm and gives added impetus to the thrown missile.

4 Palaeo-Indians (Folsom Man) stalking long-horned bison, New Mexico, about 9,000 B.C.

Whales and Walrus

Seals and Whales

Seals and Whales

Caribou

Musk Ox

Moose

Marmot

Caribou

Salmon

Hares

Caribou

Roots

Buffalo

Moose

Wild rice

Seeds

Maize

Maize

Acorns

Rabbits

Buffalo

Deer

Maize

Maize

Cactus

Maize

Fish

Game

Wild plants

Cultivated plants

Animal and wild plant food

5 Hunters, fishers, gatherers and farmers in native North America. The foods named
are mainstays and not the whole diet.

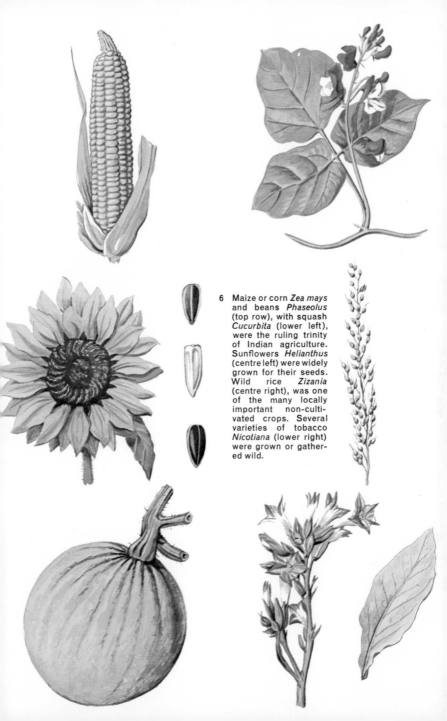

6 Maize or corn *Zea mays* and beans *Phaseolus* (top row), with squash *Cucurbita* (lower left), were the ruling trinity of Indian agriculture. Sunflowers *Helianthus* (centre left) were widely grown for their seeds. Wild rice *Zizania* (centre right), was one of the many locally important non-cultivated crops. Several varieties of tobacco *Nicotiana* (lower right) were grown or gathered wild.

7 Hohokam farmers dig irrigation networks in southern Arizona about A.D. 700. The Hohokam were the probable ancestors of the modern Pima Indians.

8 The White House, Cañon de Chelly, northern Arizona; one of many Anasazi (early Pueblo) cliff strongholds abandoned about A.D. 1300 in the face of drought and nomad raiders.

9 A thatched temple of the Taënsa (neighbours of the Natchez), standing on its earthen mound, shows a last ripple of influence from classical Mexico. Mississippian culture of the 16th century.

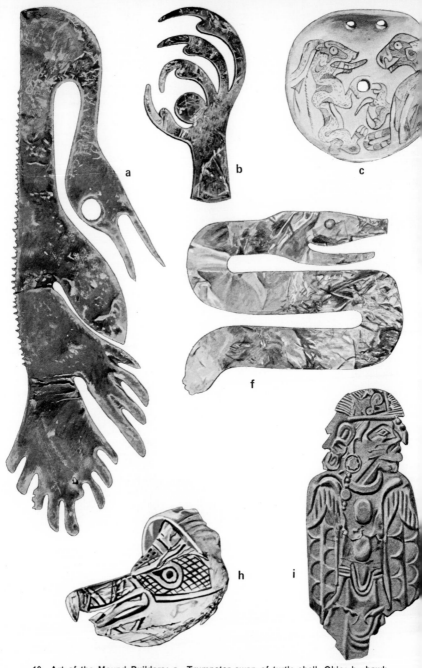

10 Art of the Mound Builders: a Trumpeter swan of turtle-shell, Ohio; b hawk
talons of mica, Ohio; c engraved shell gorget of panther and eagle motif, Texas;
d 'mother and child' jar, Illinois; e flying hawk tobacco pipe of stone, Ohio;
f snake of mica, Ohio; g pipe modelled on a warrior or priest beheading victim,
Spiro Mound, Oklahoma; h bird head engraved on shell. Spiro Mound; i wInged

man of embossed copper sheet, Missouri; j stone pipe modelled on player with stone disc for chunkee game, Oklahoma; k clay triple pot, Tennessee. a, b, d, e and f are Hopewell culture, about 300B.C. to A.D. 500; c, g-k are Mississippian, about 700-1500 A.D. (illustrated specimens mainly from middle ranges of these time spans).

Cree

Ojibwa (Chippewa)

Algonkin
Abitibi
Têtes de Boule

Micmac

Malisit
Abenaki
Penobscot

Santee

Menomini

Ottawa

Huron

1

Sauk
Fox

Yankton

Winnebago

Pota-
watomi

Tobacco

2 Mahican

Iowa

Kickapoo

Neutral

5 4 3

Wampanoag
Pequot

Oto

Mascouten

Miami

Erie

Wenro

Missouri

Illinois

Shawnee

Delaware

League of the Iroquc

1 Mohawk
2 Oneida
3 Onondaga
4 Cayuga
5 Seneca

Powhatan

Tutelo

Osage

Yuchi

Cherokee

Tuscarora
Pamlico

Quapaw

Chickasaw
Alabama

Catawba

Caddo
Tonkawa

Choctaw
Taënsa

Muskogi (Creek)

Natchez

Atakapa

Biloxi

Timucua

Chitimacha

Seminole
Calusa

11 Representative tribes
    the East and Southe
    with approxima
    localities.

Tekesta

☐ Subarctic

☐ Eastern Woodlands

☐ Plains-Prairies

☐ Southeast

| 0 | 200 | 400 | 600 | 800 | 1000 mile |

| 0 | 400 | 800 | 1200 | 1600 km |

Their rype corne

Their greene corne

Corne newly sprone.

Their sitting at meate.

the place of solemne prayer.

The house wherin the Tombe of their Herounds standeth.

SECOTON

A Ceremony in their prayers wth strange gestuts and songs dansing about posts carued on the topps lyke mens faces.

12 Maize, pumpkins and tobacco grow in the coastal Algonkian village of Secotan (North Carolina). Painted by John White in 1585.

The manner of their fishing.

mer of their attire and
...ing them felues when
...e to their generall
...es or at theire
...nne feasts.

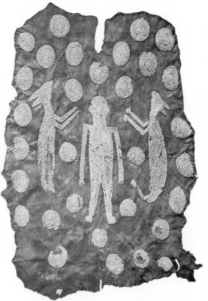

15 Deerskin robe decorated with figures in *Marginella* shells. Worn by Powhatan, father of Pocahontas and head of an Algonkian confederacy in 'Virginia' (now North Carolina) in 1610.

14 John White's famous portrait of a Secotan chief from the Pamlico River, North Carolina. Note tattooing, the bare feet, and bow guard on the left wrist.

13 (Opposite) Indians of Secotan fishing from a dugout canoe, hewn from a single log. Painted by John White in 1585.

16 Modern Seminoles in Florida.
The Seminoles, a Creek offshoot,
moved west after occupying
Florida for about a century, but a
few still live in the swamplands.
Home-made patchwork clothes
and the women's hairdo date
from about 1900.

17 Timucua warrior painted by John
White. Once masters of northern
Florida, the Timucuans collapsed
before other Indians and white
men in the 18th century. They
shared many cultural traits with
Mississippians such as the
Natchez.

18 A 15th century Iroquois village in New York State. Maize growing, hunting and skin clothing typified the various Iroquois tribes before European contact.

19 Iroquois couple of the 18th or early 19th century. European cloth, ribbons and beads were used to create distinctive styles.

20 (Below) Ritual healing masks worn by the False Face (left) and Husk Face (right) Societies of the Seneca (Iroquois). The wooden False Face mask must be cut from a living tree.

21 (Opposite) Brant, a Mohawk chief, painted by Verelst in London in 1710 while on a diplomatic visit with three other Iroquois leaders. The more famous Joseph Brant was his grandson.

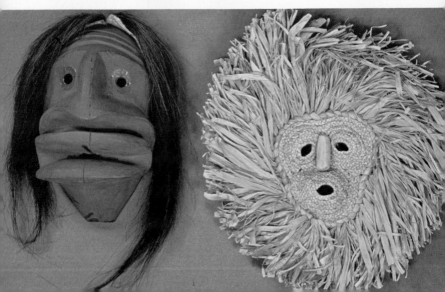

22 Eastern Woodland crafts. (Above) Micmac birchbark canoe model; pipe-tomahawk of
    English make; Huron moosehair-embroidered bark cases and moccasin of about
    1865; Ojibwa quilled bark plate, 1863. The sale of decorated trinkets to tourists began
    early at resorts like Niagara Falls where the quilled plate was bought. Tomahawks
    were exported to America from England and France.

    (Opposite page) Ojibwa-style 18th century pouch (woven quillwork); old Seneca-style
    moccasins (porcupine-quill, beads, ribbon-appliqué); pouch (woven beadwork); awl-
    cases (quilled); 'octopus' pouch (floral beadwork); Ottawa bag (basswood bark,
    dyed); Huron purse (moosehair); strings of wampum. Excepting perhaps the purse
    these examples were made for home consumption. The 'octopus' and woven-
    beadwork pouches may be Métis (Red River mixed-blood) work.

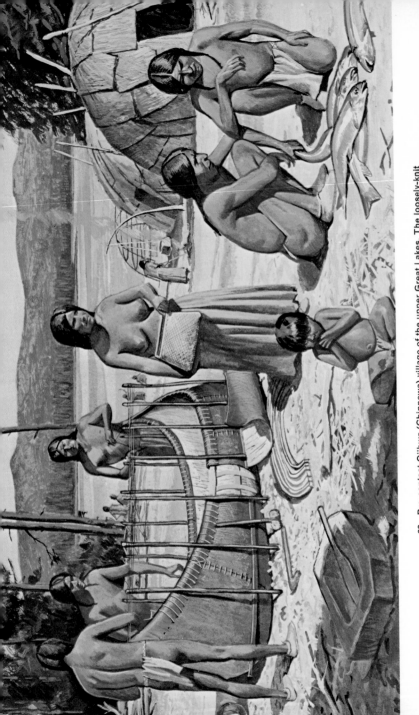

23 Pre-contact Ojibwa (Chippewa) village of the upper Great Lakes. The loosely-knit Ojibwa tribe depended on game and wild plant foods, and used birchbark for canoes, containers and their domed wigwams.

24 Gathering wild rice in the Great Lakes. Wild rice *Zizania* was an important resource for many tribes in the central lakeland region.

	Northwest Coast
	Plateau
	Plains-Prairies
	California
	Great Basin
	Greater Southwest

25 Representative tribes of the West and Southwest with approximate localities.

26 Plains Indians on the march in pre-horse days. Big dogs could drag up to 75 lb (34 kg) on travois; women's loads of 150 lb (68 kg) are reported.

27 Pawnee earthlodge village in Nebraska in 1871, based on a contemporary photo-

28 Inside a Mandan earthlodge as depicted by artist Karl Bodmer in 1833. Several tribes on the eastern margin of the plains – besides the Mandan, Hidatsa and Arikara on the upper Missouri – used these circular dwellings of logs covered with earth and up to 60 ft (18 m) across.

29 Dance of the Mandan Bull Society to attract the buffalo; painted by Karl Bodmer in Dakota, 1834.

MATO-TOPE

Geschmückt mit den Zeichen seiner Kriegsthaten.

Paré des emblêmes de ses faits d'armes.

Adorned with the insignia of his warlike deeds.

30   Mato-topé (Four Bears), a Mandan chief, painted by Karl Bodmer in 1834.

31   Plains gamblers inside a tipi of about 1890. The object of the game is to guess which moccasin holds the hidden counter; stakes were often high.

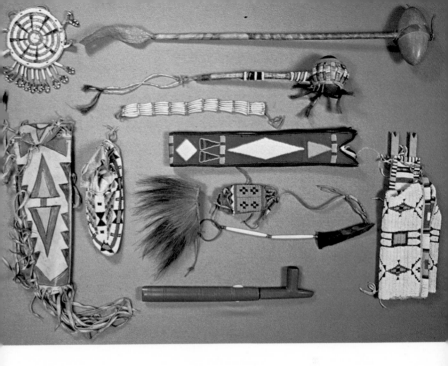

32 Plains crafts. (Opposite) Blackfoot man's shirt and leggings, 1842, and war bonnet of an undetermined tribe, about 1860.

(Above) Arápaho quilled disc pouch; stone-headed clubs; dentalium shell necklace; Crow beaded horse decoration; Shoshoni painted rawhide regalia case; Cheyenne hard-sole moccasin; deer-hair roach headdress; beaded strike-a-light pouch; Oglala model cradle; catlinite pipe.

33   A buffalo hunt painted by the American artist Frederic Remington in 1897.

34   A buffalo hunt as depicted by Northern Cheyenne artist Howling Wolf in 1876.

35 Teton Dakota or Lakota (western Sioux) as painted by Karl Bodmer in 1833. Note the buffalo robes, and funeral scaffold at right.

36 A Blood (Blackfoot) man wearing the standard modern 'war bonnet', no longer exclusive to the Plains Indians.

37 'Man-who-gives-the-war-whoop', a Plains Cree warrior of the Canadian prairies as painted by Paul Kane in 1848.

38 Traditional Pueblo dress: (from left to right) married woman, old style; Hopi maiden; Rio Grande woman; man, Hopi and most Rio Grande pueblos; Taos man of the Summer People division.

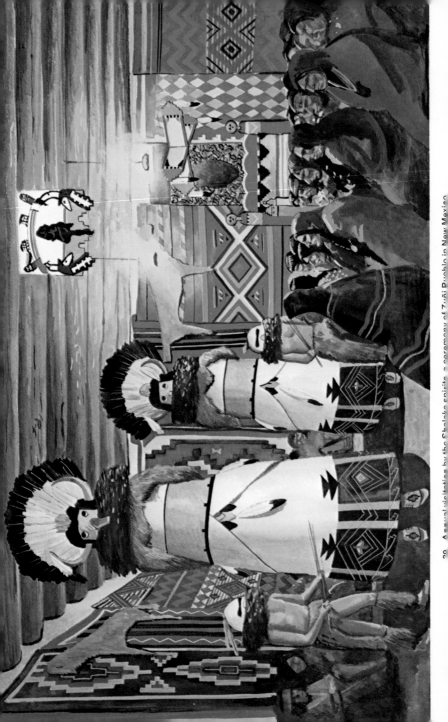

20   A royal visitation by the Shalako spirits, a ceremony of Zuñi Pueblo in New Mexico.

40 The Hopi Snake Dance, Arizona. The Antelope Priest soothes the rattlesnake
held in the Snake Priest's mouth. On the ninth day of this complex ceremony the
snakes are released to carry prayers to the gods.

41 Pueblo crafts. (Above) Hopi ritual cornmeal trays (wicker, lightning design, Tewa of Hano; coiled, kachina design, Shungopovi); pottery canteen, Hopi; kachina doll, Hano; small black pot, Santa Clara.

(Left) Dance kilt, embroidered, Hano; woman's belt Jémez; dance sash, brocade weave, Hopi. All about 1915. The Tewa people of Hano, originally refugees, are Hopi in almost all but speech. Hopi ceremonial gear is widely used by other Pueblo Indians.

42 Navajo Indians of Arizona and New Mexico. The girl wears the 'officers's wife'
style adopted after 1865, whilst the older woman shows the traditional home-woven
two-piece dress.

43 Three 19th century Navajo wool blankets. Once made for home use, good Navajo blankets are now prized by collectors. Inset shows a typical loom and weaver.

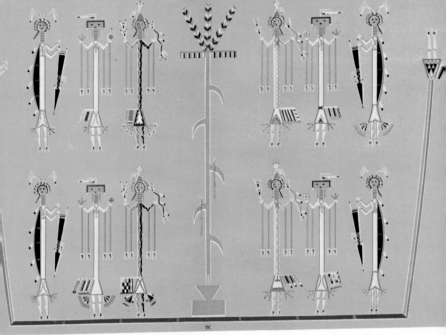

44 Navajo sand-painting as used in healing ceremonies. Made of coloured earths sprinkled dry on the ground and picturing spirits, sand-paintings must be erased the same day or night.

45 Navajo silver, turquoise and copper jewellery, including woman's belt and squash-blossom necklace, 1920–40. First learned in the 1850s, Navajo silverwork quickly attained artistic and economic importance.

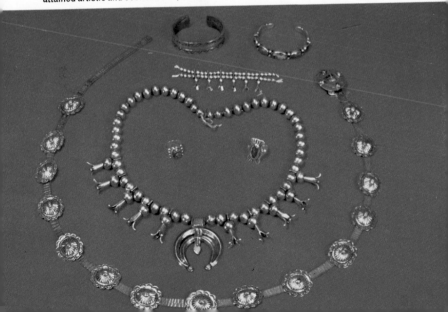

46 Chiricahua Apache couple of the 1880s. The mixture of styles (as of blood) reflects the Apaches' long history of predation on settled folk, both Indian and white, lasting until the surrender of Geronimo in 1886.

47 Pre-contact Pima Indians of Arizona-Sonora. Heirs to the Hohokam, the Pima and allied Papago continued to use the ancient irrigation systems up to modern times.

48 Pima coiled baskets of willow and black *Martynia* pod, 1890 (left), and 1935 (right).

49 Three 19th century Mohave Indians from the lower Colorado River. The woman's facial tattooing and bead collar are distinctive, but the old man's robe woven from strips of rabbit fur is widespread in the West.

50   Paiute camp in Nevada from a photograph of 1870, showing the basketry used for containers and the women's caps.

51 The plank boat (which was unique in North America) used by the Coast Chumash Indians of southern California.

52 A reed boat (balsa) in central California. Balsas occurred also on the Colorado River, in South America and in the Old World.

53 The White Deerskin Dance, a wealth display of the Hupa Indians of northern California. The leaders carry outsize ceremonial blades of obsidian.

54 (Above) String of dentalium currency; Hupa woman's apron of buckskin fringe
wrapped with bear-grass, 1842; Californian woven hemp sash with shell (currency)
beads and woodpecker scalps, Pomo of about 1830.

(Below) Californian baskets: Pomo, 1825 (originally feathered) (top); Pomo feathered, 1930s (left and right); Yurok, 1926 (old design) (bottom).

55 A Pomo village of central California. An abundance of acorns under-pinned the economy of very many Californian groups of tribelets.

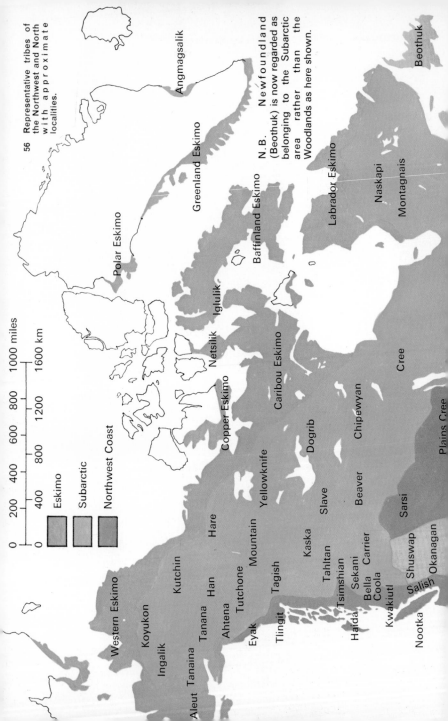

56 Representative tribes of the Northwest and North with approximate localities.

N. B. Newfoundland (Beothuk) is now regarded as belonging to the Subarctic area rather than the Woodlands as here shown.

Angmagsalik

Greenland Eskimo

Polar Eskimo

Baffinland Eskimo

Labrador Eskimo

Naskapi

Montagnais

Beothuk

Iglulik

Netsilik

Copper Eskimo

Caribou Eskimo

Cree

1000 miles

1600 km

0	200	400	600	800	1000 miles
0	400	800	1200	1600 km

Eskimo

Subarctic

Northwest Coast

Dogrib

Chipewyan

Yellowknife

Mountain

Hare

Kutchin

Han

Tanana

Ahtena

Tutchone

Kaska

Slave

Beaver

Western Eskimo

Koyukon

Ingalik

Tanaina

Aleut

Eyak

Tagish

Tahltan

Sekani

Carrier

Sarsi

Plains Cree

Tlingit

Tsimshian

Bella Coola

Shuswap

Okanagan

Haida

Kwakiutl

Salish

Nootka

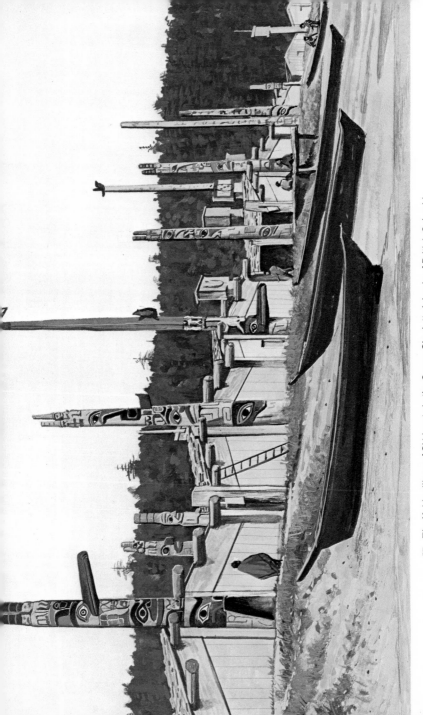

57   The Haida village of Skidegate in the Queen Charlotte Islands of British Columbia, about 1878, showing heraldic 'totem' poles and seagoing canoes.

58   A Coast Salish interior painted by Paul Kane in 1847. One woman weaves a blanket of mountain goat wool and hair from the dog (a special breed now extinct) while another spins.

59 A 19th century Tlingit couple in festive attire. The man (standing) wears a Chilkat blanket and carries a small ceremonial 'copper'; the woman wears a trade 'button blanket'.

60 Totem poles of the Tlingit of southern
    Alaska (above left) and of the Kwakiutl
    on Vancouver Island (above right). The
    contrast between the austere northern
    and exuberant southern art styles is
    apparent. Also shown is a Thunderbird
    figure, Kwakiutl (left).

61 A canoe raised high above the Pacific shore of Washington forms a tomb for a Coast Salish noble, whose widows mourn below.

62 Northwest Coast (above) Kwakiutl owl mask; Haida berry basket; Tlingit wooden
potlatch hat; Haida wooden bowls for fish oil in shape of seal and beaver. The hat
is perforated for attaching basket cylinders marking potlatch feasts given by the
wearer.

(Opposite) Wooden fish-club representing seal; 'soul-catcher' of ivory, set with
Haliotis shell; spoon of carved mountain goat horn; model totem pole of argillite.
All Haida. The soul-catcher is used by a shaman (medicine-man) to cure a patient
whose soul has wandered away.

63 Kutchin ('Loucheux') warriors of the 19th century. Among the northernmost of Indians, these scattered Athapaskan bands ranged the tundra and pine forests of Yukon and Alaska.

64 A 19th century Naskapi winter camp in northern Quebec. Essentially caribou hunters, the Naskapi and Montagnais, like other northern Indians, long ago adapted their economy to commercial fur-trapping.

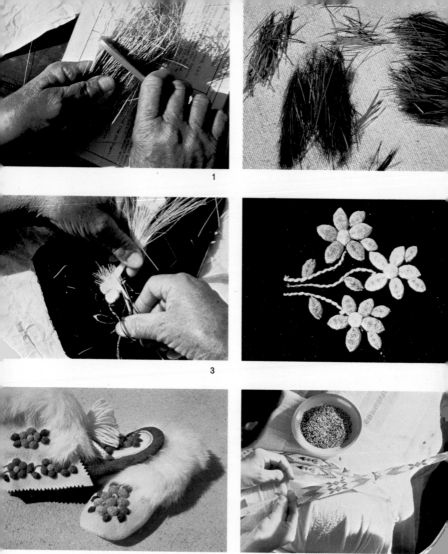

65 Northern Athapaskan crafts, 1969: 1 Preparing moose hair; 2 Hair and (centre) porcupine quills, dyed; 3 Trimming moose hair 'bristle' motif; 4 Hair embroidery completed; 5 Ready for sale; 6 Bead weaving on bow loom. 1–5 are of the Slave Indians at Forts Smith and Providence, Northwest Territories; 6 is of the Dogribs at Fort Rae, Northwest Territories.

66 A two-man kayak and Aleut hunter (top), a Labrador
Eskimo family, after John White's painting, 1587 (centre),
and a modern Greenland Eskimo woman (lower right).

67 (Above) Eskimo female and male dolls from Baffin Island, showing skilful use of different shades of caribou skin.

(Below) Model kayak from Greenland, fully equipped for seal hunt, with harpoon, inflated buoy for dead seal, etc.

(Opposite) Aleut seal-gut bag with caribou-hair embroidery; Eskimo woman's belt set with caribou teeth; fish-shaped ivory line-sinker; mammoth-ivory arrow-straightener; ivory ladle; driftwood snow-goggles; mammoth-ivory scraper with stone head; two engraved ivory bow-drill bows, all from northwest Alaska about 1825. The Central Eskimo soapstone carving of a beaver is modern.

68 Central Eskimo spearing fish which are trapped behind a stone weir at a river mouth in autumn.

69 Drum dancing is performed by the Eskimo for healing as well as for social entertainment in the long Arctic nights.

70 Indians in transition. Chief Walking Buffalo, Assiniboin (Stoney), 1871–1967, who took the peaceful road from scouting for the then North West Mounted Police to teaching and lecturing.

71 Modern Plains Indian forestry workers from the Crow Agency in Montana. The Crow, never at war with the U.S.A., are today better placed economically than many other tribes.

clouds and rain. From time to time women would break into the circle, joining hands with the men of their choice. For a while couples would be missing, the theme of the festival being fertility. The climax came on the third morning (provided no infraction of the sacred rules had prevented the liquor from fermenting), when the men drank and made formal speeches in turn. Thereafter each family turned to its own supply and by nightfall most of the village would be in a stupor. Here again we have a southern trait; hardly anywhere else in aboriginal North America was alcohol known.

Individual curing rites were held by medicine-men or shamans, whose power derived from dreams or the killing of four eagles. They cured by sucking foreign bodies – stones, cactus and so on – out of their patients, and a run of failures meant execution by clubbing.

Both hunting and warfare called for ritual preparation designed to pacify the spirit of the victims. Fighting, mostly defensive and against the Apaches, was carried on with bows and arrows tipped with stone points picked up at ruins and poisoned with putrid liver from a deer bitten by rattlesnakes, and with short cylindrical clubs. The killing of an enemy involved the killer in sixteen days of spiritual uncleanness. While the rest of the village danced in honour of the victory he fasted in seclusion and even his weapons required decontamination. When at the end of the period he was presented with the purified enemy scalp, to guard and to feed, he received with it the power to cure insanity.

Basketry

Although some decorated and plain pottery was produced, Piman craftsmanship has found its best expression in basketry. Trays and shallow bowls are made, more finely coiled than those of the Hopi. Only the sewing materials, creamy white split willow stems and black pods of

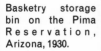
Basketry storage bin on the Pima Reservation, Arizona, 1930.

devil's-claw (*Martynia*) are visible. Traditional designs are geometric but life forms have crept in to suit the tourist market. Symbolic meanings can generally be supplied for the earnest enquirer, Indians being kindly people at heart. Wickerwork does not occur here, but plaiting, twilling and coarser coiling are employed in the making of conical shoulder-baskets (creels), and such domestic utensils as fire-fans, stirrers, winnowing trays, cradles, and storage bins for grain up to six feet high.

Entering the Modern World

Pima history has been mercifully free of epics. The first missionary contact was made about 1700 by the German Jesuit Eusebius Kühne (Padre Kino) but permanent missions, established some years later, were never very successful. The chief monument to their work is the splendid church of San Xavier del Bac (rebuilt 1797) on the Papago reservation south of Tucson, Arizona, which is still in use.

Never at war with the Americans, the Pimas and Papagos sold large quantities of grain to the California-bound, and added cattle-raising to their own economy. They served diligently as Army scouts against the Apaches who had bedevilled them for centuries. Now, however, they face a more sinister enemy: the drying-out of their lands caused by damming and over-use of the Gila river system. No amount of intoxication, ritual or otherwise, is likely to solve that problem.

The Mexican Pimans

The Piman family is far-flung. In caves and brush shelters among the crumpled mazes of the Sierra Madre in Chihuahua live the Tarahumara, whose runners are reputedly capable of 100 miles in a day. South of them, the Tepehuanes. In Sonora there is the Cáhíta group, including the Ópata, Mayo (*not* Maya) and Yaqui. Beyond them the Cora and Huichol, whose luminous 'primitive' painting and 'gods'-eye' fetishes – crossed sticks with a diamond of bright wool strands at their centre – are now invading our boutiques. All these tribes represent the southern edges of the Southwestern culture area but hardly belong in this survey, except for the Yaquis, who have established half a dozen communities on the outskirts of modern Arizona cities.

Originally farmers, gatherers and hunters like the rest, the Yaquis were notably successful in fighting, and occasionally eating, their neighbours. One hundred and fifty years of amicable labour by the Jesuits (always more pragmatic than the Franciscans and therefore banned from the New World in 1767) left them converted and remoulded, but with a lively sense of their identity. Their contempt for governmental interference kept them intermittently in arms down to 1927. Between the 1880s and the outbreak of the Mexican revolution in 1911 thousands were transported to virtual slavery in the sisal plantations of Yucatán, while others fled to the USA, but an unconquered nucleus remained. During the revolution the Yaquis acquired a journalistic reputation as the steeple-hatted, lethal hench-men of the bandit-general Pancho Villa. Eventually the new regime confirmed them in their ancestral lands. Those in Arizona live mainly by wage work and speak more Spanish than Yaqui but are unified by their synthesis of native and seventeenth century Christian religion. This finds particular expression in the week-long *Pascola* (Easter) cere-monies, wherein a doll image of the Infant Jesus is honoured by Deer dancers with drums and rattles.

The Yumans

The last old residents of the Southwest to be noticed are the Yuman tribes, who in general hold the western boundary of the Area – the Colorado River. Starting near the mid-point of the Grand Canyon in northwestern Arizona and following the river to its delta in the Gulf of California we meet in turn the Havasupai, Walapai, Mohave, Halchidhoma, Yavapai, Yuma proper, and Cócopa; the Maricopa, now Pimas by adoption, have already been noted. Yumans are not true nomads but move house fairly readily; they tend to be loosely organized and lack many of the technical resources of the Pimas and Pueblos. They have hereditary chiefs but with little power; war leaders arise spontaneously and command greater respect. Descent is through the father; clans are not important; and the number of wives is a matter of convenience.

The Havasupai are the most favoured. In summer they live at the bottom of Cataract Canyon, half a mile deep, manipulating the erratic waters of the creek to raise generous crops of corn and squash, beans, tobacco and sunflower seeds non-stop from June to September. At the end they invite their neighbours and trading partners of the Walapai, Navajo and Hopi to a week of harvest festival. In October they quit their brush-covered, earth-banked houses on the canyon floor and climb out to semi-permanent camps in the cedar thickets of the plateau for a winter of hunting and gathering. Unusually modest by nature, the Havasupai dressed from top to toe in buckskins, killed and cured by the men.

The woman's costume consisted of two deerskin aprons, generously fringed. The front one hung from the neck to the ankles while the hind one started from the waist, where a skin girdle or perhaps a Hopi sash secured them both. On the inside a skin under-girdle with deer-hoof jinglers was worn. Both sexes painted and tattooed the face.

There was no weaving but some cotton was grown for use with strike-a-lights. A few functional pots were made. Basketry forms included the conical creel for seeds and berries, carried on the back with a tumpline across the forehead, fan-like beaters for knocking the seeds into the creels, and an hourglass-shaped bottle waterproofed with piñon resin. The big horns of the bighorn sheep provided ladles.

Downstream from the Havasupai live their poor relations, the Walapai. The languages are close enough to suggest a recent separation but the Walapai lack the advantage of the fertile canyon and so subsist almost entirely on wild foods, shifting their camps more frequently and ranging further from the river than their more fortunate offshoot. Their way of life is nearer to that of the western Apache. The same is true of the Yavapai, who have drifted east and south from their earlier homes on the Colorado. The widespread use of the terms Mohave-Apache and Yuma-Apache for them has caused confusion from time to time.

The Mohave, and south of them the Yuma, are both river peoples, living on the wide flood-plain of the lower Colorado where it divides Arizona from California. Somewhere between them, but hostile to both, were once the Halchidhoma, whose survivors joined the Maricopa.

The Mohave and Yuma are closely similar and a single description will broadly fit the two of them. Clothing was minimal or absent, as befitted shade temperatures of 105–120°F. (It was a soldier of the Fort Yuma garrison who came to a bad end and after spending one night in Hades returned for his blankets.) Men wore rawhide sandals and sometimes a tiny G-string. Women made do with a pair of willow-bark fringes, the hind one ruched up into a bustle. Men used mud and piñon gum to model their hair into crowns or horns; women cut a fringe and let the rest flow free. Male foreheads and female chins were tattooed. Girls in particular loved red and yellow face paint. In cool seasons blankets of woven bark or rabbit-skin were worn. A bright yoke of netted beads was a speciality of Mohave women.

Most household activity went on under a rectangular open-sided shelter, but there was also a species of pit-house entirely covered with sand. Domed summer huts of brush were used, with a fire of dung at the door to discourage mosquitoes.

The annual re-silting of the bottomlands ensured generous yields of the usual staples, less tobacco which could be picked wild, and cotton (willow bark fibre was woven instead). Mesquite beans and other unplanted foods were important. Fish were shot with arrows or lured with crushed melon seeds into bark nets. Heads, fins and all went into the pot to be stewed with corn. Large game was scarce, which may explain why the Yumas' keen interest in horses, when they got them, was culinary.

Domestic pots and a wide variety of coiled baskets were made, including five-foot storage bins and clay bowls large enough to float infants across water. True boats were lacking; adults navigated balsas made of bundles of reeds stiffened with a pole, or simply bestrode a cottonwood log.

Boys of ten or so underwent initiation at which the nasal septum was pierced and a cord inserted. On four consecutive days they ran 10–15 miles in one of the four directions, with little or no food or sleep in between. On the fourth day the cord was replaced by a greasewood rod through the nose, which would give place later to a string of beads. A girl at puberty spent parts of four days face down on a bed of heated sand beneath a bark blanket, while guests made polite speeches. During this time she must not look about, nor talk, nor eat salt, nor touch her head except with a special scratching-stick. For four days of each month thereafter she was secluded. Boys opting for a woman's role – the berdaches we have seen in other tribes – went through a four-day adoption into the opposite sex.

With an assured food supply the Mohave and Yuma had leisure for war, which has been described as a psychological necessity among them. Their favourite weapons were the bow and the barrel-headed club, used as much for jabbing faces as smiting pates. Raiding parties were usually organized by some brave man who had dreamt of the morning star. They might fall upon an unsuspecting camp but ideally there would be a stand-up fight until two or three men had been killed. Girls were captured whenever possible, for sale or adoption, but there were no other prisoners. The heads of the slain were hacked off to be scalped at leisure. The scalps – most of the head skin – were hung on poles and danced by youths and girls, with hair painted white, for four days. Strict purification rites were essential for all who handled them. Although battle casualties were usually restricted, the Yumas and Mohaves were capable of a stubborn indifference to heavy losses by no means characteristic of all Indian warrior tribes.

Those dying of natural causes hereabouts could enjoy their own obituaries, since unrestrained mourning began as soon as death was seen to approach. Bodies were cremated over a pit which was covered with sand when the pyre fell in, and the deceased's house and property were burnt at the same time. For four days the mourners fasted and bathed in smoke to ward off supernatural sickness.

Of the river Yumans, that leaves only the Cocopa and, since in essence they are a fainter carbon copy of the Yuma, so shall we.

The Apache

The name of the Apache – Zuñi for 'enemy' – has cropped up already but they and their cousins the Navajo come last in our survey of the Southwest because they were the last to arrive. They refer to themselves by dialect variants of the term *Na-déné*, The People, which reveals their far northern origins as members of the Athapaskan stock.

The Athapaskan-speaking peoples are thought to be the most recent – but still ancient – immigrants from Asia. They spread across the north from the Pacific to the western shore of Hudson Bay – territory they still hold. Sometime in the ninth or tenth centuries A.D. bands began to leave the Subarctic and follow the historic drift south. Some became forest Indians in northern California, others trickled down the western edge of the plains. One small group, the Kiowa-Apache, tacked itself on to the Kiowa and became full-time buffalo hunters, just as did the Sarsi under the wing of the Blackfoot. The Lipan (*Lipa-N'dé*) roved independently over southwestern New Mexico and western Texas as fringe Plainsmen, raising dogs for the pot since the buffalo supply was unreliable. For the rest there is a grand confusion of group names but the people divide broadly into eastern and western. The eastern Apaches are the Jicarilla and the Mescalero. The Jicarillas hunted buffalo but also hobnobbed enough with the Pueblos to acquire some agriculture. The Mescaleros favoured the mountains further south and west but likewise ranged widely and sought the warmer lowlands in winter; their standby was the fibrous heart of the mescal. The western Apache turn up under such names as White Mountain, San Carlos, Arivaipa, and Chiricahua (sometimes treated as intermediate), each covering numerous sub-divisions.

For these restless, hardy and adaptable nomads all nature was a survival kit (barring fish, which was taboo), but the externals of their material culture were simple. The eastern Apaches lived often in tipis and dressed in Plains fashions. In the west the dwelling was a low domed hut of brushwood and grass known as a wikiup. When the band moved on, the camp was burnt. Western clothing was originally of skins and elaborately decorated buckskin dresses survive for girls' puberty ceremonies. In the nineteenth century men were likely to be wearing a long cotton breechclout, sometimes cotton pantaloons, a loose shirt, and a cloth headband or turban to confine unbraided hair, while women adopted a full calico skirt and hip-length blouse. As the Apaches neither grew nor wove cotton the source must have been trade, Government issue, or loot. The same must be true of the 'store' jackets, vests and hats which figure prominently in contemporary photographs. A distinctive moccasin was worn, having a rawhide sole with an upturned projection at the toe and a soft top gartered at the knee and lapped over to form a pocket.

A little coarse pottery was made, and a lot of very good basketry. The Jicarillas did beadwork. Corn-growing was haphazard among the western bands, mesquite beans and other wild crops being the real staples. Hunters wore antlers to stalk deer. Social organization was more formalized in the west than in the east. Numerous clans, linked in larger groupings or phratries, cut across band membership and so provided a measure of cohesion at tribal level.

Degrees of restriction in marriage partners varied, but it was usual for a man to marry his first wife's younger sisters, and a widow her deceased husband's brother. Nowhere was it permissible for a man to speak to his mother-in-law or vice-versa, but certain cousins were expected to indulge in ribald joking. Children were kindly treated but schooled in hardihood.

Girls still undergo a puberty ceremony resembling that described for the Yumans but if anything more elaborate: older women knead their figures into pleasing proportions, and sacred pollen is sprinkled on them for fertility. The Mountain Spirits (*Gans*), impersonated by masked men with head-dresses of branching wooden slats, dance round them by firelight to the sound of bullroarers and communal singing.

Both Northern and Pueblo elements are detectable in this ceremony, as in other aspects of Apache religion, with a mystical concern for beauty and harmony on the one hand and, on the other, the personal role of the shaman dedicated to the curing of disease. Witches and ghosts were equally feared.

Each band was completely autonomous, although alliances were easily made and unmade. Leadership was largely a matter of strong personalities coming to the top; it might remain within an influential family for some generations.

Raiders and Warriors

The Apaches seem to have come upon the settled tribes and the arriving Spaniards at about the same time. Both had a profound effect on the Apache standard of living. Kindly, generous and scrupulously honest among themselves, they regarded the environment as something to be fully exploited, and corn-growing Indians and horse-riding, metal-using colonists were very welcome features of this new environment. Sometimes they traded; more often they raided or just blackmailed. Horses were delicious, and enlarged their marauding range clear to the state of Jalisco (although the Chiricahuas could do very nicely on foot). Costly punitive expeditions were mounted and fragile agreements concluded. But the temptations were many, and the Apache youth was taught that it is glorious to excel in war, but not to die; circumspection was more praiseworthy than the suicidal gestures of the Plains Indians.

The Apache wars of the American era began in earnest in the early 1860s when an abortive attempt to seize the Chiricahua chief Cochise by

Goyathlay, or Geronimo (1829–1909), the Chiricahua Apache war leader, photographed in 1886, the year of his surrender.

treachery was followed by the hanging of six Apache hostages. Hostilities were kept on the boil by official ineptitude over location and re-location of tribal reservations. There were interludes of peace involving one band or another but both sides were understandably touchy and the cruel insensitivity of the whites was matched by the vengeful, and efficient, ferocity of the Indians. The names of the war leaders – Mangas Coloradas, Cochise, Nachi, Nana, Victorio, and Goyathlay, 'The Yawner', whom the Mexicans nicknamed Gerónimo – sowed terror on both sides of the border for three decades. Yet the numbers of warriors 'out' at any given time were derisory compared with the forces deployed against them. Gerónimo was the last to surrender, in September 1886, with fewer than forty men, women and children. Not only they but the faithful Apache scouts as well were shipped east, first to Florida and finally to Oklahoma, where Gerónimo spent his last quarter-century growing melons. He outlived his time long enough to dedicate his memoirs to Theodore Roosevelt and be photographed in a top-hat at the wheel of a stationary horseless carriage. The Apaches in Arizona and New Mexico turned to cattle-ranching, and latterly to professional forest fire-fighting. In Sonora the vendetta festered on until at least 1900, and there was a report of three Mexican scalps lifted in April 1930.

The Navajo

The Athapaskan immigrants who pushed towards the Four Corners of New Mexico and Arizona, Utah and Colorado were not to know that their chosen location would combine with environment and the accidents of history to make them the largest tribe in North America. The Spaniards found them (1629) near an abandoned Tewa pueblo called Nábaju – 'sowings' – and distinguished them as the Nábaju Apaches. They call themselves Dené – The People, as usual – but the world knows them as the Návajo. Or Navaho; the pronunciation is the same, but they prefer the Spanish spelling.

The Navajo arrived as hunters and gatherers, which soon enough meant hunting Pueblo slaves and gathering Pueblo corn. Spanish colonists on the Rio Grande were fair game too. When chased the predators could slip home on stolen horses, mules and donkeys to virtual immunity in the great canyons – Chaco, del Muerto or Tsegi (Chelly). Not that all contact was predatory; there was trading, and in the turbulent days of the Pueblo Revolt many Indian refugees found asylum with the Navajos. These incomers brought both techniques and ideas, and intermarriage helped to establish them. Spanish sheep and goats did well; the Pueblos taught the art of weaving, and soon Navajo women (not the men, as among their teachers) were producing woollen blankets of outstanding merit. Corn patches and peach orchards appeared among the Anasazi ruins. The northerners forgot their roots and pinpointed their tribal birthplace in the southwest. They adopted the matrilineal clans of the agriculturalists and wore masks and mud in impersonating their gods. The stark and startling magnificence of their multicoloured environment, from the Painted Desert to Monument Valley, from the banded sandstone of the canyons to the evergreen of pine and piñon in the mountains, topped eight days out of ten by a sky so blue that Sacred Turquoise stole the colour for its own – all this nourished a near-mystical reverence for beauty in the Navajos. Their chosen location brought them into the light of Pueblo sophistication but left them too far from the Mexican border to play cat-and-mouse with the military, so that when the final reckoning came in 1863 they could but bow to enforced peace and pastoralism. The isolation of their country minimized the pressure from white land-seekers, while their artistic skills, expressed in wool and silver, created an important cash resource.

Internment

By the time the American Civil War broke out the Navajos were already growing a considerable amount of corn and pasturing a great many sheep. The preoccupation of the Union troops with Confederate invaders gave them opportunities to augment their flocks; a single raid in 1863 netted them 20,000. But the Confederates departed and to combat boredom the Union men were set against marauding Indians, under the reluctant leadership of the one-time mountain man Kit Carson, now a colonel of militia. A tract of forty square miles in eastern New Mexico, with Fort Sumner in the middle, was set aside as a military reservation and called the Bosque Redondo from the Round Grove of cottonwoods which was its landmark. Nine hundred Mescalero Apaches were forcibly settled there to raise corn.

In 1863–64 Carson scorched the earth of the Cañon de Chelly and marched eight and a half thousand Navajos the 300 miles to the Bosque. The two tribes bickered and pillaged each other's crops until in 1865 the Mescaleros decamped. Pests, drought, floods, and Comanches lurking on the sidelines reduced the Navajos to destitution and in 1868 they were returned to their own country with $100,000 worth of sheep and equipment.

Housing and Clothing

Hogán is the Navajo word for house. The older hogan is an earth-covered, conical structure with a framework of three interlocking poles, north, west, and south, and two poles, separated, fronting east and enclosing a low porch. The floor is dug out about a foot deep, leaving a bench round the wall, and there is a hole in the roof for the passage of smoke and draughts. Blankets, sheepskins and utensils are the only furnishings. Where timber is easily come by a polygonal hogan is built of logs laid up horizontally and roofed with poles and dirt. Outside will be the usual brush ramadas, windbreaks and corrals. Dwellings tend to be widely scattered, and a death means instant abandonment.

Early photographs show Navajo men wearing shirts of buckskin or cotton. Nether garments were either loose cotton trousers, long or short, skin knee-breeches, or close-fitting skin leggings with a row of silver buttons from thigh to ankle. The head-band of fur or cloth was replaced in war by a skin cap with a pompom of owl or eagle feathers (also an

Old-style Navajo house or *hogán*, built of earth on a pole and brushwood foundation, Arizona, 1930.

Apache fashion). The woman's dress was made up of two rectangles of dark woollen cloth sewn together at top and sides except for the neck and arm holes. It differed from the Pueblo manta in not leaving one shoulder bare. Footware echoed Pueblo styles. During internment at Bosque Redondo the women observed the ladies at the Army post and proceeded to adopt a style which has lasted to this day, consisting of a dark velveteen blouse and a pale, flounced calico skirt. The velveteen shirt became popular with men, worn outside cotton trousers slashed below the knee, but nowadays denim has just about taken over. Both sexes wear the hair in a club but only the men use a headband, often surmounted by a wide-brimmed hat. Sparse moustaches and beards are sometimes allowed to grow. Men and women alike wear silverwork and blankets. The first is their own; the second, unhappily, seldom so. By the end of the eighteenth century Navajo blankets were being eagerly sought by Spaniards and other Indians. A Franco-Mexican commentator of 1830 compared them favourably with the finest sarapes of Saltillo, and in these days the weavers can no longer afford to be wearers.

The Navajo Blanket

The wool, sheared and carded with white man's tools, is washed in yucca suds and spun on a native wooden spindle. Half a dozen spinnings may be needed to produce a fine, hard yarn. Weaving is done out of doors on a vertical loom slung on a pole frame. The weaver kneels before it and works upward, lowering the upper bar as she proceeds. She uses no shuttle, passing the weft threads through the warp with fingers and a small rod. Vigorous thumping with the batten forces the weft home. Weft strands of a given colour are carried across the work only as far as the design requires, when a separate strand of the next colour is introduced. The finest-spun, hardest-woven blankets are reputedly waterproof, but the grades of weaving depend on the purpose. Blankets are or were used for apparel, for sleeping, and as saddle-cloths.

Navajo women seem always to have been more adventurous in colour and design than Pueblo or the New Mexican treadle-loom weavers of the Chimayó tradition whose work is superficially similar. Colours were obtained from vegetable and mineral dyes, set with alum, urine or ashes as mordants, and full advantage was taken of the natural shades of the wool. Red was difficult until, around 1800, the Spanish traders brought in heavy English flannel of military scarlet. This material, called *bayeta* (baize) was lovingly ravelled and respun, to be combined with native yarns of, predominantly, black, white and indigo. Bayeta seems to have inspired the golden age of Navajo weaving, which lasted nearly three quarters of a century. When the trade channel shifted to the eastern USA and the use of aniline dyes spread, true bayeta gave way to cheaper American yarns of lower quality, although some was imported direct from Manchester and Huddersfield.

For about thirty years from 1880 many blankets were woven in ready-dyed commercial yarn from Germantown, Pennsylvania. These 'Germantowns' often have warps of cotton parcel string.

Design elements include vertical and horizontal stripes, parallel-ograms, diamonds, triangles and zigzags. An early style known as the Chief blanket showed the same basic pattern when folded into halves or quarters. Blankets woven for home use had no borders; those came when the trading posts opened the market for rugs for white homes. It was the (less scrupulous) traders too who persuaded the weavers to reproduce figures of the *Yei* or *Yeibichai* spirits from the sacred sandpaintings, shocking the more devout. Perhaps they were not quite perfect copies; in even simple designs an intentional flaw will be made, to avoid imprisoning the soul of the figure – a widespread practice applying equally to basketry and pottery.

Reputable traders in the Navajo country, such as the Hubbells at Ganado and the Wetherills of Kayenta, not only built up a valuable outside market but worked hard to preserve standards. One result has been to put the Navajo blanket beyond the reach of the average Navajo Indian. By no means all of them sell for thousands of dollars (some do), but most Navajo ladies now weave for export only and themselves wear trade blankets machine-woven by the Pendleton Mills at Portland, Oregon. Their quality is good and their designs, while pleasing to the Indian taste, are not counterfeit Indian.

Narrow red and green wool belts figured in white cotton are woven on a Pueblo-style waist-loom and sold in large quantities to the Pueblos. Saddle-girths are woven directly on to the cinch-rings. Men knit and wear footless stockings.

Silverwork

The Navajos secured the silver buttons and buckles of Spanish colonial finery long before they learned to make their own. It is said that one Atsidi Sani, 'Old Smith', who had already taken up blacksmithing, was taught to work in silver by a Mexican craftsman, probably about 1868. Atsidi Sani taught his sons and the craft spread rapidly. The Zuñis had been making jewellery in brass and copper wire since the 1830s but went into silver later than the Navajos – who themselves used copper alongside silver for many years.

The raw material was US coinage until in 1890 the Treasury objected and the traders supplied Mexican pesos; nowadays they sell one-ounce slugs refined in California. Equipment was copied from Mexican models: clay forge and crucibles, charcoal for fuel, sheep- or goatskin bellows, and an assortment of trade hammers, punches, pliers and files, with an axe-head or some such for an anvil. Modern smiths have added such refinements as blow-torches and nitric acid. Borax is used in solder.

Silverwork is either cast or hammered and filed into shape, or a combination of both. Moulds are of clay or soft sandstone, greased with tallow. Early buttons were coins hammered into half-globes; two soldered together made a hollow bead. Single cup-shapes equipped with a tiny clapper made bells of the wedding-cake variety which women might wear on sashes to warn sons-in-law of their approach.

Conchas ('shells'), the engraved or embossed oval, convex plaques worn on belts, have already been mentioned. Other large pieces for home consumption include heavy wrist-guards, *ketohs*, for protection against the released bowstring; bridle mountings; buckles; and pendants in the shape of an inverted crescent, single or double (*najahe*). Such pendants usually hang from a necklace of globular beads, some of which will have a flower-like projection which the Navajos call a squash-blossom. In fact the shape is a perfect model of a pomegranate, which betrays its Spanish origin. The crescentic najahe itself stems from the Middle East, and the tiny hands which sometimes sprout from the tips strongly suggest the hand of Fatima which one has seen painted on Moroccan doors against the evil eye.

About 1880, after experimenting with glass and coral, the Navajo smiths began setting their silverwork with turquoise. Much of the stone used is greenish and veined with the matrix but the clear blue, regarded as male, is more highly prized. Turquoise occurs locally, and some is traded from Santo Domingo Pueblo, but Persian and even Chinese stones have been imported.

The marriage of silver and turquoise stimulated the demand for finger-rings, bracelets, brooches and ear-bobs, and enhanced the saleability of Navajo jewellery to the white public. In 1940 the number of silversmiths was estimated at 600, including a handful of women. Pop culture has widened the market and Navajo work is snapped up in London. Unlike home-woven blankets, however, silverwork is still commonly used by the Indians themselves, both for adornment and as an economic tool. All the trading posts hold great quantities of jewellery in pawn, to be redeemed usually after the spring wool sales and the autumn lamb sales; little is ever forfeited.

The sheep concerned are herded and largely owned by the women, who wield great influence in Navajo society. Farming is mostly men's work, and so is the conduct of religious affairs.

The Healing Chants

The beliefs which the People brought south centred on healing, practised by individual medicine-men or shamans. Under the influence of the regimented Pueblos the shaman was reduced to a diagnostician, whose function is to determine the cause of the illness and prescribe the appropriate ritual. He sings and prays with a hand extended, and ponders the various chants available. When he lights upon the correct treatment his hand will tremble uncontrollably. It is then up to the sufferer to approach a Singer qualified to mount the particular

Navajo priests chanting at a healing ceremony in Arizona. The patient sits on a blanket at the door of the hogan, into which she will be taken for ritual treatment on a sand-painting. Photographed in 1930.

The patient's husband distributing $500-worth of gifts at the end of the healing rite.

ceremony, be it the Night Chant, Mountain Chant, Wind Way, or some other, which he will have spent years in studying. He and his helpers will assemble the necessary masks, paint, coloured earths and prayer-sticks, which here are reeds packed with sacred pollen and turquoise fragments. The patient's family and clan gather property for distribution to participants and onlookers.

The major chants last nine days. The first four are spent in purification by sweating and emetics, and beseeching the Supernaturals to attend. During the second four the gods are said to arrive, to enter their likenesses in the sand-paintings on the hogan floor: elongated 'matchstick' figures, kilted and bearing rattles or garlands, shielded perhaps by Rainbow and guarded by Fly or Bear. These are made by dribbling coloured sands, ochres and charcoal on to a bed of clean sand that may measure eighteen feet across. The patient is seated in the middle of this altar while the priests intone the long cycle of prayer-songs recounting the relevant myth. Handfuls of the sacred sand are pressed against the affected parts, and at the end of the session the whole picture will be scooped up and carried away; a new design will be used on each of the four nights. The ninth night sees the priests dancing in public, masked a little like the Pueblo kachinas but with less decorum. Everyone sings, the women distribute food and there are gifts for all. The cost may be enormous for what might have been cured by a few cents' worth of bicarbonate; but think on the concluding lines of the Blessing Way:

> May it be beautiful before me
> May it be beautiful behind me . . .
> May it be beautiful all around me
> In beauty may I walk
> In beauty it is finished . . .

It is not just the patient but all the People who are fortified. Even in these days the Navajos need reassurance; ghosts and witches still menace them, and when the hospital fails the sick may still appeal to the Earth Mother, Changing Woman, and the Hero Twins she bore to the Sun.

In beauty or otherwise, the Navajo story is by no means finished. The reservation has been progressively enlarged to 25,000 square miles but still cannot support a population pushing on 140,000 – more than ten times the figure for pre-Bosque days. At least the Navajo Nation has since 1972 controlled its own affairs. Even so the Tribal Council at Window Rock is not finding it easy to plot the Trail of Beauty between the alternatives of poverty and the prostitution of the Land to open-cast mining.

Chapter 7

Great Basin: The Living Past

Cross the Colorado River and you leave agriculture behind. The acorn and the whale, the salmon and the seal, will feed men in the west and north, but on the rim of the Great Basin the Corn Maidens bow out for good. Rain and sun lie beyond but never in the right seasons and proportions for fickle maize.

The Basin is a huge, arid region of parallel ridges and alkali plains lying between the Rockies and the Sierra Nevada, and it is leakproof. What water there is drains inland to evaporate, leaving a few saline marshes and small lakes, plus the Great Salt Lake, last remnant of a postglacial captive sea. The obvious vegetation is saltbush and sagebrush on the flats and piñón in the hills, but the Indians knew of much more. In the south the Basin merges with the Californian desert and in the north with the Plateau area in Oregon and Idaho, whose rivers seek the sea.

There is no need here to step back in time, because for man time has stood still: the typical Basin culture is the Desert Archaic of 10,000 years ago, externally simple but fundamentally efficient and enduring. White pioneers, noticing only that women scrabbled for edible roots, coined the scornful term 'Digger Indians', but we know them by such names as Paiute, Paviotso, Gosiute, Chemehuevi, Kawaiisu, Washo. These denote linguistic and local groups, not tribes as such. Because the food supply was thinly spread so were the people. Families moved independently for most of the year, coming together only for autumn rabbit and antelope drives which called for cooperative effort and incidentally brought opportunities for courting and recreational dancing. Speakers of any one of the half-dozen languages (all of them Shoshonean bar the Hokan Washo) recognized their affinity but shared no overall chiefs.

Priesthoods and ritual dances were likewise unknown but shamans played an important role, summoning game, curing ills, neutralizing witchcraft, and entertaining the laity with feats of fire-magic. Wolf and his brother Coyote had jointly created the world but it was Coyote whose exploits, sly, bawdy or beneficent, made up the verbal testament of the people. Coyotes, alone of the animal kingdom, were never eaten.

In summer windbreaks or shelters of reed matting might suffice for housing. For the extremely cold winters various types of dwelling were constructed of brushwood, grass, bark or earth, supported by dead branches since there was no means of chopping down living trees. Household equipment included a little simple pottery, stone metates, reed mats, the essential digging-stick or dibber, and excellent basketry utensils in which food could be boiled by the hot-stone method.

Aboriginal clothing consisted of the G-string for men and a pair of fringe aprons for women, with the rabbitskin robe in cold weather. Moccasins were occasionally worn, and simple snowshoes. Hair fell to the shoulders and was daubed with red and white clay. Ears and noses were pierced for ornaments, and faces were tattooed and painted with earth pigments mixed in bone-marrow. In the historic period, as ideas seeped in from the Plains, some Paiute groups made fairly simple shirts, dresses and leggings of poorly-dressed buckskin. For women a finely woven basketry skull cap, perhaps developed to prevent chafing from the brow-band of a tumpline, was characteristic.

Seeds and roots were the major foods and survival depended on precise knowledge of the distribution and ripening of the plants exploited. Each family group kept to a particular area, through which it worked as the annual cycle of cropping required.

Over seventy-five species of food plants have been noted, of which the piñón (pine nut), ripening in autumn in the hills, is the single most important. Pronghorn 'antelopes', never common, were taken in communal drives. Rabbits were driven into fibre nets a foot or two high, stretched up to a mile across the width of a canyon, and there clubbed in their hundreds. The jackrabbit population, however, like those of many other rodents is subject to periodic decimation, and the Basin peoples were prepared to eat virtually anything that moved – except Coyote, for the reason stated. Snakes, lizards, small rodents, caterpillars and even plump bees were laid under tribute. The grasshopper 'plagues' of the white settlers were bonanzas for the Indians.

With so diversified a bill of fare there were no public harvest rituals. All living things had souls which could be coerced by qualified shamans, but that was all.

Social Life

Marriages were normally arranged by the families. It was common for a man to marry two or more sisters as they matured, and to take on a brother's widow; two brothers would occasionally share one wife. There were no clan restrictions on the choice of partners, but Basin society within its standards was notably puritanical.

The notion of a guardian spirit for men was present but not seriously pursued. For girls puberty involved seclusion for up to thirty days. A birth saddled both mother and father with precautionary taboos: the father of an unborn child must not twist himself a cord lest the babe be strangled in the womb. Unwanted or deformed infants were destroyed but healthy ones spent their time swathed in buckskin and absorbent sage bark on basketry cradleboards and were 'changed' twice daily. Personal names were altered according to age.

Such leisure time as the food quest allowed was spent in gambling with dice or the moccasin game, or that universal favourite, hurling poles at a rolling hoop. At night the story-tellers came into their own.

Petty quarrels might arise but among such well-spaced, small communities motives for war hardly existed. Slaves would have been a liability and scalping was not seen to serve any useful purpose. One's enemies worked more subtly, through magic (no death was ever 'natural'), and one paid a shaman to combat that. The dead were dangerous, and the dying abandoned if possible as a matter of safety, but bereaved spouses observed mourning for a whole year. Corpses were either buried or burned along with the house and all property except a few family keepsakes.

The Marginal Utes

Such was the essential Basin culture: almost the irreducible minimum, and indestructible as long as the environment and the isolation lasted. Change began on the northeastern periphery in Colorado where the Utes held pastures adequate for horses and so became a link in the spread of equestrianism to the Plains and Plateau. They adopted many Plains ways (even the Sun Dance but not till the 1890s), raided widely, and emerged as a tribe. But their tipis remained small and their women still went out with the seed baskets. Their wily leader Ouray (1820–80) contrived to keep the Utes out of major collisions with the whites despite the constant paring down of their lands. The single explosion occurred at White River in 1879 when the Indians expressed impatience with the

Ute couple photographed in the Wasatch Mountains of Utah during the Powell Expedition of 1871–5. The warrior is painted from head to foot.

reforming zeal of Agent Nathaniel Meeker by killing him and seven Agency employees and then inflicting a dozen casualties on the Army column sent against them. Their reward was an even less congenial reservation in Utah.

In and around southern Idaho the Bannocks likewise took on a Plains cast and likewise, in 1878, had a shortlived war with the USA. For this they engaged the sympathy of some Northern Paiutes led by Winnemucca the Younger. However, the Paiute penchant for peace was dramatically vindicated by Winnemucca's daughter Sarah, who had had a brief spell at a California ladies' college before becoming an Army wife, interpreter and scout. Foreseeing disaster for her people, Sarah penetrated enemy lines and succeeded in bringing out her father and his warriors before battle commenced. (Deserted by her first officer-husband, Sarah married another and opened a school for Indian children, but faded into obscurity after being widowed.)

The Desert Prophet

Without doubt the most influential personality known from the Basin was Wóvoka or Jack Wilson, the apostle of the Ghost Dance cult which has been described in the Plains chapter. Wóvoka at the time of his vision in 1888 was a respected and peaceable employee on the Wilson ranch. He had already received shamanistic power through dreams. The great revelation came to him during an eclipse and while he was in the throes of fever – a perfect conjunction of circumstances – but it was not original. The concept of divine deliverance from oppression is a recurring theme in human history, and messiahs had already been promised in other regions of native America, North and South. The Paiute version dated from perhaps 1870, when already the Indians were harried by white miners and their seed-destroying stock. By 1888 communications were better in the West and Wóvoka's message – essentially a spin-off from Christianity – was to spread far and wide, with ugly consequences for the Sioux. But the massacre at Wounded Knee resulted from the Sioux misinterpretation of the doctrine; Basin culture was a peaceful culture, and Wóvoka's message was one of peace and faith. His influence outstripped and betrayed him.

Chapter 8

California : The Brittle Eden

The Yahi Example

The Neolithic Era came to an end in North America on August 29, 1911, when a bedraggled scarecrow of an Indian was found crouching exhausted in Oroville, California. Through all his fifty years of life he had depended on stone-tipped arrows to get him meat, and on acorns and wild grass seeds to supplement it. His hair, cropped short in mourning, had been singed off, not cut with a blade. He spoke only his own Yahi tongue. By nightfall he was dressed in white man's clothes and lodged in the town jail for protection from the curious. Days later he was whisked off to San Francisco as the protégé of two eminent anthropologists, Professors T. T. Waterman and A. L. Kroeber of the University of California. There he stayed until his death from tuberculosis in 1916, working as an assistant janitor in the Museum of Anthropology and earning the respect and affection of his associates both academic and manual.* They called him Ishi, the word for 'man' in his own language.

Ishi continued to make bows and stone arrowheads, fish-spears and fire-drills, but no longer of necessity. His mastery of such skills and his willingness to demonstrate them, as well as to impart knowledge of his language and beliefs, made him an invaluable ethnological informant. Indeed a unique informant, for when Ishi died the Yahi people really were extinct.

There had been perhaps 400 Yahis, the southern dialect division of the Yana people who ranged in prescribed order across two and a half thousand square miles of northern California below the volcanic peak of Mt. Lassen. In spring they gathered wild clover, and later the seeds of

---

*The story of Ishi is movingly told in Theodora Kroeber's *Ishi in Two Worlds* (Univ. California Press, Berkeley, and Cambridge U.P., London, 1961 and later editions).

Ishi, the last surviving Yahi Indian (died 1916) preparing a salmon-harpoon or leister; rotating the wooden fire-drill in a tinder-filled notch in the hearth board held firm by a knee and a foot; blowing on the tinder to ignite grass.

many grasses, but their vegetable staple was the acorn. In the rivers
there were salmon to be taken on two-pronged harpoons. Deer could be
snared, or lured into arrow-range by miming with the stuffed head of an
antlered buck. The food quest was constant but rewarding enough in
normal seasons. The balance, however, was easily upset. For the Yana
disturbance began in the 1850s, when their trails became roads for white
immigrants seeking goldfields and farms. Soon they were in competition
with sheep and cattle which cropped their clover and seed-bearing
grasses, while the salmon runs were interrupted by silt poured into the
rivers by hydraulic mining. Hunger led to sporadic stock-killing and
barn-robbing. The shooting of pilferers provoked reprisal murders and
many settlers considered themselves – rather too gleefully – justified in
treating Indians as vermin to be exterminated. By 1870 the Yana
population was down to about thirty souls. A dozen Yahis were left, but
until 1884 no one realized that; they had simply faded into their
shrinking wilderness. Then began a decade of petty thieving from
ranchmen's line camps, and silence once more. In November 1908 the
sole Yahi village was stumbled upon. The population was four: Ishi, who
got away, his sister and a crippled old man who both apparently
drowned in flight, and a bedridden old woman who was left behind but
spirited away overnight. Two and a half years later Ishi took the white
man's road, and was astounded that it did not lead to his immediate
death.

If Ishi's story does not sum up the whole history of Indian California it
is none the less a consistent variation on a tragic theme. Everywhere a
reasonably comfortable livelihood could be gained by a hardworking
population with simple equipment. The environment encouraged the
growth of small local communities, mainly self-sufficient. There was no
scope for grand alliances such as might face up to invaders. When the
aliens arrived the northern Indians were destroyed by cruelty, the
southern by mis-handled piety. Californian cities today shelter big
Indian populations but few of them are of Californian stock.

The Amicable Babel

California as a culture area is nearly as big as the modern state. The
southern end, with the peninsula of Baja California, is sometimes
awarded to the Basin or the Greater Southwest, and before the Oregon
border is reached there are hints of the Northwest Coast and Plateau
areas. The land between, spread across two mountain systems and a
central valley to the Pacific shore, supported perhaps 150,000 Indians –

by far the highest density in North America. But density did not imply unity: well over a hundred languages and dialects were spoken, belonging to six distinct stocks. Two stocks are exclusively Californian; the other four between them turn up from the Arctic to southern Mexico and away to the Atlantic coast. California seems always to have been a haven for wanderers and a seducer of migrants.

As in the Basin and Plateau, the people were primarily gatherers, with hunting or fishing in various degrees of secondary importance. The difference here is that the food resources were generous enough to foster more local specialization, both material and intellectual. Political organization seldom reached beyond the village, even among groups of similar language, and so we cannot speak of tribes but only of tribelets. One such might be made up of a village of say 200 people with a couple of smaller satellites. Perhaps for that reason there was very little warfare. Trade was preferred, and gave rise to a rare development: a financial system based on shell money. Communities were too small to support priesthoods and ceremonialism on the Pueblo scale but they had a wealth of myths and stories and made a great formal to-do over puberty and death. And baskets created by their womenfolk are reckoned among the best in the world.

Least studied are the Indians who inhabited the long, mostly incandescent finger of Lower California, with its tip in the Tropics. (It was for this supposed island that the Spanish borrowed from their own literature the name 'California', the Furnace-hot Land.) Most of them were Yuman-speaking but their names have a southern ring: Guaicura, Pericú, Cochimí, Akwa'ala-Paipai, and on Tiburón Island the Seri. They lived very close to the sand, on cactus fruit and seafood, wore mostly paint and never built roofed dwellings, although they could navigate log rafts well out to sea. Eighteenth century missions have possibly obscured finer points in their original culture.

The Acorn People

In southern 'mainland' California we first meet the pattern of living sketched for the Yahi, made possible by the acorn. The coastal plain teemed with units of 2–300 people, more or less differentiated by dialect but identified by locality. Each tribelet had its range of up to thirty square miles running back from the sea to the oak groves. There, when the acorns were ripe, boys knocked them down for the women to carry home in two-bushel baskets slung on the shoulders in a net. The nuts were shelled, split, dried and stored. For use they were pounded into meal in a stone mortar often pecked into a convenient boulder and fitted with a basket hopper sealed to the rock with native asphalt. Acorns of all the seven species gathered have a high tannic acid content, which was leached out by pouring water through the meal in a porous basket or a simple depression in the sand. Acorn meal was eaten as porridge or mush, drunk as gruel, or made into cakes.

Grass seeds were parched, ground on a slab, mixed with water and consumed cold. More exciting to the palate was the honeydew exuded by aphids, zealously collected and rolled into pellets. Over the year there was in fact a wide range of fruits, roots, nuts, greens and salads to be enjoyed, none of it cultivated except a little tobacco. Deer were in moderate supply but rabbits abounded and the sea offered clams, fish, and sometimes seals and otters. Young grasshopper swarms were driven into pits and roasted. Caterpillars boiled with salt were a delicacy.

Men often dispensed entirely with clothing but women were never seen without the fringe aprons back and front. Both sexes wore their hair unconfined, women topping it with the usual basket cap. Men's faces and women's faces, wrists and breasts were tattooed. Pads of yucca fibre were the only footwear. Robes of rabbitskin were sometimes outshone by robes of sea-otter fur.

The usual house was a conical affair eight feet or so in diameter, of heavy poles thatched with grass or reeds and sometimes earthed partway up. It had a separate door and smokehole, and the floor was dug out to a depth of two feet. Rectangular roofs without walls provided shade for most daytime activities. Small sweat-houses were built, for sweating only.

The Chumash Boat

Dugout canoes and reed balsas or rafts were the usual watercraft, but an intriguing puzzle is set by the Chumash of the Santa Barbara Channel coast and offshore islands. Alone of all the peoples in North America, the Chumash built seagoing boats of planks lashed together, caulked with asphalt and capable of carrying from three to twenty persons. Double-bladed paddles served to propel them. The timbers were split with relative ease from fallen or fire-felled cedars by the use of antler wedges, and smoothed with shell blades and abrasive stones. Planks were used elsewhere in California for houses and other purposes but the idea of joining them into a watertight hull seems to whisper of inspiration from the far side of the Pacific. We shall see later that Japanese wrecks brought iron to the coast further north in pre-European times – but it is never altogether safe to doubt Man's native ingenuity.

Southern Californian crafts included the making of simple pots and flared tubular tobacco pipes of clay, bowls of soapstone, and basketry utensils of many shapes and sizes. Sea shells, broken small, were pierced, strung and rolled over abrasives until worn down into even-sized discs. Besides serving locally as a medium of exchange these shell beads were traded far inland beyond the Colorado.

Villages were normally made up of more or less interrelated families, presided over by a fatherly figure whose responsibility was to ensure harmony by oratory and good example. The office tended to be hereditary. Heads of families saw to the conduct of religious affairs and kept the matting bundles in which the group's sacred objects were preserved. War chiefs did not exist, for lack of need. When fighting did occur no scalps were taken.

Initiation and Death

Ritualism came to the fore at the initiation of boys and girls. Boys were drugged with Jimson or Jamestown weed (*Datura*) and lay for several days in a stupor during which guardian spirits revealed themselves and sometimes vouchsafed special power-giving songs. This recalls the vision quest of the Plains, where suffering rather than narcotics was used to induce hallucinations. For Californian lads the matter did not end there. Painted, they stood around a large sandpainting while the significance of the various natural phenomena it represented was explained to them. One by one they lay in an open grave and leapt out again in token of death and rebirth. In another pit biting ants were poured over them, to be whipped away with nettles. Another sandpainting, a foot-race, and moral harangues followed.

Girls lay on a warm sand bed and suffered restrictions and lecturing much as did those in the Southwest. Their most testing ordeal was perhaps keeping down a pellet of tobacco swallowed in water, as a proof of virtue. Their sandpainting ceremony was followed by a race to a flat rock on which they painted designs. Only after this initiation could they be tattooed.

The dead were cremated and their effects burnt with them. A year more or less after death, full-sized images were made of a number of the departed, with reeds and buckskin and human hair. After seven nights of mourning the images were burned together. In the memorial ceremony for a headman captive eagles were surreptitiously pressed to death by dancers circling the fire, and their bodies cremated. Paint, feather kilts and feather topknots were the usual ceremonial attire.

Central California

This style of life persists as one goes north, with local adjustments according to terrain, vegetation and distance from salt water. The people just described are often, for historical reasons, classed together as Mission Indians. The labels given to those beyond them refer essentially to language groups (remember that no sense of nationality exists). Yokuts, Mono, Maidu, Wintun, Yuki and Yana are but some of them, with the Achomawi and Atsugewi who together make up the Pit Rivers. The Pomo, north of San Francisco Bay, dressed – or not – as in the south; women left out the basket cap but men found hairnets a convenience. For ceremonies they wore beautifully-worked head-dresses of black and yellow woodpecker feathers and kilts of vulture plumes. Besides conical bark lodges they built domed houses of reed thatch thirty feet across, and semi-subterranean sweat-houses which were also clubrooms for the men. A larger-still version of the sweat-house was used for ceremonies.

Here where rivers held water the whole year round, fishing methods included angling with shell hooks, weirs with basket traps, and drugging the waters with soap-root to bring trout to the surface belly upwards. Dogs helped to drive deer towards hidden marksmen, and birds were killed with clay pellets from a sling.

In a country of highly-skilled basket makers the Pomo women stand supreme. Twining and coiling techniques were employed about equally. In addition to everyday utensils, containers of special elongated shapes were made for rituals. All were tastefully decorated with rhythmic geometrical designs. Most beautiful of all were the tightly coiled bowls studded with shell discs or pendants of iridescent abalone (*Haliotis*) or sprouting brilliant tiny feathers from the crowns of quail, woodpecker and hummingbird. Many of these – too many, one might sigh – were expressly made as gifts for the dead and perished in the cremation fire.

War was still uncommon, but slings and obsidian (volcanic glass) stabbing-spears were added to the weaponry, with body armour of parallel rods which most warriors found too restricting. Scalps *were* taken, and included the ears. Initiation rites were less rigorous, but children of both sexes had to lie unflinching while old men scored their backs with shell blades. Four days' seclusion was imposed on the father of a newborn child. On the lighter side the Pomo and their neighbours were ardent swimmers, runners and gamblers.

The Wealth-conscious North

The material scene changes relatively little, but the social a great deal, in the northernmost reaches of the area. Among the almost identical but totally unrelated Hupa (Athapaskan), Karok (Hokan) and Yurok (Algonkian), acorns are still the staff of life, with venison and fish – salmon, steelhead trout and lampreys. Sturgeon are prized for glue rather than caviare. Tattooing and the basket cap are still in evidence but the men wear a deerskin round the loins, and a few scanty beards speak of Northwestern origins. Women wear a fringed wrap-around skirt, open in the front, where the gap is closed by a double-thickness apron of skin thongs, wound with shining bear-grass and hung with nut shells.

Houses are massive rectangles of cedar planks with pitched roofs and sunken floors, with a tiny circular door in the gable end. Some have stone-paved forecourts for lounging. Dugout canoes are supplied by the Yurok and the same people bring in marine fish and seaweed for salt.

Partly subterranean house of timber with three-pitched roof and round door, used in north-western California. The type shows Northwest Coast influence.

There is the same lack of political cohesion as in the south. The new feature is the cult of wealth. The Hupa and their associates were money-minded. Clamshell beads were worn, yes, but the coin of the Hupa realm was dentalium. This tubular, fang- or tusk-like shell is widely distributed but in Pacific waters was most accessible to the Indians on the west coast of Vancouver Island, whence trade carried it far into the prairies and the desert. Matched for size and strung end to end (wide to wide and narrow to narrow so as not to telescope), dentalia were so precisely valued by the Hupa that men had lines tattooed at measured distances on the left arm against which to check the value of the string. Purses were carved from antler.

Money could buy anything, from house sites to indemnity for murder or bad language. Practically all crimes and misdemeanours had their recommended price; it was the job of go-betweens to secure the most face-saving terms possible within the limits. Even the infrequent wars, brief and savage, usually ended in protracted haggles over mutual reparation. Such awareness of value developed in these Indians, as in those who used the clamshell currency in strings of many thousands, a grasp of numbers uncommon among preliterate peoples.

The goal for a man was the accumulation of wealth, to be passed on to his heir. One did not gain prestige by spectacular giving, as is more general in the Indian world, and the idea of burning all property at death was incomprehensible to the Hupa. But wealth had its obligations. Lacking Rembrandts, the Hupa rich man invested in other rarities, particularly in beautifully flaked blades of imported obsidian, far too big to be functional, in choice featherwork, and in the skins of albino or melanic deer. These treasures were shown to the public in the Deerskin Dance, which might last two weeks, or in the shorter Jumping Dance. Men in wolfskin crowns and buckskin or civet cat fur kilts, with condor plumes in their hair, waved the deerskins aloft on poles. The heads of the deer were stuffed, and embellished with scarlet woodpecker scalps. Other men wearing wildcat skins and chaplets of sea-lion tusks paraded the obsidian blades. The myth justifying the ceremony was sung at great length, and the whole community derived blessing from its performance.

A rich man might afford the bride-price (scaled according to her status) for an extra wife. Yet there was a notion that the spirits of wealth were straitlaced. Men did not sleep at home, where their wives and treasures lay, but in the kin-group's sweat-house. Only on the summer food-gathering expeditions away from the village could spouses consort freely. Births tended to be concentrated in the spring.

It may be that the Yurok-Karok-Hupa acceptance of a world for rich and poor has enabled them to adapt to the American Dream, but they have been helped by their relative isolation and the presence for many years of a protective military post. None are rich now, but they have survived better than many California Indians, farming their own country. Elsewhere the story has been different. The fate of the Yana and Yahi has already been noted, and is all too typical of the areas affected by the Gold Rush and ensuing land booms. Many thousands of Indians were indentured as labourers up to 1861; a shockingly high proportion of them died of venereal diseases. Small wonder that those who were left grasped vainly at the promise of the first Ghost Dance of 1870.

The Missions

For the Southern Californians regular contact with white men began with the Franciscan mission of San Diego de Alcalá in 1769. Others followed in quick succession: San Gabriel, San Luis Obispo, Santa Clara,

San Carlos Borromeo at Monterey, sometime provincial capital. The worrying presence of Russian outposts at Fort Ross (Rossiya) and Bodega Bay encouraged the movement and the full list of twenty-one missions was completed with the building of San Francisco Solano at Sonoma, north of the Golden Gate, in 1823. It was however the southern missions which had the greatest impact on the Indians, and in the south that the Spanish settlers established their cattle-ranching empires.

Indians were gathered into the missions in droves, without violence if without volition. Village identities were lost and the people became Diegueños, Luiseños, or Gabrielinos according to their mission, and are so classified today. They were decently clothed and taught to tend vineyards and cattle, and cut stone for the splendid mission churches and outbuildings. They were adequately fed, and died of discipline, claustrophobia and epidemics; the unborn from deliberate abortion. Yet some loyalty developed, and much dependence. When in 1834 the republican government of Mexico secularized the missions they were lost utterly; a mission population of some 31,000 had shrunk by the turn of the century to just about 2,000. Those who survive today, on numerous tiny reservations belatedly established, know that Paradise once lost is gone forever.

Chapter 9

The Impressionable Plateau

The relatively simple life, based wholly on wild foods, does not change abruptly at the upper edge of eastern California and the Great Basin. Stretching through Idaho, eastern Oregon and Washington and far up into central British Columbia is the Plateau area. It is walled east and west by the same mountain systems as the Basin but neither presents impossible obstacles. It has its share of dry treeless plains with sagebrush and even cactus but is watered by two great rivers, the Columbia and the Fraser, and their tributaries, which call the salmon up from the Pacific. Timbered hills are nowhere beyond reasonable access.

Over two dozen language groups occupied the area, most of them from two main families. The Salish-speakers hold roughly the northern half of the region and include, among others, the Shuswap, Ntlakyapamuk (more conveniently dubbed Thompsons), Okanagan, Sanpoil, Kalispel and the Flatheads who were so called because they did not practise cranial deformation like the coastal Salishans. The Sahaptin-Klamath group ranged south of the Canadian border and included the Cayuse, Nez Percé, Klikitat, Yakima, Umatilla, Wallawalla and Modoc. The Kutenai or Kootenay, in between, are now assigned to the Algonkian stock. (Salishan and Algonkian may indeed spring from a common stem.)

People lived in round semi-subterranean lodges, entered through the smokehole in the earth-packed log roof, with a notched log for the inside staircase. Such lodges varied in diameter from ten to forty-odd feet, according to locality and the number of families accommodated. A second house type resembled a high pitched roof set at ground level, covered with bark and partly earthed up, sometimes sixty feet in length. As in the Iroquois longhouse, several families occupied apartments off the central corridor. The whole dwelling was dismantled at the end of the winter, or burnt after a death within. Villages were small and usually near rivers or creeks. Tipis covered with reed mats were used on summer

197

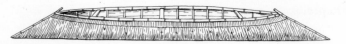

'Sturgeon-nose' canoe used in shallow waters by the Kutenai and Plateau Salish tribes. It was built usually of spruce bark but of birchbark where available.

gathering trips. Transport was provided by dugouts, blunt or sharp according to local river conditions, and in the north by a characteristic bark canoe pointed at both ends below the waterline. On overland journeys pack-dogs helped the women.

Clothing for men was scanty even in the north. The breechcloth seems to have arrived late but fur or buckskin leggings were worn, with robes of rabbitskin or woven grass. For women skin dresses replaced hemp ponchos towards the north. There was no headgear. Bark utensils appear, but basketry was everywhere important. The Salish tribes and the Klikitat in particular are noted for their coiled cedar-root baskets, tall and often rectangular or oval, decorated by imbrication. In this process a third element overlies the stitching of the coil to give a tiled effect to geometrical designs. Mats – tough, of reed, or soft, of grass – were used for many purposes.

On the Plateau roots took the place of acorns as the staple plant food. The commonest was the camas (*Quamasia* sp.), a relative of the hyacinth, whose starchy bulb was eaten raw, boiled, roasted or made into cakes. The Klamath, living in a specialized tract of lake and marshland, depended on *Nymphaea* (lily) seeds. Kouse or kowish (*Peucedanum*), 'biscuit root', was valued as a supplement to camas along the Columbia, and the more arid regions yielded prickly pears. While the women were digging the year's root supply in the spring the men went after birds, rabbits and mussels. Beavers and marmots were relished and deer, sometimes driven over a cliff, were important, but almost everywhere the mainstay was salmon. Platforms were built out over rivers, especially at rapids, from which the fish were dip-netted or speared by men working in controlled rotas. White stones were sometimes sunk below the platforms to show up the quarry. Women were not allowed near the salmon waters for fear of ritual contamination, although it was they who split, dried and cooked the catch. Many villages appointed a seasonal Salmon Chief to administer the fishery and if necessary frustrate the witchcraft of some malevolent down-river community responsible for non-appearance of the fish. First-fruits ceremonies, recalling our harvest festivals, were held for both fish and wild root crops.

An In-between Land

What are thought of as typically Plateau-culture groups showed the same lack of cohesion as the Californians. Villages or hamlets were guided by a father figure, and war leaders elected for the duration of the conflict. The Nespelim and Sanpoil were noted for peace at any price, but less pacific neighbours used armour, poisoned war-arrows with rattlesnake venom or ranunculus, skinned the whole head as a trophy, and took female prisoners as slaves for trade. Organized religious observances were not prominent. Boys dreamed for guardian spirits; the seclusion of adolescent girls might last for two years, or even four in the north. But Plateau culture, simple in itself, was absorbent, and by the time the white man arrived was already strongly affected by outside

The Appaloosa horse. The 'Heavenly Horse' of ancient China, this spotted breed found its way via the Netherlands and Mexico to eastern Washington and Idaho, where the Nez Percé Indians specialized in its selective breeding for war and prestige. The name comes from a neighbouring tribe, the Palus.

influences. From the sophisticated dwellers on the North Pacific shore came a preoccupation with wealth and the division of society into nobles, commoners and slaves; clans and moieties to dictate on marriage, inheritance and personal obligations; masked dances and a plaguy cannibal demon; and the institution of the potlatch, wherein one gains glory and shames one's rival by outdoing him in prodigal benefactions. These ideas were adopted to a varying extent by the Plateau tribes nearest to the western mountains, who carried on a regular trade with the Coast in such commodities as berries, bark, skins and mountain-goat wool for weaving, in exchange for woven blankets, sea-shells, dugout canoes and slaves.

Over the middle and eastern half of the Plateau, it was the Equestrian Revolution that made itself felt after about 1750. The country of the Cayuse, Nez Percé and Palus, as we have seen, was good for large-scale horse-raising. The horse gave direct access to the buffalo for those strong enough to venture out into the plains (the Kutenai and Okanagan may have dared it on foot) and provided an irresistible commodity for trade and raid with the Blackfoot and other tipi-dwellers. As a result a veneer of Plains culture spread far into the Plateau, with skin shirts and horned bonnets, tipis, and pemmican to eat, although for obvious reasons roots and fish kept their place in the diet. The tipis may well have spread more rapidly after traders' canvas became available. Inevitably, of course, the picture was never identical for all the groups. The Upper Kutenai, for instance, adopted the Plains sun cult, lived in (brush-covered) tipis and harried the Blackfoot for female slaves, while the Lower Kutenai spent their time fishing and paddling pointed canoes in good Salish style.

Small and Desperate Wars

White penetration of the area began towards the end of the eighteenth century with the probings of the Hudson's Bay and North-West Company fur-traders, and in time lower Columbia became a highway to the trading establishment on the coast. The dispute with Britain over sovereignty led the United States to encourage settlement in 'Oregon' in the early 1840s, with predictable consequences. The first small war flared in 1847–48 when the Cayuse, dying off from measles and blaming Dr. Whitman's mission at Waiilatpu, slaughtered him and fourteen of his people. In 1855–56 the Yakima, Klikitat and sundry allies were embroiled in a 'war' of brutal skirmishing and destruction on both sides, in which the military operations were bedevilled – very literally – by volunteer companies bent on extermination. From November to June,

Chief Joseph (Hinmaton-yalatkit, Thunder-coming-up-from-the-Water-over-the-Land), 1840–1904, half Cayuse, half Nez Percé. Peaceable by nature, he led the brilliant fighting exodus of the Nez Percés from Idaho to the Canadian border in 1877, being forced to surrender 40 miles short of sanctuary. A handful of his followers did reach Canada.

1872–73, all fifty Modoc warriors, victims as well as perpetrators of treachery, held off a thousand troops and artillery in the vicious moonscape of the Lava Beds. That well-photographed campaign ended with the hanging of their leader, Captain Jack, and three others for killing General Canby under flag of truce. The desperate bid of the Nez Percés to reach Canada has already been mentioned.

On the Canadian side some groups have fared better than others. The Kutenai have just about maintained their numbers as cattlemen and fruit pickers; the Salish have declined by 80 per cent. Disease and disruption have done their work here unaided by violence. There have of course been openings for the Indian fighting spirit: a treasured personal memory from 1940 is of watching with two Ntlakyapamuk warriors in Canadian Army battledress for a hippo to surface in London Zoo.

Chapter 10

Northwest Coast: American Gothic

The Northwest Coast area is very long, very steep and very narrow; its climate is perennially mild and very wet. Backed by high mountains which keep out the continental cold and fronting a sea warmed by the Japanese Current, it receives 100 inches and more of rain a year and is densely forested. The shoreline pitches abruptly into a maze of inlets and rocky islands, with no coastal plain; beaches are limited in length, breadth and number, and travel between them is easier by water than over the tangled land. The forests are of fir, spruce, and best of all the red and yellow cedars, splendid materials for the craftsman in wood. Game abounded: the fine-woolled Rocky Mountain goat on the heights, deer, squirrels and martens in the woods, beaver and mink along the rivers, lorded over by black/brown and grizzly bears, pumas and wolves. Jackrabbits (like the acorn) were missing, and so were rattlesnakes. Wildfowl swarmed through on migration. The waters were richer still, with whales, sealions, fur seals, sea otters, halibut, herring, smelt and candlefish in the sea and five species of salmon crowding annually into the rivers to spawn. The region has no parallel in America, and neither had the people.

For here was affluence *without* agriculture – a sedentary life ruled by class privileges and social obligations of immense complexity, supporting highly sophisticated plastic and dramatic arts, and all of it wholly dependent on wild foods. The food indeed was free, but its taking called for cooperative effort and keen ingenuity; and it is evident that the necessary skills, once learned, were cultivated for their own sake and beyond the requirements of mere survival.

Archaeological information on the Coast is sparse but does indicate that man has exploited the resources of the shoreline for some 4,000 years, and that the culture as we know it has been fully formed for a very long time. Work still uncompleted at Ozette on the Washington coast promises to illuminate with exciting clarity the developments of the past five centuries. The site, a Makah Indian village abandoned in the 1920s, contains middens going back at least 2,000 years but its particular importance stems from a catastrophe which struck it much more recently. About 1450 A.D. a landslip engulfed whole houses in a soft mud that preserved virtually everything not made of animal tissue. The assemblage of objects recovered proves its age by including nothing whatever of European origin, but is nonetheless instantly recognizable as 'Northwest Coast'. Later deposits sealed by minor mud flows illustrate the growing influence of trade goods down to the present century.*

On the Coast as elsewhere the Indians who shared the common culture were not of common language, or even physical type. Three major linguistic stocks are represented, none of them neatly segregated. In the north the Tlingit and Haida belong to the Greater Athapaskan (Na-Déné) stock, but their neighbours the Tsimshian, like the distant Chinook, to the Penutian. The rest are divided between two branches of the Mosan (?Macro-Algonkian) stock: the Wakashan, including the Kwakiutl, Haisla, Heiltsuk, Bella Bella, Nootka and Makah; and the Salishan, with the Bella Coola, Comox, Quinault, Quileute, and numerous small groups on and south of Puget Sound. Local bodily variations affect stature and proportions. The nose may be narrow and prominent, or low-bridged, concave and of decidedly Asiatic appearance.

Although from the mouth of the Columbia to the armpit of Alaska the way of life is remarkably consistent, three major groupings can be seen. The Tlingit, Tsimshian, Haida and Haisla together make up the northern group, which is credited with the fullest expression of the culture. South of them the Heiltsuk, Kwakiutl, Nootka, Bella Coola, Quinault and other Salishan units represent the central group, whose lower limit can be drawn near the southern shore of Puget Sound. The third group comprises the Chinookans of the lower Columbia and numerous Coast Salish bands. From there onwards the peoples – Alsea, Siuslaw, Coos, Kalapuya and others – begin to share Plateau and Californian traits and their classification becomes debatable. As elsewhere in this book we shall try to describe the life in broad outlines, which will not necessarily apply to each and every tribe.

Art in Coastal Life

In all the area heraldic art is so closely interwoven with everyday life

*I am greatly indebted to Dr. Richard D. Daugherty of Washington State University, director of the excavations, for these details.

that a word must be said about it here to make the rest intelligible. Despite differences in the forms of inheritance all Coast peoples were passionately concerned with their descent. The basic unit was the lineage, roughly a group of kinsfolk tracing their origin to a common ancestor associated with creatures of great power, such Bear, Raven or Killer Whale. Family histories preserved the exploits of ancestors, in the course of which they had gained the right to display representations of such spirit helpers, as heraldic devices. Families had their crests, so did clans, and so did moieties, the dual divisions which made up a village or group of villages. This preoccupation with crest figures must have had an important influence on the development of artistic expression, both stimulating its practice and limiting its field. Carving, painting and weaving repeat endlessly the figures of Wolf, Whale, Octopus, Beaver and other characters from the myths, and sometimes human actors and demons. Not all the figures are expressly symbolic, of course, but the repertory is fairly rigidly established. Figures may be carved in the round with a degree of naturalism, but repetition has led to conventions not only in shapes but, particularly, in the treatment of flat surfaces. Fins, paws, eyes, cross-hatched beaver tails and so on are rearranged on textiles and low-relief carvings. Whole animals are often split down the front and opened out so as to show both right and left sides, hinged as it were at the spine. Regional styles exist but it is rare indeed to find a Northwest Coast object that does not immediately proclaim its origin.

Dress and Undress

Men's summer dress in this mild climate consisted of ear and nose pendants, and in the north a wooden or bone plug through the lower lip. In the rain everyone added a brimmed hat and a circular cape; the hat woven of spruce root and the cape of cedar bark. Women never appeared in less than an apron; cloaks kept out the chill. Buckskin is no asset when rain-sodden, nor were Coast women very good at curing it; only the northerly Tlingit adopted, and often bought, the tailored skin garments of their Subarctic neighbours. For the same reason moccasins were mainly restricted to the north. Men's hair fell loose to the shoulders, women's in braids down the back. Beards were not always plucked. Women's chins were tattooed in the south, while highborn Haida ladies might have family crests tattooed over most of the face, trunk and backs of hands. Red, black and blue paint was favoured for feast days, again perhaps in heraldic designs, and bear's grease plain or coloured was much worn for skin protection. Scintillating flakes of mica were added to it long before our cosmeticians dreamed of glitter make-up.

From the Chinook to the Kwakiutl an artifically tapered skull and a sloping brow were marks of beauty and respectability. The deformation was effected by compressing the infant cranium between padded boards on the cradle, with no apparent damage to the brain.

Ceremonial attire was of utmost importance to these socially conscious people. Festal occasions were marked by the wearing of red cedar-bark head rings filled with loose white down, and stiff, tyre-like bark collars. Chiefs and shamans wore head-dresses bearing carved figures, painted and inlaid with iridescent shell, spiked with sealion whiskers and hung with ermine tails. Cloaks were of softly-woven bark or wool, or costly sea otter fur. During the nineteenth century nudity was banished and some painted skin breechcloths, leggings, tunics and dresses came to vie with European cloth garments. Trade blankets, dark blue with a red border, were embellished with heraldic beasts outlined in pearl buttons. 'Button blankets' became universal favourites and immense numbers of them changed hands as formal gifts.

Houses

Northwest Coast houses, often huge, were built entirely of cedar wood without benefit of nails or pegs. Normally they sat side by side in a continuous street facing the sea (or in some places the river). Predictably the details of construction varied according to locality, but all were rectangular and supported by a permanent framework of massive posts or planks. Walls and roof were detachable and could be borrowed for seasonal use at other sites, since a household might move nearer to a particular fishing ground in summer. In the north and centre the ground plan was nearly square, from 20' × 30' up to 50' × 60' or even, among the Kwakiutl, much larger. These houses were gabled, with a gentle pitch to the roof. Walls consisted of vertical planks, slotted or lashed on; or horizontal planks, either resting one upon another between supporting poles or slung in loops and overlapping. Ventilation was controlled by shifting the roof boards. The small round or oval doorway was set in the gable end, sometimes forming the mouth of a figure carved on a centre-post or totem pole.

The Nootka and Salish house was an even bigger affair, if less impressive architecturally, with horizontal walling and a penthouse roof sloping down from a mere fifteen feet to ten or so. Gaps in the planking served as doors and windows. In such dwellings numerous families were

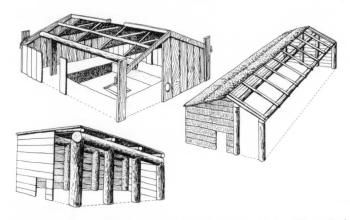

Basic Northwest Coast house types: northern – gabled, with vertical planking; central – gabled, with horizontal planking; southern – shed-roofed, with horizontal planking. All three types might be very much longer than shown here.

Yakutat (Tlingit) interior, about 1890, showing sunken floor, central fire-place, and the use of chests and racks for storage. (The recumbent man is said to have been mauled by a bear, possibly the one whose skin hangs beside him.)

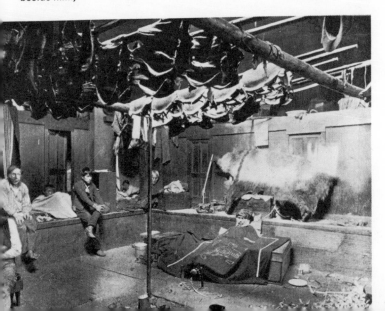

assigned spaces on either side of a central passage, an arrangement which put Capt. Cook in mind of 'a long stable, with a double range of stalls'.

All interiors were floored with planks, and in northern houses the central area was excavated into two or more levels, with the fireplace in the middle. Platforms for sleeping and storage were next to the walls, which were hung with mats against draught. The house chief's quarters might boast internal walls, but the usual demarcation of family limits was a mat curtain or a pile of the wooden chests in which household effects were kept. On the seaward side of the village street wooden platforms provided a venue for outdoor activities.

Totem Poles and other Woodwork

The heavy timbers of the house frame, as well as the centre post of the gable, were traditionally carved and painted, and it was from them that the much-misunderstood totem pole evolved. The free-standing pole is a relatively recent and short-lived phenomenon, hardly known before the

Totem poles showing Thunderbird and Bear crests outside a modified Kwakiutl Indian house on Vancouver Island, about 1900.

beginning of the nineteenth century, and is peculiar to this area. It was valued but not venerated, having nothing to do with religion. Its purpose was to advertise the crests and titles of the owner and his family, or on occasion to commemorate a dead kinsman by displaying his honours. The sudden flowering of totem poles is attributable to the general availability of iron cutting tools resulting from the fur trade, and the increased wealth and heightened rivalries that went with it. Poles continued to be erected until the 1890s – the Skeena River Tsimshians did not adopt them until the 1870s – but wood rot and Christian revulsion took a heavy toll. Once having gained the status of an endangered species, however, they inspired conservation measures up to university and governmental level, and valuable work has been done on reconstruction and the carving of new poles. At the heart of this effort was the late and sincerely lamented Kwakiutl craftsman and hereditary chief, Mungo Martin, Naka'penkim. Martin carved the splendid pole, now standing in Windsor Great Park, which the Province of British Columbia presented to the Queen to mark its centennial in 1958.

A vital product of the woodcarver was the watercraft upon which all travel and much food-getting depended. Canoes from sixteen to sixty-odd feet in length were made from single logs. Those used for river work or seal hunting were small, silent and easily manoeuvrable. The largest were the so-called war canoes, in which crews of fifty and more undertook coastwise voyages of several hundred miles. Adzed and smoothed to beautiful symmetry, these seagoing craft were equipped with projecting prows to deal with rough water, and were propelled with short, crutched paddles; sails came with the white man. For state visits, or freighting home the summer's catch from the fishing camps, two such canoes would be lashed together and decked over with house planks.

Wood was the true servant of the Northwest Coast craftsman. His tools included antler and hardwood wedges for plank-splitting, stone and shell adzes and knives, beaver-tooth chisels, sharkskin for smoothing, and hot water for bending. Archaeological digs show that small iron tools, though rare, were not entirely lacking in pre-contact times. Their most likely source was wreckage from across the Pacific such as the Japanese Current still dumps on the American shore. Besides houses and canoes, wood provided cradles and clubs, rattles and masks, platters and helmets, cooking pots and chamber pots and boxes to hold everything from dice to the dead. Food vessels were carved in the round, plain for everyday, in animal form for feasts. The four walls of boxes and

Dugout canoes arriving for a Kwakiutl wedding feast. Sails were adopted after contact with white voyagers.

chests were made in one piece, a flat board being grooved in three places and then steamed to flexibility and folded at the grooves. The outer ends, bevelled to fit tightly together, were secured by stitches that did not penetrate the outside surface. A bevelled bottom was fixed in the same way and a fitting lid provided.

Other Crafts

Pottery was wholly absent.

The most striking products of the basketmakers were the twined spruce-root hats worn for rain or vanity. The Nootka type resembled an inverted bowl, with or without an onion-shaped dome on top and whaling scenes round the brim. Further north the brim flared trumpet-wise from a flat, narrow crown and was painted with 'totemic' figures. A chief might add a cylinder to the crown for each potlatch he gave.

Basketry utensils were of minor importance here, but some very delicate work was achieved.

Woven blankets were truly native to the Coast, owing nothing to Old World models or materials. The wool came from the wild mountain goat, sometimes the mountain sheep (bighorn), and among the Salish from a special breed of small white dog now lost. Dog hair, with admixtures, was woven under tension on a true loom to produce rectangular blankets in simple checkered patterns mixing red, blue and black with natural white. The so-called Chilkat (Tlingit) blanket, made also by some Tsimshians, was typically six feet long, two feet wide at the ends and three in the middle, with heavy fringes except along the straight upper edge. It was finger-woven with the warp hanging loosely from a single bar. Shredded cedar bark made a strong core for the warp and the rest was goat wool. Black, white, yellow and blue-green were the usual colours, and within wide borders the whole field was covered with dissected animal motifs.

Stocking the Larder

Food on the Coast meant fish. Salmon was paramount, and taken in vast quantities by harpoon, nets and traps. Weirs were built across wide rivers as well as small streams to funnel the annual 'runs'. Shoals of herring came inshore to spawn, so closely packed that a man with a herring-rake – a pole with a row of bone teeth – could impale several fish at one sweep, shake them into the canoe and repeat the act in continuous motion. Branches sunk below buoys over the spawning grounds caught the greatly relished herring eggs. At the northerly rivermouths a highly important fish crop was the olachen (oolakan, eulachon, candlefish, *Thaleichthys*), a small salmonid so full of oil that strings of them dried would burn brightly enough to provide almost the only lamplight known to Indian America. The fish was taken in bag nets, allowed to putrefy slightly, and boiled in the well of a canoe to render the oil. The lady skimmers squeezed out the last drops against their breasts, which must not be washed until the season ended. The oil, filling important nutritional gaps in the diet, was traded far down the coast and over the 'Grease Trails' to interior tribes.

At sea, halibut and cod were taken with bone hooks on kelp lines, while the Nootka went after whales with great harpoons and earnest prayer. Whaling, carried on from special canoes manned by half a dozen men, called for special knowledge and equipment; its rewards lay as much in the excitement and prestige as in the blubber and hide. Wives

A Nootka whaler holding a harpoon with (*lower left*) a sealskin float attached.

as well as whalers observed strict taboos.

Land game was taken by the usual snares, deadfalls and stalking. Bears, the object of a cult in some areas, were treed by dogs. Vegetable food was limited to a few green plants such as clover and skunk cabbage, roots, and some berries. Fish was eaten fresh or dried, broiled or boiled, and almost everything was dipped in fish oil. The heads and roes of fish split for drying were set aside to rot awhile before being eaten as a delicacy. From down-wind the proximity of a village was seldom in doubt.

The Social Scale

Social equality had no meaning on the Coast. There was no divine king as among the Natchez but society was rigidly stratified into chiefs, nobles, commoners and slaves. Chiefs were the heads of family lines who by inheritance, purchase and judicious choice of wives from other highborn families held the greatest number of honorific titles, crests, rights to superior fishing grounds or clover patches and so forth. Their heirs were sons in the south, sister's sons in the north (where, however, marriages could be manipulated to restore the heritage to the male line). A chief was expected to treat his own people with benevolence and work constantly to enhance their prestige by increasing his own; to outsiders he must display the arrogance of his superiority. Nobles were those of more moderate means, who had some chance of bettering themselves within their own jealously graded class without aspiring to chiefly status. Commoners were the poor relations who, holding no rights to sources of wealth, had no hope of accumulating the surplus necessary for advancement. Slaves were war captives and their offspring, and were treated as chattels. They lived well enough but could be bartered, given away or killed at their owner's whim. Corpses of slaves were buried under the posts of new Tlingit houses. Alive, they could be used as rollers over which a great chief's canoe was drawn up the beach. An enslaved chief even when rescued by his own people could never lose the stigma.

Political organization seldom reached beyond one village, although a few were loosely confederated (and clan or moiety membership might forge links throughout an entire language group). The rivalry of chiefs encouraged inter-village bickering over fancied or studied insults, sometimes precipitating savage revenge raids. Slave raids needed no other excuse. War parties travelled by canoe and attacked at dawn. They wore protective corslets of rods or hide and wooden helmets, and fought with spears and clubs and double-bladed daggers of stone or copper. Whole heads were taken as trophies. Peace treaties hinged on critically assessed reparations.

The Potlatch

More often, however, rivalries were fought out by potlatching. A potlatch is a formal distribution of gifts to guests from outside the donor's own group, accompanied by lavish feasting, speechmaking and dancing displays. Potlatches were given to mark such events as the initiation of boys and the maturity of girls, betrothals, weddings and, even more important, the subsequent repayment with interest of the bride price. Names and privileges, whether inherited or acquired by other means, required public validation by a potlatch. Disposal of the dead and the building of a new house were matters entrusted to one's opposite moiety, recompensed at a potlatch. The food and gifts needed could take years to amass, but the giver's kinsmen were expected to contribute actively and care for their own status ensured that they did so. Truly staggering amounts of property were distributed: canoes, furs, slaves, blankets, chests, horn spoons and other items specially carved to luxury standards, even intangible privileges. Guests were seated and treated in strict accordance with their rank – and close account was kept by both sides of what changed hands. The donor might have impoverished himself and his dependants economically in return for higher standing and a new name, but the principal guest departed under obligation to respond by even wilder prodigality. The food provided, not reckoned among the gifts, might with malice aforethought include fare normally considered repugnant, such as dog or slave.

It will be clear that the potlatch supplied incentives for families to cooperate and ensured a measure of circulation for wealth. The sense of occasion too was psychologically valuable. The less acceptable aspect of the system was seen more especially among the Kwakiutl where the humiliation of rivals was actively pursued. To show aristocratic indifference to vast wealth a host might sink canoes, slaughter slaves, and break one or more 'coppers', the enormously costly copper shields treasured for their implications of prestige. Not to accept such a challenge, crippling as the aftermath might be, meant dire loss of face. Death brought no waiver; the obligation to repay with interest fell upon the heirs. It is hardly surprising that the apparently irresponsible redistribution of Indian Service grants and equipment and its reinforcement of 'pagan' attitudes led the Canadian government to ban

Haida 'copper', length 31 in. These extravagantly valued tokens of prestige were made from native copper, supplemented later by metal from the sheathing and boilers of merchant ships.

the potlatch in 1884. The blow to Indian morale was nearly fatal. The ban was withdrawn in 1951 and potlatches of sorts are held today, with five-dollar bills and refrigerators replacing button blankets and canoes.

Ritual and Drama

Coast religion allowed for some guardian spirits, here and there a vaguely conceived creator, and the usual contractual relationship with the supernatural world of Nature. Shamans could cure bodily disease and the more subtle disorders due to the wandering away of the soul. The sombre, gothic art of the region mirrors the sinister nature of the spirits which haunted the dark forests and fjords, inspiring terror mingled with fascination. Giants, sea monsters and ogres abounded. The Wild Woman, Dsonoqua of the protruding lips, whose diet was roasted babies, appears regularly in Kwakiutl carving. Societies existed to impersonate the supernaturals and re-enact the myths, working with consummate stagecraft and a licence to behave outrageously. All Nootka boys were kidnapped by the Wolf Spirits and secreted for days while they learned Wolf songs and dances before being rescued in a mock battle and laboriously schooled back to human behaviour. The Kwakiutl youth disappeared into the forest under the tutelage of the Cannibal Society, to reappear at a public gathering in a state of spirit possession, biting flesh from spectators' arms while Society members fed on human

215

Members of the Hámatsa Society of the Koskimo branch of the Kwakiutl at a winter feast in 1894. Formal dress includes down-filled bark head-rings for men and button-blankets for women. The woman on left with head turned shows the artificially tapered skull required by fashion.

corpses (in recent times, and perhaps always, simulated). The masks worn for impersonations inspired some of the best work of carvers in both realistic and fantastic veins. Great ingenuity was employed in making 'transformation' masks which could fly open to reveal the face of a different creature within. Winter, when there was only casual fishing to be done, was the high season for performances by the so-called secret societies, given indoors by the flicker of firelight.

The Chinook Jargon

In Alaska the true Northwest Coast culture is separated from the Eskimo by one small transitional group, but in the south it becomes progressively attenuated towards California. At the mouth of the Columbia the Chinook lived in communal houses, deformed their skulls and held slaves, but seemingly lacked social and artistic complexity. Active traders, they appear to have evolved a simplified mixture of local languages for commercial intercourse. British and American trading ships plied the coast from the 1780s, in the wake of naval exploration, and J. J. Astor established a shore post in 1811; the trade language was exposed to English. Astoria soon passed from American to Canadian hands and so French was heard in the land. The Chinook Jargon grew and spread abroad from California to Alaska, where it is still remembered by a few nostalgic old-timers. At the heart of its fluctuating vocabulary of 700–1,200 words were Chinookan and Nootkan roots, shorn of inflections and reinforced by a growing proportion of English and French, more or less transmogrified. Such terms as potlatch (Nootka, *give*), Siwash, 'Indian' (French *sauvage*) and cheechako, 'newcomer, tenderfoot' (Chinook + Nootka) may attain local immortality, but kingchautch, 'English' (*King George*), is no longer relevant.

A Foot in the Past

The Northwest Coast saw no wars between Indians and white men. The loudest explosion in the record came in 1811 when Nootkas seized Astor's ship, the *Tonquin*, slaughtering all hands save one who reached the powder magazine and blew ship, Indians and himself to perdition. Disease and intermarriage have nevertheless reduced the Indian population, while missionary and administrative efforts and economic temptations have sapped the culture. But not all is lost. Many Indians work in or operate salmon canneries, with the Native Brotherhood functioning as a sort of intertribal trade union vis-à-vis the Indian Affairs Branch in Ottawa. (In Washington State, on the other hand, salmon are the crux of bitter hostility between Indians and sporting and conservation interests.) Traditional designs etched on copper and silver jewellery command a ready market, and the Haida, who for 150 years have carved delicate miniature totem poles and trinkets in gleaming black argillite, have acted to protect their fading craft from Oriental plastic imitations. On the Skeena River at Templeton, B.C., the Gitksan, an up-stream Tsimshian group, have combined promotional expertise with pride in their past at the 'Ksan Historic Indian Village, incorporating an outdoor/indoor museum, dance displays, a training centre for craft workers and a retail outlet for their creations.

217

Chapter 11

The Wide Subarctic

A single Indian tribe separates the Coast-culture, Tlingit, from the southernmost Eskimo on the Pacific shore: the Eyak. Once thought to be Indianized Eskimos, they are now recognized as Athapaskans with their roots in the Subarctic culture area. That area spans the whole continent, touching the sea again at the bottom of Hudson Bay and reaching the Atlantic on the Gulf of St. Lawrence. Elsewhere the whole northern coast is Eskimo. With few pretensions of its own, the Subarctic culture has absorbed ideas from beyond its western and southern margins. It can be divided into sub-areas: the Yukon, the Mackenzie, the Central below Hudson Bay, and the Eastern on the Labrador Peninsula. All we need to notice is a language line running southwest from the Churchill River on the Manitoba shore of Hudson Bay. West of it the languages are Athapaskan, east of it Algonkian.

The land, once clear of the mountains of northern Alaska, is mainly flat, studded with lakes large and small and areas of muskeg bog, and frozen hard through the long and severe winters. A great part of it is covered by the boreal forest (taiga) of spruce, birch and willow, giving way in the north to open tundra – the Barren Grounds. Caribou, migrating across the Barrens in countless thousands, were the mainspring of the Subarctic culture. They are still there and still significant in Indian life, although both numbers and importance are in decline. In the forests the more stable woodland caribou is joined by the moose and some woods buffalo, while in the far north there are musk oxen. The hare, or 'snowshoe rabbit', occurs everywhere but is subject to the ten-year cycle of build-up/crash in numbers which can seriously affect the human population. Fish teem in the waters and wildfowl flock north to breed.

The tribes inhabiting this vast territory are thinly scattered; and once again we can use the word 'tribe' only to denote small groups of families

A northern Athapaskan couple photographed at Rocher River, Great Slave Lake, in 1952.

united by dialect, not by any sort of political organization. In Alaska they include the Ahtena, Ingalik, Tanana and Tanaina, Koyukon and Kutchin ('Loucheux') whose numerous small bands straddle the border far into Yukon Territory. (The Han Kutchin were hosts, willy-nilly, to the Klondike Gold Rush.) Along the eastern foothills of the Rockies are the Tahltan, Tsetsaut, Sekani, Carrier and Chilcotin, some of whom, trading skins and wool for fish-oil and blankets with the Coasters, have borrowed notions of wealth and pride in ancestry. The Tagish, on the borderline, are themselves Tlingits turned inlanders. The heartland of the Western Subarctic lies on both sides of the Great Bear, Great Slave, Athabasca and Reindeer Lakes. Here roved the Hare, Dogrib, Slave and Chipewyan, who included the Yellowknives ('yellow' meaning copper). These Chipewyan – not to be confused with the Chippewa/Ojibwa – had a narrow outlet to the west shore of Hudson Bay, sandwiched between the Eskimo and the Cree. From there eastwards we are with Algonkian-speakers, the aggressive Cree holding the land as far as the Labrador Peninsula where the Montagnais-Naskapi take over. South of the Cree the Ojibwa and Algonkin proper grasp the hem of the Eastern Woodlands. A complete listing of 'tribes' is not attempted here because there has been a good deal of name-swapping by earnest students and reshuffling of bands by the Indians themselves.

Material Life

Common to them all were a meat and fish diet, skin clothing, bark canoes, guardian spirits, seclusion of girls, inequality of the sexes, a high

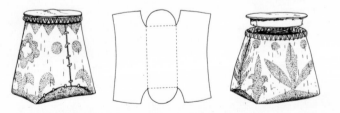

Birchbark *mokoks*, the general-purpose receptacles of the north woods, with pattern of folding. The upper rims may be bound with cherry-bark or dyed goose-quill, and the outer layer of the bark cut away to leave negative designs.

risk of famine, and an unusually delicate taste in decorative art. A new feature in the material inventory is dependence on bark for containers of all sorts in place of wood, pottery or baskets. Housing everywhere was simple and fairly constant in type. The Kutchin built domed lodges covered with skins. The Cree sometimes used bark-covered domes. Everywhere else the lodge – in Algonkian country we can properly use the word 'wigwam' – was a conical tent like the Plains tipi, covered with bark in the forests and hides on the tundra. There was a fireplace in the middle, with a smokehole at the apex. Door coverings were absent or inadequate, and some people preferred skin sleeping bags in the open air during the bitterest weather because of the icy draughts induced by the escape of warm air from the top of the lodge.

Clothing becomes more elaborate from south to north, starting with moccasins, leggings, and a sleeveless shirt sometimes tied between the thighs before breechcloths were adopted, and a rabbitskin blanket. Women wore shorter leggings and longer shirts. In the east detachable sleeves were added. The most characteristic costume of the Subarctic Athapaskans consisted of leggings or fully-seated trousers with moccasins attached, topped by a tailored, sleeved shirt with triangular tails back and front. A hood might be added, and mittens were carried on a neck cord. Decoration included bands of fine geometrical figures woven in porcupine quills, with pendants of dentalium, silver-grey *Eleagnus* seeds or beads, and fringes. For women the same general style of shirt or dress reached nearly to the ground. In winter some fur garments were worn, hair side in or as underwear. Athapaskan men braided their hair and plastered it with ochre, and wore feathers at the nape. Noses and ears were pierced for pendants, and faces tattooed. An effective if painful method of producing straight tattoo lines was to push an awl as far as possible just below the surface of the skin and then draw a sinew thread dipped in charcoal through the channel.

Cree men wore tight hip-length leggings, a long breechcloth, separate moccasins, a robe and a fur cap, and one must assume a shirt, fringed but not pointed. Robes might be of beaver fur. Women wore the usual short leggings and long dresses, and covered the head with a hood-like affair tied under the chin and reaching to the belt at the back.

The distinctive garment of the Naskapi men was a well-cut, gored frockcoat of caribou skin, without buttons or pockets, adorned not with fringes or beads but with symmetrical panels of lines, dots and lozenges in red and blue paint. The origins of this style have inspired much theorizing but it is hard to dismiss early French colonial models from the mind. Naskapi ladies of more recent years have favoured a mushroom-shaped cloth bonnet or tam-o'-shanter, and they roll their hair on wooden cylinders like large cotton-reels below the ears.

Decorative Art

The artistic speciality of the interior Northwest is porcupine quillwork woven into a warp of sinew on a loom resembling a miniature bow with many strings. Designs were necessarily angular, made up of tiny squares of different colours. Cree styles were somewhat bolder than the Athapaskan and executed with wider quills somewhat resembling the Woodlands quillwork described earlier. The work was used for belts and garters and as panels on garments, pouches, quivers and gun-cases. Some appliqué quillwork was done in floral patterns also, especially by the Cree. Dyed moose hair was occasionally incorporated into both woven and appliqué quillwork, or applied independently to pouches and moccasins. Bristly flower or berry designs, made by stitching a small bunch of moose or caribou hairs to the groundwork, bending up the ends and trimming them with scissors, are still to be seen on moccasins produced by Slave and Kutchin women. This particular technique is possibly a late import from the Huron and lacks the finesse of earlier work.

Moccasins are about the last item of native wear to disappear, especially in the north. Here the prevailing style is made of smoked moosehide in one piece, seamed up the toe and having an oval insertion over the instep. This insertion, or vamp, is commonly covered with dark velvet or bleached caribou skin, sometimes embroidered in moosehair or silk thread but almost invariably edged with two or more coils of glistening dyed horsehair wound on a core of the same. The horsehair, sold ready-dyed by the Hudson's Bay Company, has replaced piping of split bird quill.

Dyed bird quill was a favourite binding for the upper rims of birch bark containers (mokoks). The vessels themselves might be decorated with negative figures cut away from the outer surface of the bark.

Trade beads were used in conjunction with quills before supplanting them. They are woven on the bow loom or couched in bold floral patterns, besides serving as margins (white) for designs in red and blue cloth. The Naskapi-Montagnais used them on caps, pouches and moccasins, and in the form of small squares as hunting charms worn at the neck.

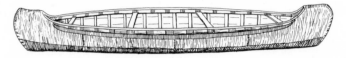

Chipewyan spruce-bark canoe. Birchbark was also used but needed ribs more narrowly spaced than shown above.

Travel

The Subarctic peoples moved a great deal within prescribed territories, often 'owned' by families. The more northerly summered out on the Barrens. They travelled on foot, with dogs and women as porters, and canoes were carried in summer for ferrying. In winter the flat-bottomed toboggan, of narrow boards curled up in front, was pushed and hauled by the women, rarely by dogs. Returning hunters sometimes made do with a frozen hide on which to slide the load. Neighbours of the Eskimo had true sledges with runners. Snowshoes, either circular ('bear-paw') or boat-shaped, were essential. Their wooden frames were netted with *babiche*. This was the rawhide thong which in the absence of vegetable fibre cordage was used everywhere in the north for lashing and tying things together. Finely cut babiche was made into netted game bags and snares; heavier grades provided tow-lines, burden-straps, and the mile-long fence 'wires' along which caribou were stampeded into pounds for slaughter.

Woman's Lot

Athapaskan babies were born in seclusion. Mothers sometimes killed daughters at birth to save them from a life of notable drudgery; only one or two groups were reported to treat their womenfolk with kindness. Marriage took place early, the bridegroom joining his wife's parents and hunting for them for the first year. He might however lose his wife at any time if successfully challenged to a wrestling match by another man. The wife was expected to accompany the victor without question, and there are records of a woman being lost and won seven times in a single day's wrestling. A man had the number of wives he could support by his hunting (and retain by his prowess). Occasionally several men shared one wife.

Dealing with the Supernatural

Of formal religion there was virtually none. Each man dealt directly with the spirits of the animal and natural world, taking care not to offend them lest his hunting and fishing fail, and followed the guidance received in dreams. Witchcraft was a danger to be neutralized by charms or the counter-measures of shamans, who also dealt in prediction and lost property. The speciality of the Algonkian shaman was to enter a small, closed lodge and summon thereto the spirits, whose many pronouncements in strange and strident tongues overawed the surrounding laymen no less than the violent rocking of the lodge as if battered by a tempest. Some of the interpretations pronounced by shamans at the end of a séance have proved accurate to a degree not readily explained.

Naskapi hunters assessed their prospects by various magical means, chief among them being scapulimancy. That involves reading the heat-cracks in a moose or caribou blade-bone held over a fire, rather as some European ladies read tea-leaves but with much greater conviction.

The Subarctic too was the home of the *Wi'tigo* (Windigo), another cannibal ogre whose particular victims for possession were those whom famine had forced to preserve their own lives by eating the flesh of the dead. The stories have a Dracula-like quality, even to the necessity for a stake through the heart to lay the spirit. Windigo killings have occupied Canadian courts within the present century, but the existence of the psychosis reflects the precarious nature of life in earlier days when an irregularity in the caribou migration – especially if coinciding with the periodic crash in hare numbers – could mean widespread death from starvation. Letters written from the north in the 1840s show that tales of survival by cannibalism were still rife. It is also clear that the Indians who were sometimes driven to such cannibalism were themselves deeply repelled by it.

The Vanished Beothuk

Culturally attached to the Subarctic area were the Beothuk of Newfoundland, whose habit of daubing themselves and their belongings with red ochre is said to have originated the term 'Red Indians'. The Beothuk language has finally been classified as Algonkian, but the fact that it was long in doubt indicates that it must have diverged early on from the parent stock. The Beothuk way of life seems to fit well enough into the pattern for the area except for an interest in sea mammal hunting, learnt possibly from the Eskimo who formerly occupied the northern tip of the island. For it they used a seagoing birchbark canoe of unique design, V-shaped in section and with gunwhales raised high amidships.

Their pestering of white fishermen led the French to place a bounty on Beothuk heads which immigrant Micmac Indians eagerly collected. When in 1810 the British governor issued orders for their protection it was already too late; the Beothic Society for the Civilization of the Native Savages combed the island in 1827 and found none. It is just possible that a few found refuge on the mainland with their old trading partners the Naskapi.

The Fur Traders

The pattern of development for the Northern Indians in general was fixed on May 2, 1670, when the Governor and Company of Adventurers of England Trading into Hudson's Bay received the charter giving them commercial sovereignty over about half the continent of North America. The Company's business was fur, which it bought but did not catch; the trapping was up to the Indians. In return it offered knives and kettles, firearms, coloured cloth and woollen blankets of high quality – comforts irresistible to a Stone Age people in a harsh land. The Indians rearranged activities to concentrate on beaver, marten and muskrat, and to make long trips with the catch to Company 'forts' and 'factories' on the Bay. Not until 1779, when the H.B.C. monopoly was challenged by the North-West Company of Montreal, did any serious penetration of the interior begin. The Nor'-Westers, Highland Scots with French-Canadian *voyageurs* for canoemen, set off a burst of exploration that spanned the continent. Alexander Mackenzie followed the river of his name to the Arctic Ocean in 1789, and in 1793 crossed the Rockies to the Pacific. His starting point for both expeditions was Fort Chipewyan on Lake Athabasca, one of the many trading posts which began to dot the area.

Rivalry between the fur companies led to some less than scrupulous practices in wooing the Indian, including the liberal and near-disastrous outlay of dilute rum, and culminated in exchanges of shots between traders. In 1821 the contenders amalgamated under the H.B.C. flag. Alcohol was withdrawn from the trade, and the Company's pioneering efforts in vaccination saved the Cree from the near-extinction visited on the Upper Missouri tribes. Company paternalism may have been commercial good sense (only a wilful misunderstanding of the Victorian spirit would suggest that it was nothing more) but it provided a bulwark against recurrent famine and put an end to warfare. Mostly pious men, the traders married Indian wives whom they sometimes carried back to Scotland on retirement after raising large families of halfbreed children who generally stayed behind. Mission schools followed the fur posts, and later the Mounted Police in detachments of one. After Confederation the Canadian government made treaties with a number of northern groups – the last was with the Dogrib in 1921 – guaranteeing annuities and services in return for land cessions. The yearly payment of 'treaty' had the effect of bringing scattered families together regularly, and a measure of political cohesion was imposed by the nomination of band 'chiefs'.

The H.B.C. surrendered its monopoly in 1869 but stayed in the field (the initials, they do say, stand for Here Before Columbus). It weathered a further period of competition with 'free-traders' but not before depletion of fur stocks by over-trapping had brought many Indians close to destitution. Licensing of trap-lines and the enlistment of Indians in imaginative conservation measures did much to stabilize the situation down to 1940, but since the war the pace of change has accelerated drastically. Transport, once confined to dog teams, canoes and a few river steamers, has been revolutionized by snowmobiles, outboard motors, the Alaska Highway, and most of all aircraft. Mining, oilfields, power schemes and defence installations afford a living for some Indians but hardly ever on a par with that of the transient white specialists whose skills they are too seldom fitted by education, language and temperament to emulate. Some still trap for a shrinking fur market; some drink. Some are turning back to subsistence hunting in preference to an apathetic half-life around the post offices where their welfare cheques and old age pensions are issued.

Chapter 12

The Resourceful Eskimo

The Eskimo were the first Americans to discover the white man and about the only ones to see him off. It happened in Greenland between the tenth and fifteenth centuries, and the details are veiled in a seductive mist of uncertainty. We know that Eirik the Red brought fourteen longship-loads of colonists from Iceland in 986 A.D. to establish the New World's first Christian republic, but Eskimos do not figure in the earliest Norse records. It is possible that the settlements were founded during a suggested break in Eskimo occupation, between the departure of the Dorset Eskimo and the arrival of the Thule. When contact was made it seems to have been concerned with exchanging red cloth for furs, punctuated by skirmishing. But the Norsemen were strong in their farms and pastures and the Eskimos more interested in the edge of the sea-ice – further north then than now.

In 1261 the republic rendered allegiance to Norway and the Greenland trade was allowed to falter and die; no ship came (legitimately) from Europe after 1410. Elizabethan voyagers found a ruin or two, a handful of nails, and a cross on a grave. The colonists had vanished. They had arrived during a prolonged warm period, which was followed after 1200 by an extremely cold phase affecting most of the northern hemisphere. The sea ice moved south, and with it presumably the Eskimo. The white Greenlanders must have been increasingly in competition with them for seals and narwhals – which the Eskimos were the more adept at catching – to supplement their shrinking resources. It has been suggested that they perished from privation and disease, that they were killed off in raids, or that they joined what they could not beat and merged into the Eskimo population. Whatever the process, it was completed at just about the time when Columbus was making the last discovery of the New World. But until the eighteenth century Greenland was once more to be wholly Eskimo land.

What then constitutes an Eskimo, as distinct from an Indian? Bodily he is recognizable by a short stature, stocky build, long head and short face, and well-marked Mongol eyefold. Temperamentally he is mercurial but long-suffering, resourceful, a good mechanic, and much given to laughter and banter. His language is distinct and, within three divisions recognized, remarkably constant: from northwestern Alaska to eastern Greenland the dialects vary so little that men from opposite ends can understand one another. And everywhere the Eskimo is a hunter – with few exceptions a shore-dwelling sea hunter – and wholly carnivorous. It is in fact his failure to use to the full the scant vegetable resources available that separates the Eskimo from the Archaic tradition of total efficiency, meaning the exploitation of everything edible. The Eskimo did not need to do so; efficient enough in his chosen sphere, blessed with a gift for ingenious equipment, he could win all the food he required from the sea and its margins, seldom falling prey to the famines which plagued his land-locked neighbours. Having no squeamish reluctance to eating 'offal' he obtained all the nutritive elements necessary for health.

The Eskimo-Aleut range covers over 3,000 miles in an air line from west to east – much more if one follows the coast and islands. From north to south the distance is something like 2,000 miles, from the Polar Eskimo at 79°N to the now abandoned outposts on the Gulf of St. Lawrence around 50°N; roughly level with London. This tremendous line, broken only on the inner shores of Hudson Bay, was thinly garrisoned by a population that never reached 100,000 souls.

Proto-Eskimo, Eskimo and Aleut

In the west the record of Eskimoid culture patterns dates back 3,000 years and more. A phase of tiny stone blade manufacture in Alaska, labelled the Arctic Small Tool Tradition, seems to go back that far and to have developed into a culture named after a site at Cape Dorset. An important acquisition of the Dorset people was the stone lamp, an open tray in which seal oil could burn through a moss wick, making life possible out on the treeless tundra and on the shoreline where driftwood was too precious for fuel. Dorset then was at least proto-Eskimo, and the people spread eastwards and south to the upper tip of Newfoundland. Behind them, from roughly the same nursery, came the Thule people, fully-developed seal hunters who pushed all along the northern coasts, replacing, destroying or absorbing the Dorset tenants. Along the western coasts of Alaska a slightly different pattern arose, based on hunting whales and walrus from open skin-covered boats. The languages spoken by the Pacific and northern groups vary sufficiently to be classified in two separate divisions. A third division is the Aleut, whose divergence from the Eskimo proper goes much further back in time. The Aleut take that name from the long chain of islands, kept relatively mild and perpetually rainy by the Japanese Current, stretching far into the Pacific from the Alaska Peninsula.

Along these western coasts local cultures have flowered and died, mostly within the Christian era, leaving evidence of high artistic skills in stone, bone and ivory. Old Bering Sea, Okvik, Ipiutak and Punuk craftsmen produced carvings of striking originality and aesthetic impact – all of them, from whichever age or area, bearing the stamp of a personality distinctively Eskimo.

The modern Eskimo call themselves 'Inuit', meaning, as usual, 'humans'. 'Eskimo' is an Algonkian word and means 'raw meat eaters'. That is sometimes appropriate but not much more so than among Indians, even in a land of little fuel. Raw liver is a delicacy far south of the Arctic.

Igloos, Tents and Cabins

One thing everyone knows about Eskimos is that they live in igloos built of snow. They do, but not all of them and not all the time. The snow house is the winter dwelling of the Central Eskimo of the Canadian north, and may be set far out on the sea ice. Circular in plan, sometimes clumped together in threes to give a living room, bedroom and store and entered through a covered passage, it would seem to have developed out of the beehive stone huts of earlier days. It is itself however an architectural achievement of no mean order. The blocks of which it is built must be of snow compacted to an exact consistency, cut to precise shapes, and accurately spiralled to form a dome supported by a key block – a principle unknown elsewhere in North America. The walls are chinked with soft snow and a window of ice admits light. The heat generated within by oil lamps and bodies produces an interior shell of frozen condensation and the temperature can rise high enough to allow the occupants to shed all or most of their clothing. Small overnight igloos for travellers can be put up in under an hour. Very large ones are built for drum dances, and small annexes for dogs.

The summer substitute for the snowhouse is a tent of caribou skin, which in some cases, packed with snow for insulation, serves for winter as well. In Alaska and the east, and in Greenland too, houses were more solid affairs of logs, turf, stones and timber as the supply allowed. Whale

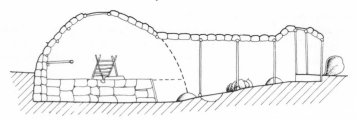

Point Barrow Eskimo house in cross-section. It is stone-paved, semi-subterranean, and entered (on all fours) through a sloping passage with recesses for storage. The dome of sod is supported by whale ribs and driftwood. The domed snow-house differs in construction by being built up spirally of angled blocks, with a key block at the apex where the sod house has a square skylight.

ribs made useful joists, and sheets of gut made windows. Frequently the floor was sunk to leave a bench at ground level for sitting and sleeping. Snow houses also had this sleeping platform; even though itself of snow it afforded greater comfort than the floor, where the coldest air accumulated. Best housed were the Aleut, who could afford to use wood enough for a fully timbered pit-house, earth-banked and entered by a passage or through the smokehole.

Warm Clothing

The seal-oil lamp has been mentioned as a liberating factor which allowed permanent residence beyond the tree line. No less vital to existence in high latitudes is wind-tight – which means tailored – clothing. Caribou skin with the hair left on was preferred almost everywhere for the shirt (*parka* in the west, *anorak* further east, and *dicky* in Labrador), trousers and boot tops. Tough seal hide, chewed into shape, made the boot soles. Seal skin was used for garments too in specific circumstances, and occasionally dog skin. The feathered skins of cormorants and waterfowl could be made up into shirts. Southwestern Alaskan men wore suits and caps of ground squirrel fur, and Labrador girls favoured moleskin trousers. Polar bear trousers belong to the eastern Arctic and Greenland.

The principle of insulation was understood or at least practised: cold weather clothing consisted of two suits, the inner one turned fur-side-inside and the other fur-side-outside, trapping a layer of air between the tanned surfaces of the garments. Attached hoods were general.

The Resourceful Eskimo

Numerous regional styles existed in both cut and decoration. Elaborate contrasts of white and various shades of brown were achieved by the Central Eskimo by applying strips cut from different parts or colour phases of the caribou pelt. The Copper Eskimo favoured a close hood with a sharp peak for men and a voluminous, overhanging hood for women, and the anorak had narrow tails reaching to the ankles. Tails fore and aft, of varying width, length and bulk, are found right to the Atlantic; the utility of the posterior one, in a land of cold, cold ground and no chairs, is easy to appreciate. Women's hoods everywhere were adapted for carrying babies who, wearing only moss pads, shared the warmth of the mother's body. Hoods in the west were edged with fur, wolf or wolverine preferred.

In the rain-soaked Aleutian Islands waterproofing was as urgent as cold-proofing. Translucent seal intestines, cut in strips and pieced into frocks, met the need. These Aleut gut waterproofs often have a tunic-like collar, copied perhaps from Russian officers, and are decorated along seams and hem with tufts of bristle or strips of dyed parchment stitched with caribou hair in minute patterns of extraordinary delicacy. The same style of decoration, unhappily difficult to illustrate without photographic enlargement, occurs on waterproof bags. The Aleut hunter's outfit was completed by a wood or bark helmet streamlined to a long peak before the eyes, with ivory amulets attached. The Alaskan Eskimo also used this helmet, or a plain visor.

Some Canadian Eskimo costumes have in relatively recent years been heavily adorned with beads. Sophisticated Greenland ladies wear netted yokes of beads recalling the patterned shoulders of Scandinavian knitwear.

Hair styles are not elaborate where the head is mostly covered out of doors. Women generally wear two braids, but Greenland fashion leans toward a tight topknot bound with gay ribbon. Some men went cropped or even tonsured. Beards were often left unplucked. Face paint is lacking but tattoing was until recently widespread among both sexes, on chin, cheeks, brow, arms and breasts. A girl's chin was tattooed when she became marriageable. In Alaska little girls wore beads hanging from the nose but in adult years treated the hole in the septum merely as a convenient place to carry needles. Long ear pendants were popular with women, but the characteristic Eskimo facial adornment was the lip-plug or labret. Lips were pierced in childhood and small ivory pins inserted, to be replaced by ivory or stone studs of increasing size, up to four in number. Labrets were prized possessions, lovingly carved by the men in the leisurely winter days.

The Kayak

An outstanding example of Eskimo ingenuity is the kayak. Skin boats belong to many parts of the world but the one-man kayak, fully decked, slim as a racing shell but infinitely more seaworthy, is unique. (The Koryak version in Siberia we take to be an inferior borrowing.) It is a hunting craft, affording the advantages of speed and manoeuvrability enjoyed by a horseman on land. The standard eastern and northern model is pointed at both ends, with a single cockpit amidships or slightly aft. This manhole is rimmed by a wooden collar around which the occupant's anorak can be sealed. With his hood and sleeves tightly closed by drawstrings the paddler and his craft form a single watertight unit. Capsizing then is of little consequence since the kayak can be righted by sidelong thrusts of the paddle. Rolling the kayak on its own axis is deliberately practised and I have seen one Greenland Eskimo kayaker remain bottom-up while a second sped over his keel like a waterborne steeplechaser.

Kayak frames were made of driftwood and covered with seal skins, ivory or bone being sometimes used for reinforcement. The double paddle, another Eskimo speciality, was/is of wood with its narrow blades similarly reinforced. Regular applications of oil were needed to

Greenland kayak with hunting weapons, found at sea off Aberdeen in about 1700 with a dying Eskimo aboard. This, and a few other Eskimo kayaks found in British waters in the 17th and 18th centuries, were ascribed to 'Finn-men', i.e. the Lapps of Norwegian Finnmark (who do not use skin boats) but are now thought to have escaped from whalers bringing them to Europe as curiosities. (Now in possession of the University of Aberdeen.)

Eskimo umiak, the so-called women's boat, used for transport and also for whaling. The length may exceed 40 ft. The light wood frame is covered with walrus or seal hides kept watertight by constant oiling and if possible a daily drying-out on land.

keep the skin hull waterproof and sufficiently flexible to withstand the impact of floating ice. The average length here is around eighteen feet.

The Aleut kayak, or *baidarka*, was relatively short, square-sterned and snub-nosed. The bow might be divided like an open beak or pierced by a round hole serving the magical purpose of an eye and the practical one of a handle. The baidarka often had one manhole forward for the hunter and another aft for the paddler, who used a single-bladed paddle. The Aleut style was seen all along the Bering coast.

Fully equipped for seal hunting, the kayak would carry on its deck the harpoon and throwing-board, stabbing spear, inflated sealskin buoy and a circular sieve-like drag for attachment to the quarry, and wound-plugs to prevent loss of valuable blood and buoyancy. In post-contact times a small screen of white cloth might be added, not as a sail but to camouflage the hunter on an ice-strewn sea.

The oldest specimen of a kayak now in England would seem to be one found at sea off Hull, containing a dead paddler, in the year 1613. This one was only about twelve feet long, with a framework of bone. One or two more appeared in Scottish waters in the eighteenth century, and about 1700 an Eskimo kayaker died in Aberdeen three days after being brought ashore. Contemporary opinion dubbed them 'Finn Men', meaning Lapps from Norwegian Finnmark, but the Lapps never had skin boats. The more recent theory is that they had escaped from whaling ships bringing them home as curiosities. The distance from east Greenland is not less than 2,000 miles.

The Umiak

For family transport, and in the Bering region for whaling, there was the ungraceful umiak. This was an open boat of seal or walrus hide up to forty feet long, with a flattish bottom and flaring sides. It differed from, and probably excelled, the Irish curragh in having a tougher and more elastic skin than the Celtic cowhide and a lighter and less rigid frame. Single-bladed paddles (later oars) were used, but along level shores or up rivers it could be towed by husky dogs.

The Komatik

Northern Indians drag the flat-bottomed toboggan but the Eskimo has his komatik, a true sled with runners. The light wooden frame is lashed together with rawhide for flexibility, and the bed is an open grid of slats. The bone-shod runners are given a coating of ice or frozen mud before a journey. Sizes vary with purpose; from five to nine dogs can draw loads of 400 lb on a big one, and a good team in ideal conditions can cover forty miles a day. In Alaska dogs are harnessed in line, two abreast. This, the 'Nome hitch', is probably a legacy from the Russians; the older, 'native', rig is the fan hitch wherein each dog pulls on his own trace. It needs only an altercation among the dogs to weave the traces into a tangled rawhide skein of great strength, but the Eskimo husky-driver prides himself on meticulous accuracy with the whip. Men going after seals on broken ice drag their own light sleds with a kayak aboard, reversing the load to cross from one floe to another.

The Food Quest

The Eskimo ate all creatures great and small (bar the doughty killer-whale), but seal and caribou were the real staples. Caribou pushed out to the seashore in summer, in flight from the solid fog of mosquitoes and gadflies over the tundra. Besides meat and vegetable stomach-contents they yielded antler and bone for tools, sinew for sewing, and the essential furs for clothing and sleeping-bags. West of Hudson Bay, between the Athapaskans and northern coast dwellers, ranged the Padlermiut or Caribou Eskimos, the only truly inland group. Linked to herds whose movements were sometimes erratic, and without the back-up of sea mammal food, these people lived with the menace of famine. The food they had was cooked over fires of heather and creeping plants in separate tents or huts; the caribou grease which they burned in lamps was, unlike seal oil, inadequate for boiling pots. Caribou were stalked or driven into pounds and shot with arrows, or stampeded into water and speared from kayaks. Coastal Eskimos made summer hunting trips into the Barrens, sometimes leaving their womenfolk to fish down-river.

In summer, seals were harpooned from kayaks or stalked by men crawling seal-like on their bellies across the floes. Some were netted (fish never were). In winter, dogs helped hunters to find holes in the snow-covered ice where seals came up to breathe. Each animal used several such holes and a long vigil might be necessary before it returned to the one being watched. A downyfeather was laid on the small circle of water to give a warning quiver as the animal approached. Then – a more or less blind jab of the harpoon into the hole and with luck the quarry could be hauled out. Before dragging it home the hunter must release its spirit through a cut on the head and offer it a drink of fresh water kept thawed in a mitten inside his clothing. Walrus, less evenly distributed than seals, were hunted on or between the ice floes.

Whaling along the Arctic coast was a matter of trapping and grounding the 18-foot beluga or white whale in the estuaries. In Alaska it meant going out in umiaks after the formidable bowhead, or Greenland right whale, of anything up to seventy feet. Crews cooperated, and the hunt was subject to strict propriety and magical observances recalling those of the Nootka whalers. The initial attack was made with harpoons, each attached to an inflated buoy to hinder diving. As the victim tired the hunters moved in close to stab with spears. When the whale was finally beached the principal hunter's wife made the ritual proffer of water before butchering could begin.*

Fish were speared behind weirs or caught on bone and ivory hooks and gorges through holes in the ice. Wildfowl were shot with blunt arrows or entangled in skilfully thrown *bolas* – three cords knotted together with stones on the ends. Other game harried according to locality included bears, polar and otherwise, musk oxen, mountain sheep, hares, beaver and ground squirrels. Wolves, foxes and wolverines were unkindly killed by scattering balls of fat about containing pointed strips of dried baleen folded small. Moistened in the stomach, the baleen straightened to its full nine inches.

---

*Efforts by the International Whaling Commission to ban or restrict the taking of bowheads (*Balaena mysticetus*) have caused much bitterness in Alaska where the Eskimos, sucked into a world of television and packaged foods, cling to the whale hunt as an affirmation of racial identity. Unfortunately their use of harpoon guns and explosive missiles has dulled the edge of ancient skills, so that many more whales are maimed than caught. The Eskimo quota for 1979 was fixed at 18 bowheads landed with a margin of up to nine unsuccessful strikings, a one-third increase over 1978. The annual catch of belugas (*Delphinapterus leucas*) in the Alaskan and Canadian Arctic still runs into thousands.

Tools and Toys

Baleen, bone, beaver teeth, ivory from walrus and extinct mammoth, soapstone and chalcedony, surface copper and even meteoric iron furnished the hardware of Eskimo life. A genius for gadgetry turned these materials, with rawhide and sinew for lashing, into a tremendous range of specialized tools. There were compound harpoon heads designed to detach from the shaft and turn in the wound while still tied to a retaining line, snow-knives for igloo building, probes like ski-sticks for detecting thin ice ahead of the walker, ivory crampons against skidding, ivory boot-sole crimpers, bow-drills and bodkins, thimbles and shovels, fish hooks and dragging hooks, sinkers and net-shuttles, pestles, chisels, steam-folded wooden pails and all manner of engraving tools. One distinctive implement was and still is the ulu or 'women's knife', with a half-moon blade and a T-shaped grip. It is used with a rocking motion except at meal times, when a quick stroke of the ulu separates a mouthful of meat or blubber clenched in the teeth (Eskimo noses are not as a rule prominent).

Mechanical toys were not lacking. A piece of fur on an endless thong threaded in and out of holes in a board made a mouse that vanished and reappeared when the thong was pulled, and a wooden bird on a flexible quill leg could be made to peck at food painted on his stand. Tops and rotating buzzers, dolls and miniatures of all kinds were popular, and books have been devoted to Eskimo cat's-cradles.

Recreation

One may wonder whether the Eskimo's capacity for fun enabled him to endure the long twilights of the high north in the first place, or was developed in the face of them. Men are ardent wrestlers, and tossing in a walrus skin is much enjoyed. Many villages contain outsize buildings, of snow or otherwise, where people meet for singing, dancing and drumming, the recital of traditional stories and pointed commentaries on local events, or shamanistic performances with or without a patient. Rows of seated women 'dance' with their arms and bare torsos in a unison better known from Indonesia. In Alaska dances both derisory and devout are performed by men wearing masks of wood and feathers. Some masks are caricatures but others, based on dream experiences, have a hauntingly surrealistic quality.

Tobacco, which circled the globe to reach the Eskimo from Siberia, is smoked in pipes of Asiatic design or chewed by men in pellets mixed with a dried fungus bought from the Indians.

Social Life and Death

The Aleut seem to have adapted their social and governmental systems from the class-conscious Tlingit, but among the Eskimo organization was minimal. Outstanding personalities might wield influence but aspiring tyrants were likely to be disposed of by common consent, preferably by the man's own family to cancel the obligations of blood revenge. The essential unit was the family, which included relatives by marriage. Family cooperation was important in crises and in communal hunting, and a man marrying outside his immediate group enlarged the network of family support. On hunting or trading trips it was well to have kinsfolk along the way in a land that was generally, and sometimes homicidally, suspicious of strangers. Marriage like divorce was devoid of ceremony. Boys of 17 or 18 settled in with girls a year or so younger at the house of one or other's parents, and were considered married when a child was born. The wife was liable to be carried or enticed away by an older, stronger man and whether the aggrieved husband could do anything about it depended on the backing of his relatives. A man might keep the number of wives he could feed, or share just one with other men. A not unimportant aspect of hospitality was the loan of the host's wife to a guest. It was normal too for a close partnership to grow up between two men, one sharing the other's wife with no emotional consequences other than pleasure felt for pleasure given. Such partners had mutual obligations of assistance in any emergency. All children belonged to the mother and her official husband and questions of paternity were not regarded as important. Jealousies could and did arise when consent was lacking, and end in murder. Murder meant blood feud, unless the victim was in the uncommon position of having no kin to avenge him. The preferred avenger was the son of the dead man, even if vengeance had to wait till the boy grew big enough for the deed.

Corpses were more dreaded than killing. Burial being difficult in the permafrost, the dead were covered over as well as might be, or not at all. Practical necessity might lead to the abandonment or killing, often at their own request, of the aged and infirm. Some girl babies too were 'thrown away'; male hunters and female seamstresses were essential to one another but in that relentless environment the accident rate for males was high and too great an imbalance of the sexes was to be avoided.

Warfare as such was fairly unorganized, although Eskimo and Indian neighbours alternated between trading and trying to exterminate one another. Inter-Eskimo strife belonged mainly to the Bering area (like other cultural refinements) and involved the surprise raid and slaughter of all males that we have seen further south. Plate armour was of walrus ivory stitched with rawhide. Any unavoidable pitched battles could be interrupted by an agreed 'half-time' for recuperation.

Regular contact with white men was resumed in Greenland on the return of the Scandinavians in 1721. As a Danish dependency Greenland was closely and paternalistically governed for the wellbeing of the Eskimos down to the Nazi occupation of Denmark in 1940, when a United States protectorate was established over the island. The population at that time comprised 17,000 natives and 500 whites. A handful of Eskimos clung to old ways in the north, and on the east coast at Angmagsalik and Scoresby Sound (resettled in 1925), but nowadays one speaks rather of 'Greenlanders'. Modern housing and schools serve a literate people, proud of its identity. Packages of a popular Danish flour have cake recipes printed on them in Eskimo as well as Danish.

On the Pacific side the Aleut suffered horribly at the hands of Russian fur seal hunters from about 1745 until the trade was brought under control by the Czar. It is reckoned that exploitation and disease reduced the Aleut population to ten per cent of its original 20,000; Orthodox priests converted the survivors. The Alaskan mainlanders were more resistant. Along the Labrador coast the Eskimos once harried the white fisherfolk as gleefully as they harried the Naskapi but have long lived at peace with the paleface 'Live-yeres' under the eyes of the Moravian Brethren and the Grenfell Medical Mission. Behind them the Hudson's Bay Company has maintained a string of trading posts reaching far into the Arctic archipelago and across to the Alaska boundary (once upon a time they crossed the Strait into Siberia). Most of these date from the late nineteenth century or after, and as in Indian country their influence is waning. Eskimos still trap the Arctic fox and other choice furs but new generations are less and less willing to espouse the rigours of living off the land (or sea), even with power-driven canvas canoes in place of kayaks and snowmobiles instead of dog-sleds. Year-round camping has just about come to an end. Epidemic diseases which halved the original population are probably no longer a serious threat. The Canadian Eskimo, or Inuit as the government now officially styles them, are steadily increasing, but opportunities for employment in the 'New North' are not enough to go round. Such is the Eskimo temperament, however, that it is hard to abandon optimism.

Chapter 13

The Indian Discovers
Himself

This book is primarily about the Indians as they were, before they lost the freedom to act as they pleased and go wherever it was safe for them to venture. A lot is being written today about what has happened since then and much of it makes uncomfortable reading. Only a summary of recent developments can be given here.

The British Crown sought in 1763 to reserve all lands west of the Alleghenies for the use of the Indians. That proved to be no more realistic than the huge reservations later proposed for the Plains Indians or the new native homeland of Indian Territory. The reservation Indians, despondent and confused, were seen not to be using the land to the full and that, to the prairie farmer and the cattleman, was ample justification for taking it from them. Reservations were progressively reduced (by purchase), and Oklahoma Territory was lopped from Indian Territory before swallowing it altogether. Under the Allotment Act of 1887 the United States began the process of dividing reservation lands among individuals, in the belief that personal possession of 160 acres* would encourage self-sufficiency and pride of ownership. It seldom did so. It was assumed by those in authority that the Indians were in any case due to disappear, partly by the absorption of those sufficiently advanced into the white population. Education and legislation were all designed to fit the Indian to take his place in the modern world, the 'main-stream', whether he liked it or not.

But the Indians did not disappear. Instead, from a low point in 1900 when the US Indian population was down to 237,000, they began to

*(per head of family, with diminishing scale for minors and the unattached. White buyers strove to ensure that such holdings did not long remain in Indian lands, and inheritance raised intractable problems. The Reorganization Act sought to restore allotted lands to tribal ownership.)

increase at twice the average rate for the white population. The US census for 1970 reported 792,730 Indians, and the 1971 figure for Canada, including Eskimos, was 312,765. Together they add up to 1,105,495, compared with a widely accepted estimate of a little over one million* on the eve of discovery. There is a difference in that the million in 1492 was wholly Indian, whereas the million in 1970 includes a great many who have only a small amount of Indian blood. No attempt is made nowadays by the census takers to ascertain degrees of racial admixture, but in 1927 only 61% of Indians in the USA were reckoned to be full-bloods, ranging from the Menomini at 15% and the Kiowa at 49% to the Navajo at a slightly optimistic 100%. In the East and South runaway slaves contributed extensively to the mixed-blood population, and the Five Civilized Tribes admitted their own emancipated slaves (freedmen) to full membership, as well as white spouses. More recently large communities of mixed ancestry such as the Carolina Lumbees have opted for recognition as Indians.

However that may be, a million people in North America now classify themselves as Indian or Eskimo, and begin to see themselves as a significant minority group. US Indians have had the vote since 1924, and only a third of them live on reservations – often because there is no longer room for them. Sadly, in areas where the two races meet the white man is not always prepared to accept the Indian on equal terms. Prejudice stemming from early hostilities, reinforced by popular fiction and impatience with the uncouth and indigent, dies hard. For their part the Indians resent being reminded of their material shortcomings and are bitter about what they regard as manipulation by outsiders, whether that means blatant cheating or measures intended for their own good. There has long been a great fund of goodwill towards Indians, born well behind the lines, but all too often the Indians have been unwilling or unable to take its manifestations at face value. Under the Indian Reorganization Act of 1934, passed while the idealistic John Collier was Commissioner of Indian Affairs, many tribes elected to become legal corporations; but factionalism is a fact of Indian life and those who cooperate in Government-inspired improvement programmes risk being labelled Washington puppets.

Of the urban majority of Indians many make periodic visits to the home reservation to attend ceremonies or merely to recharge their batteries from the traditional current of family relationships. Such

*(Some students favour a somewhat higher figure.)

Ed Burnstick, Cree, Director of the Canadian branch of the American Indian
Movement (AIM), 1976.

absences are no help to long-term regular employment, and the Indians'
different sense of time is one of the reasons why they find jobs harder to
come by than do workers of other colours. Federal aid supports those
without earnings but cannot of itself check demoralization. It is largely
among the non-reservation people that movements such as the moderate
National Congress of American Indians and the radical National Indian
Youth Council have arisen. The most powerful now is perhaps the well-
organized and militant American Indian Movement – AIM. Their
various views are expounded in a lively Indian press and range from
thoughtful analyses of legal rights to profane lampoons having as much
to do with world revolution as with specifically Indian problems. Major
demonstrations have included the taking over of the island of Alcatraz,
the occupation of the Indian Affairs building in Washington, and in

Indian militants occupying the Bureau of Indian Affairs building in Washington, D.C., in June 1972, at the climax of a massive demonstration called 'The Trail of Broken Treaties'.

1973 the theatrically symbolic capture of the hamlet of Wounded Knee on the Pine Ridge (Oglala) Reservation. Indian militants have generally kept aloof from Black Power activists but some seek to make common cause with discontented Canadian Métis and the Chicanos, the Mexican (largely Indian and largely illegal) immigrant workers. They do not speak with one voice. Some demand the complete abolition of the Indian Service, which they claim is discriminatory. Others have campaigned equally fiercely against Congress's own proposals to 'set the Indian free', seeing in the Service their only hope of maintaining the tax-free status they enjoy as Indians.

In Canada where the westward pressures were later and lighter (and a Mounted Police force, as often in makeshift uniforms as in scarlet tunics and white helmets, created by sheer naïvety a mystique of the Pax Britannica), Indian wars as such did not occur and there was room for generosity in the provision of reserves. Full citizenship was granted in

Chief David Crowchild, an elder of the Sarcee Indians of Alberta.

1954. Irritations have nevertheless given rise to considerable activism by such bodies as the National Indian Brotherhood of Canada. The Canadian Parliament's proposal to hand over Indian administration to the Provinces caused much alarm. At least one group has demanded that each tribe be recognized an an independent nation answerable only to the United Nations. A minor right claimed is freedom to pass to and fro across the US–Canadian border without the Customs and other restrictions placed on white citizens.

What all this means is that, thanks to the white man's communications and compulsory peace-keeping, Indians have become aware of other Indians – not just as allies in the next valley or scalpable enemies over the mountain but as people beset by common problems even though scattered over the length and breadth of the continent. The Indian, in short, is in process of discovering himself.

But, one may ask, looking back at the tremendous diversity of life-styles and attitudes, is there such a thing as a common Indian identity ? If there is not, now is the time to forge one, for the Indian of today. One hears much talk about 'our beautiful old culture' and accusations against administrators and educationalists of 'cultural genocide', but no culture can be sacrosanct because no culture is static, once in contact with another; our own has changed irrevocably in the course of this century. Every people treasures a myth of the Good Old Days, but myths of the past whether good or bad can have a malign influence on the present. If there is to be harmony both sides must learn to judge and be judged in terms of the present alone and to trim their behaviour accordingly. Greater flexibility of outlook is needed, not only on the part of the white man. Away from the sound and fury of Indian militancy there are many cooperative enterprises that are solidly established, in farming, stockraising, forestry, craftwork and tourism. In the United States the Indian Claims Commission has by now paid out several million dollars to tribes able to prove past injustices connected with land cessions. Many reservation families can afford to spend the summer driving from one Indian fair to another on the 'Powwow Circuit', to nourish their Indian-ness by learning new dances in costumes more gorgeous than the tartan panoply of a Burns Night in Canberra or Chicago and just as excusable. It is known that a silent minority of persons of Indian blood have assimilated themselves quietly and successfully into the anonymous, competitive world around them. But still there are the unemployed and the alcoholics to fan the prejudice of the self-righteous and the despair of the concerned.

It is hardly more possible to make any general statement about the American Indians of today than it is about those of yesterday. One can only hope fervently that the qualities of courage, adaptability and resource which enabled them to discover and populate a vast and varied continent will not now desert them, nor be stifled, for they are as greatly needed as ever in the past.

Further Reading

The sea of literature on American Indians is bottomless; these titles are offered as a specimen mixture of the scientific, the historical, the polemical, and the 'popular'. Almost all afford bibliographies. Driver (1969), Jennings (1974), and Spencer (1977), below, are the essential textbooks. For descriptive monographs based mainly on personal observation, the *Annual Reports* and *Bulletins* of the Bureau of American Ethnology, Washington, contain the accumulated treasure of nearly a century. The *Civilization of the American Indian Series* of the University of Oklahoma Press, Norman, Oklahoma, comprises a long list of eminently readable books, part ethnography and part history.

Barrett, S. M. (Ed.) *Geronimo, his own story* London, 1974.

Birket-Smith, K. *The Eskimo* (2nd edn.) New York, 1958; London, 1959.

Brasser, Ted J. *'Bou'jou, Neejee!' Profiles of Canadian Indian Art* National Museum of Man, Ottawa, 1976.

Burland, C. *Eskimo Art* London, New York, Sydney, 1973.

Dockstader, Frederick J. *Indian Art in America* Greenwich, Conn., 1967.

Downs, James F. *The Two Worlds of the Washo* New York and London, 1966.

Dozier, Edward P. *The Pueblo Indians of North America* New York and London, 1970.

Driver, Harold E. *Indians of North America* (2nd edn.) Chicago and London, 1969.

Drucker, Philip. *Cultures of the North Pacific Coast* San Francisco, 1965.

Dumond, Don E. *The Eskimos and Aleuts* London, 1977.

Dunn, J. P. *Massacres of the Mountains: a History of the Indian Wars of the Far West* New York, 1886.

Dunning, R. W. *Social and Economic Change among the Northern Ojibwa* Toronto and London, 1959.

Ewers, John C. *The Horse in Blackfoot Indian Culture* Bureau of American Ethnology, *Bulletin* 169. Washington, 1955.

Fox, Robin. *Encounter with Anthropology* Penguin, Harmondsworth, 1975.

Gidley, M. *The Vanishing Race: Selections from Edward S. Curtis's The North American Indian* New York, 1977.

Goble, Paul and Dorothy. (Three brief episodes brilliantly illustrated): *Custer's Last Battle* (1969); *The Hundred in the Hands* (1972); *Lone Bull's Horse Raid* (1973) London, Melbourne, Toronto.

Hoebel, E. Adamson. *The Cheyennes* New York and London, 1964.

Holm, Bill. *Northwest Coast Indian Art: an Analysis of Form* Seattle and London, 1965.

Inverarity, Robert B. *Art of the Northwest Coast Indians* Berkeley and London, 1959.

Jennings, Jesse D. *Prehistory of North America* (2nd edn.) New York and London, 1974.

Josephy, Alvin M. *The Indian Heritage of America* Harmondsworth, 1975.

Kroeber, A. L. *Cultural and Natural Areas of Native North America* Berkeley and London, 1939.

Kroeber, Theodora. *Ishi in Two Worlds* Berkeley and London, 1962.

Leacock, Eleanor B., and Lurie, Nancy O. (Eds.) *North American Indians in Historical Perspective* New York and Toronto, 1971.

Murdock, G. P. *Ethnographic Bibliography of North America* (4th edn.) New Haven, 1975.

Neihardt, John G. *Black Elk Speaks* London, 1974.

Opler, Morris E. *Apache Odyssey: a Journey between Two Worlds* New York and London, 1969.

Orchard, William C. *Beads and Beadwork of the American Indians* (Revised edn.) New York, Museum of the American Indian, Heye Foundation, 1975.

Orchard, William C. *The Technique of Porcupine Quill Decoration among the Indians of North America* New York, Museum of the American Indian, Heye Foundation, *Contributions, IV*, 1, 1916.

Scherer, Joanna C. *Indians: the Great Photographs that Reveal North American Indian Life, 1847–1929* London and New York, 1974.

Snow, D. *The American Indians: their Archaeology and Prehistory* London, 1976.

Speck, Frank G. *Penobscot Man: the Life History of a Forest Tribe in Maine* Philadelphia and London, 1940.

Spencer, Robert F., Jennings, Jesse D., *et al. The Native Americans:*

Ethnology and Backgrounds of the North American Indians (2nd edn.) New York and London, 1977.

Stands in Timber, John, and Liberty, Margot. *Cheyenne Memories* New Haven and London, 1967.

Taylor, Colin. *Warriors of the Plains* London, New York and Sydney, 1975.

The Athapaskans: Strangers of the North National Museum of Man, Ottawa, 1974.

Thomas, D., and Ronnefeldt, Karin (Eds.). *People of the First Man: the Firsthand Account of Prince Maximilian's Expedition up the Missouri River, 1833–34* [Watercolors by Karl Bodmer] New York, 1976 (London: Phaidon).

Trigger, Bruce G. *The Huron: Farmers of the North* New York and London, 1969.

Turner, Geoffrey. *Hair Embroidery in Siberia and North America* Pitt Rivers Museum, Oxford, 1955, 1976.

Underhill, Ruth M. *Red Man's America* Chicago and London, 1971.

Underhill, Ruth M. *Red Man's Religion* Chicago and London, 1965.

Vestal, Stanley. *Sitting Bull: Champion of the Sioux. A Biography* Norman, Oklahoma, 1957.

Washburn, Wilcomb E. *The Indian in America* New York and London, 1975.

Waubageshig (Ed.). *The Only Good Indian: Essays by Canadian Indians* Toronto and Chicago, 1970.

Weltfish, Gene. *The Lost Universe* [The Pawnee] New York and London, 1965.

Tribal Index

This index lists some 320 recorded tribes, with their respective culture areas, language groups, and *estimated* populations before disturbance. The system used in the index is described immediately below.*

Culture Areas

The capital letters (CAL, ESK, etc.) after each name indicate the area. The letters used, and the relevant coloured maps and descriptive chapters, are:

Code	Area	Plate	Chapter
CAL	California	25	8
ESK	Eskimo-Aleut	57	12
EW	Eastern Woodlands	11	3
GB	Great Basin	25	7
NWC	Northwest Coast	25, 57	10
PAU	Plateau	25, 57	9
PNS	Plains-Prairies	11, 25, 57	4
SBA	Subarctic	57	11
SE	Southeast	11	2
SW	Greater Southwest	25	5, 6

Language Groups

The overall language groups are indicated by the following Roman numerals, and sub-groups by the addition of a, b, etc.:

- I   Eskimaleut

  Ia Eskimo;   Ib Aleut
- II Na-Déné

  IIa Athapaskan;   IIb Tlingit;   IIc Haida
- III Macro-Algonkian

  IIIa Algonkian;   IIIb Gulf, including Muskogean;   IIIc Mosan, including Salishan
- IV Aztec-Tanoan

  IVa Shoshonean;   IVb Tanoan;   IVc Kiowan
- V   Penutian (mainly California)
- VI Hokan-Coahuiltecan

  VIa Hokan;   VIb Yuman;   VIc Coahuiltecan

*(See also Preface)

248

VII   Keresan (isolated)
VIII   Macro-Siouan
        VIIIa Siouan;   VIIIb Iroquoian;   VIIIc Caddoan;   VIIId Yuchi
  IX   Yukian (isolated)

Estimated Populations
The population estimated for each tribe before disturbance (not available for tribes in Mexico other than Yaqui) is shown by the *numbers in brackets*. Tribes not mentioned in this index, or mentioned but not enumerated, account for possibly 17% of the total aboriginal population.

References
Figures in **bold** type are the plate numbers of coloured illustrations. Other figures are page numbers: ordinary figures indicate text references and *italics* indicate black-and-white illustrations.

Abitibi   SBA, IIIa   *see* Algonkin

Abnaki   EW, IIIa (3,800)   39

Achómawi   PAU, VIa (3,000 with Atsugewi)   193

Ahtena   SBA, IIa (500)   220

Alabama   SE, IIIb (700)

Aleut   ESK, Ib (20,000)   230, 231, 233, 237, 238, **66, 67**

Algonkin   SBA, IIIa (7,300 with Abitibi, Ottawa etc.)   220

Alsea   NWC, V (6,000 with Siuslaw, Yaquina, etc.)   204

Angmágsalik   ESK, Ia   *see* Eskimo

Apache   SW, IIa (6,500, *includes* Chiricahua, Jicarilla, Mescalero, San Carlos, White Mountain and others)   48, 82, 165, 170–4, *172*, **46**

Arápaho   PNS, IIIa (3,000)   50, 51, 67, *70, 71, 72*, **32**

Aríkara (Ree)   PNS, VIIIc (3,000)   48, 49, 63–4, 68

Assiniboin (Stoney)   PNS, VIIIa (10,000)   50, 51, **70**

Atakapa   SE, IIIb (1,500)   48

Atsina (Gros Ventres of the Prairies)   PNS, IIIa (3,000)   50, 51

Bannock   GB, IVa (3,000 with N. Paiute, etc.)   185

Beaver   SBA, IIa (1,250)

Bella Bella   NWC, IIIc (600)   204

Bella Coola   NWC, IIIc (1,400)   204

Beothuk   SBA (Newfoundland), IIIa (500)   224–5

Biloxi   SE, VIIIa (1,000 with Pascagula)

Blackfoot (Siksika)   PNS, IIIa (15,000 with Blood, Piegan)   48, 50, 51, 55, 60, *62*, **32**

Blackfoot (Sihasapa)   *see* Teton

Blood (Kaina)   PNS, IIIa (*see* Blackfoot/Siksika)   50, **36**

Caddo   PNS, VIIIc (13,400 with Tawakoni, Wichita, Waco, etc.)   48

Cahuilla (Kawia)   CAL, IVa (2,500)

California Athapaskans   CAL, IIa (5,500, including Mattole, Nongatl, Sinkyone, Lassik-Wailaki, Kato and Tolowa)

Calusa   SE, ? IIIb (3,000)   26

Caribou Eskimo   ESK, Ia (700)   234

Carrier   SBA, IIa (8,500)   220

Catawba   SE, VIIIa (4,000)   37
Cayuse   PAU, V (500)   49, 197, 200, *201*
Central Eskimo   ESK, Ia (16,300, including Baffinland, Copper, Iglulik, Netsilik, etc.)   *see* Eskimo
Chemehuevi   GB, IVa (500)   182
Cherokee   SE, VIIIb (22,000)   26–30
Cheyenne   PNS, IIIa (3,500)   50, 51, 55, 58, 60, 67, 69, **32**, **34**
Chickasaw   SE, IIIb (8,000)   26, 28, 30
Chilcotin   PAU, IIa (2,500)   220
Chilkat   NWC, IIb (*see* Tlingit) *211*, **59**
Chinook   NWC, V (22,000 – many bands)   204, 206, 216–17
Chipewyan   SBA, IIa (2,250)   220, *223*
Chippewa   *see* Ojibwa
Chiricahua   SW, IIa (*see* Apache) 170–3, *172*, **46**
Chitimacha   SE, IIIb (3,000)   26
Choctaw   SE, IIIb (15,000)   26, 28, 30
Chumash   CAL, VIa (10,000   191, **51**
Coahuiltec   SW, VIc (15,000 + ? in Mexico)
Coastal Algonkians   EW, IIIa (? 55,000, including Conoy, Massachuset, Metoac, Nanticoke, Narraganset, Pennacook and others)   37–8, **13, 14, 15**
Cochimí   CAL (Lower), VIb   190
Cócopa   SW, VIb (3,000)   167, 170
Comanche   PNS, IVa (7,000)   48, 49, 51, 66, 82, 174
Coos   NWC, V (2,000)   204
Cora   SW (Mexico). IVa   166
Costano   CAL, V (7,000)
Cree   SBA, IIIa (7,000)   48, 220, 221, 222, 225, *241*

See also Plains Cree
Creek (Muskogi)   SE, IIIb (18,000, including Hitchiti)   26–30, 44
Crow (Absároka)   PNS, VIIIa (4,000)   1, 50, 51, 68, **32, 71**

Dakota (Sioux)   48, 49
See also Santee, Teton, Yankton, Yanktonai
Delaware (Lenape)   EW, IIIa (8,000)
Diegueño   CAL, VIb (3,000 + ? in Mexico)   195–6
Dogrib   SBA, IIa (1,250)   220, 226, **65**

Eastern Eskimo   ESK, Ia (10,000, including Angmagsalik, West Greenland)   *see* Eskimo
Erie   EW, VIIIb (4,000)   37
Eskimo (Inuit)   ESK, Ia (73,700, excluding Aleut)   220, 227–38, *230, 232, 233*, 240, **66, 67, 68, 69**
See also Caribou, Central, Eastern, Pacific Coast, Polar, and Western Eskimo
Eyak   NWC/SBA, IIa (500)   218

Flathead   PAU, IIIc (2,800 with Coeur d'Alène, Kalispel, Pend d'Oreille)   50, 197
Fox   EW, IIIa (3,000) Often linked with Sauk as 'Sac and Fox'.   41, 44

Gabrielino   CAL, IVa (5,000) (190–3), 195–6
Gitksan   NWC (Tsimshian), V (3,500 with Niska)   217
Gosiute   GB, IVa (4,500 with Ute) 182
Gros Ventre   *see* Atsina, Hidatsa
Guaicura   CAL (Lower), VIb

Haida   NWC, IIc (9,800)   204, *215*, 217, **57, 62**

Haisla   NWC, IIIc (1,300)   204
Halchidhoma   SW, VIb (3,000)   167
Han   SBA, IIa (750)   220
Hare   SBA, IIa (750)   220
Havasupai   SW, VIb (300)   167–8
Heiltsuk   NWC, IIIc (1,400)   204
Hidatsa (Gros Ventres of the River)
   PNS, VIIIa (2,100)   48, 55, 63–4
Hitchiti   SE, IIIb   *see* Creek
Hopi   SW (Pueblo), IVa (2,800,
   includes pueblos of
   Mishóngnovi, Oraibi,
   Shipáulovi, Shongópovi,
   Sichómovi and Walpi, with (IVb)
   Hano)   82, *83*, 84–97, 167, **38**,
   40, **41**
Houma   SE, IIIb (1,000)   26
Huichol   SW (Mexico), IVa   166
Hupa   CAL, IIa (1,500)   194–5, **53**,
   54
Huron   EW, VIIIb (18,000 with
   Tionontati)   31, 34, 37, *37*, 22,
   22

Illinois   EW, IIIa (9,500)   38, 41
Ingalik   SBA, IIa (450)   220
Iowa   PNS, VIIIa (1,200)   48
Iroquois   EW, VIIIb (5,500, *includes*
   Cayuga, Mohawk, Oneida,
   Onondaga, Seneca; joined later
   by Tuscarora, *q.v.*)   31–8, 44,
   18, **19**, **20**, **21**, **22**

Jémez   SW (Pueblo), IVb (Towa)
   (2,500)   84–97, *83*, *86*, **38**, **41**
Jicarilla   SW, IIa (*see* Apache)   170

Kalapuya   NWC, V (3,000)   204
Kansa (Kaw)   PNS, VIIIa (2,000)   48
Karánkawa   PNS, VIc (2,800)   48
Karok   CAL, VIa (1,500)   194–5
Kaska   SBA, IIa (500)
Kawaiisu   CAL, IVa (500)   182
Keres (Queres)   SW (Pueblo), VII
   (4,000, includes pueblos of

Ácoma, Cochití, Laguna, San
   Felipe, Santa Ana, Santo
   Domingo, Sía)   82, *83*, 84–97,
   91, **38**
Kickapoo   EW, IIIa (Some now in
   Mexico [Chihuahua])(2,000)   44
Kiowa   PNS, IVc (2,000)   48, 51, 66,
   240
Kiowa-Apache   PNS, IIa (300)   170
Klamath   PAU, V (1,200 with
   Modoc)   198
Klikitat   PAU, V (1,200 with
   Wanapum)   197, 198, 200
Koyukon   SBA, IIa (750)   220
Kutchin (Loucheux)   SBA, IIa
   (4,600)   220, 221, 222, **63**
Kutenai   PAU, IIIa (1,200)   50, 197,
   198, 200, 202
Kwakiutl   NWC, IIIc (4,000)   204,
   206, *208*, 209, *210*, 214–15, *216*,
   60, **62**

Labrador Eskimo   ESK, Ia (3,600)
   see Eskimo
Lillooet   PAU, IIIc (4,000)
Lipán   PNS, IIa (500)   66, 170
Luiseño   CAL, IVa (5,500 with
   Cupeño, Juaneño)   (190–3),
   195–6
Lumbee   SE, mixed ('new' tribe)
   240

Mahican (Mohican)   EW, IIIa
   (3,000)   39
Maidu   CAL, V (5,000 with
   Nisenan)   193
Makah   NWC, IIIc (4,000 with
   Quileute, Quinault)   204
Malisit (Malecite)   EW, IIIa (800)
   39
Mandan   PNS, VIIIa (5,000)   48, 49,
   51, 63–4, **28**, **29**, **30**
Maricopa   SW, VIb (2,000)   98, 167
Mascouten   EW, IIIa (1,500)   41
Menómini   EW, IIIa (3,000)   41, 240

Mescalero   SW, IIa (*see* Apache)
    170, 174
Miami   EW, IIIa (4,500)   41
Micmac   EW, IIIa (3,500)   39, 225,
    22
Mission Indians   CAL (13,500) *Here
    used only for* Diegueño,
    Gabrielino, Luiseño, *q.v.*
    190–3, 195–6
Missouri   PNS, VIIIa (1,000)   48
Miwok   CAL, V (12,000 with
    Wappo)
Modoc   PAU, V (1,200 with
    Klamath)   64, 197, 202
Mohave (Mojave)   SW, VIb (3,000)
    167, 168–70, **49**
Mono   CAL, IVa (2,000) *and* GB
    (2,000)   193
Montagnais   SBA, IIIa (5,500 with
    Naskapi, Têtes de Boule)   220,
    222
Mountain   SBA, IIa (400)
Muskogi   *see* Creek

Naskapi   SBA, IIIa (*see*
    Montagnais)   220, 221, 222,
    224, 225, **64**
Natchez   SE, IIIb (4,500)   21–26
Návajo   SW, IIa (8,000)   82, 167,
    173–81, *175, 179, 180,* **42, 43, 44,
    45**
Nespelem   PAU, IIIc (1,100 with
    Sanpoil)   197, 199
Neutral (Attiwándaronk)   EW, VIIIb
    (10,000)   37
Nez Percé   PAU, V (4,000)   48, 50,
    69, 197, 200, *201*
Nootka   NWC, IIIc (6,000)   204,
    206, 210, 211, *212,* 215, 217

Ojibwa (Chippewa)   EW/SBA, IIIa
    (33,000)   *40,* 41, *43,* 48, 220, **22,
    23**
    See also Plains Ojibwa
Okanágan   PAU, IIIc (2,200 with

    Lake)   197, 200
Omaha   PNS, VIIIa (2,800)   48
Ópata   SW (Mexico), IVa   166
Osage   PNS, VIIIa (6,200)   *45,* 48
Oto   PNS, VIIIa (900)   48
Ottawa   EW, IIIa (*see* Algonkin)
    38, 41, 44, **22**

Pacific Coast Eskimo   ESK, Ia
    (11,300)   *see* Eskimo
Paiute   GB, IVa (7,500 with Paviotso,
    Bannock etc.)   69, 182–6, **50**
Palús   PAU, V (1,600)   (*199*), 200
Pamlico   SE, IIIa (4,500 with
    Secotan)
Pápago   SW, IVa (6,600)   98, 100,
    166
Passamaquoddy   EW, IIIa (*part of
    Abnaki)   39
Patwin   CAL, V (6,000)
Paviotso   GB, IVa (*see* Paiute)   182
Pawnee   PNS, VIIIc (10,000,
    includes Chaui, Kitkehahki,
    Pitahauerat, Skidi)   48, 64, *65,*
    66, **27**
Pend d'Oreille   PAU, IIIc (*see*
    Flathead)
Penobscot   EW, IIIa (*part of*
    Abnaki)   39
Pequot   EW, IIIa (2,200)   39
Pericú   CAL (Lower), VIb   190
Piegan   PNS, IIIa (*see*
    Blackfoot/Siksika)   50
Pima   SW, IVa (4,000 + ? in
    Mexico)   79, 98–100, *99, 165,*
    165–6, **47, 48**
Plains Cree   PNS, IIIa (3,000)   50,
    37
Plains Ojibwa (Bungi)   PNS, IIIa
    (2,000)
Plateau Salishans   PAU, IIIc (20,000,
    includes Flathead, Kalispel, Pend
    d'Oreille, Lillooet, Nespelem,
    Sanpoil, Shuswap, Spokan,
    Thompson [Ntlakyapamuk],

Wallawalla and others) 197–202

Polar Eskimo   ESK, Ia (300)   *see* Eskimo

Pomo   CAL, VIa (8,000)   193, **50**, **54**

Ponca   PNS, VIIIa (800)   48

Potawátomi   EW, IIIa (4,000)   41

Powhatan   EW, IIIa (9,000, *includes* Chickahominy, Mattapony, Pamunkey, Rappahannock and others)   26, **15**

Pueblo   SW   77, 79–97, *80*, *83*, *85*, *86*, *88*, *91*, *94*, *95*, 174, **38**, **39**, **40**, **41**

   See also Hopi, Jémez, Keres, Tano, Zuñi

Quapaw   SE/PNS, VIIIa (2,500)   48

Quileute   NWC, IIIc (4,000 with Makah, Quinault)   204

Quinault   NWC, IIIc (4,000 with Makah, Quileute)   204

Salinan   CAL, V (3,000)

Salish (coastal)   NWC, IIIc (31,500. Over 20 groups *including* Comox, Cowlish, Duwamish, Klallam, Nisqually, Puyallup, Sechelt, Snoqualmi)   204, 211, **58**, **61**

San Carlos Apache   SW, IIa   *see* Apache

Santee Dakota (Eastern Sioux)   EW/PNS, VIIIa (15,000 with Yankton, Yantonai. Santee *includes* Mdewakanton, Wahpekute, Wahpeton, *sometimes* Sisseton)   41

Sarsi   PNS, IIa (700)   50, 170, 243

Sauk   EW, IIIa (3,500)   41

Secotan   EW, IIIa (4,500 with Pamlico, Weapemeoc)   **12**, **13**, **14**

Sekani   SBA, IIa (3,200)   220

Seminole   SE, IIIb (Part of Creek until about 1775. In 1970 there were 4,480 in Oklahoma, 575 in Florida)   29, *29*, 30, *30*, **16**

Seri   CAL (Lower)/SW (Mexico), VIb   190

Serrano   CAL, IVb (3,500)

Shasta   CAL, VIa (3,000 with Chimariko)

Shawnee   EW, IIIa (3,000)   44

Shoshoni (western)   GB, IVa (7,500 with Paiute etc.)   (182)

Shoshoni, Wind River   GB/PNS, IVa (2,500)   48, 50, **32**

Shuswap   PAU, IIIc (5,300)   197

Sioux   *see* Dakota

Sisseton   EW/PNS, VIIIa *see* Santee

Skidi   64–66

   See also Pawnee

Slave   SBA, IIa (1,250)   220, 222, **65**

Sobaipuri   SW, IVa (merged with Pima)   98

Spokan   PAU, IIIc (2,400 with Wenatchi)

Stoney   *see* Assiniboin

Susquehanna (Conestoga)   EW, VIIIb (5,000)   38

Sutaio   PNS, IIIa (merged with Cheyenne)

Siwash   Chinook Jargon word for 'Indian' (*sauvage*)   217

Taënsa   SE, IIIb (800)   22, 26, **9**

Tagish   SBA, IIb (400)   220

Tahltan   SBA, IIa (2,500 with Taku)   220

Tanaina   SBA, IIa (450)   220

Tanana   SBA, IIa (450)   220

Tanoan Pueblos   SW, IVb (15,500)
   Subdivided into:
   Tewa   Pueblos of Hano, Nambé, Pojoaque, San Ildefonso, San Juan, Santa Clara, Tesuque
   Tiwa   Pueblos of Isleta, Picurís, Sandía, Taos
   Towa   Pueblos of Jémez and (until 1838) Pecos

See also Pueblo

Tarahumara   SW (Mexico), IVa 166

Tawákoni   PNS, VIIIc (*see* Caddo)

Tekesta   SE, ? IIIb (1,000)

Tepehuán   SW (Mexico), IVa   166

Têtes de Boule   SBA, IIIa (*see* Montagnais)

Teton Dakota   PNS, VIIIa (10,000) *includes* Brulé, Hunkpapa, Miniconjou, Oglala, Sans Arc, Sihasapa [Blackfoot], Two Kettles   50, 51, 55, *56*, 60, 61, 66–72, *67*, *68*, **32**, **35**

Tewa   *see* Tanoan Pueblos

Thompson (Ntlakyapamuk)   PAU, IIIc (5,150 with Nicola)   197

Timucua   SE, IIIb (8,000)   26, **17**

Tionontati (Tobacco, Pétun)   EW, VIIIb (1,500, *see* Huron)   37

Tiwa (Tigua)   *see* Tanoan Pueblos

Tlingit   NWC, IIb (10,000)   204, *207*, 211, **59**, **60**, **62**

Tolowa   NWC, IIa (1,000)

Tónkawa   PNS, IIIb (1,600)   48

Towa   *see* Jémez, Tanoan Pueblos

Tsetsaut   SBA, IIa (500)   220

Tsimshian   NWC, V (3,500)   204, 209, 211

Tübatulabal   CAL, IVa (1,000)

Tunica   SE, IIIb (2,000 with Ofo) 26

Tuscarora   EW, VIIIb (5,000)   37, 64

Tutchone   SBA, IIa (1,000)

Tútelo   EW, VIIIa (1,200)   37

Umatilla   PAU, V (2,900 with Tenino, Wallawalla)   197

Ute   GB, IVa (4,500 with Gosiute) 48, 184–5, *185*

Walapai   SW, VIb (700)   167, 168

Wampanoag   EW, IIIa (2,400)   39

Wappinger   EW, IIIa (5,000)   34

Washo   GB, VIb (1,000)   182

Wenro   EW, VIIIb (1,500)

Western Eskimo (*in* Alaska)   ESK, Ia (31,500)   *see* Eskimo

White Mountain Apache   SW, IIa (*see* Apache)

Wíchita   PNS, VIIIc (*see* Caddo) 47, 48, *54*

Winnebago   EW, IIIa (3,800)   41

Wintun   CAL, V (6,000)   193

Wishram   PAU, V (400)

Wiyot   CAL, IIIa (1,000)

Wyandot   Dispersed groups of Huron, *q.v.*, with other Iroquoian remnants.

Yahi   CAL, VIa (*see* Yana)   167, *188*, 189

Yakima   PAU, V (1,200)   197, 200

Yakutat   NWC, IIb (2,500 of Tlingit total)   *217*

Yana   CAL, VIa (1,500 with Yahi) 187, 189, 193

Yankton Dakota   EW/PNS, VIIIa (*see* Santee)

Yanktonai Dakota   EW/PNS, VIIIa *see* Santee

Yaqui   SW (Mexico, some now settled in Arizona), IVa (30,000)   166–7

Yavapai ('Mohave-Apache')   SW, VIb (600)   167, 168

Yellowknife   SBA, IIa (430)   220

Yokuts (Valley, and Foothill)   CAL, V (18,000)   193

Yuchi   SE, VIIId (1,500)

Yuki   CAL, IX (3,000)   193

Yuma   SW, VIb (3,000)   167, 168–70

Yurok   CAL, IIIa (2,500)   194–5, **54**

Zuñi   SW (Pueblo), V (2,500) 73, 79, *80*, 80–1, 82, *83*, 84–97, **38**, **39**

General Index

Persons, subjects, and prehistoric peoples. (For tribes of the historical period see Tribal Index.)

Page numbers in *italics* refer to illustrations in the text. Figures in **bold** type are plate numbers in the colour section.

acorns 187, 190, 194, **55**
Adena culture *16*, 16–17
agriculture 12, chapters 2–6, 170
    See also maize
Allotment Act, 1887 239
amaranth 12
AIM (American Indian Movement) 241, *241*, *242*
Anasazi culture 77, *78*, 79, **8**
antelope (pronghorn) 6, 10, 61, 100, 182
Appaloosa horse *199*
Archaic Tradition 9–10, 73, 182, 228
argillite carvings 217, **62**
armour 193, 199, 213, 238
Army, US 66, 67–8, 71, 173, 174, 185, 195, 200, 202
arrow poison 165, 199
art, Northwest Coast 204–5, 216, 217, **60, 62**
atlatl *see* spear-thrower
Awátobi Pueblo, destruction of 82

babiche 223
Bacon Rind, Osage *45*
ball courts 27, 76
balsas 11, 169, 191, **52**
barbecue 24
bark (birch, elm, spruce) 32, 40, *40*, 193, *198*, 198, *220*, 221, 222, *223*, **22, 23**

Basket-Maker culture 77
    See also Anasazi
basketry 10, 74, 77, 96, *165*, 165–6, 168, 171, 183, 190, 192, 193, 198, 210–11, **41, 48, 50, 54, 55, 62**
beads and beadwork 32, 34–5, 53, 55, *95*, 99, 168, 171, 192, 194, 222, 231, **22, 32, 49, 54, 65**
beans 12, 27, 47, 49, 51, 74, 100, **6**
bears 23, 203, 205, *207*, 213, 235
beaver 22, 36–7, 51, 100, 198, 203, 205, 221, 225–6
berdache 58, 109
Bering Strait 1, 4, 11, 233, **1**
Beringía, continent of 1, 5, 11, **1**
Big Foot, Miniconjou chief 71
bird-quill decoration 222
biscuit-root (kouse) 198
Bison antiquus *2*, 3, 5, 6, 7, 8–9, **2, 4**
blankets: Navajo and Pueblo, 95–6, *95*, 713–4, 176–7, **43**; Chimayó, 176; Pendleton, 177; Northwest Coast, 206, 211, *216*, 220, **58, 59**
blowgun 26
Bosque Redondo 174, 176
bow and arrows, early absence of 6
Brant, Mohawk chief **21**
Brant, Joseph (Thayendenagea) 38
buffalo 7, 9, 10, 24, 46 *seq.*, 170, 200, 218, **29, 33, 34**
    See also Bison antiquus
bundles, sacred 60, 61, 192
Busk (Creek festival) 28

Cabeza de Vaca, Álvar Núñez 80
Cahokia 19–20, *20*
camas root 198
camels (New World) 5, 6, 9, **2**
candle-fish (olachen) 211
cannibalism 26, 43, 48, 66, 214, 215, 224
canoes
  bark, 32, 38, 41, 198, *198*, 200, 220, *223*, 225, **24**
  canvas, 238
  dugout, 24, 38, 191, 198, 200, 209, *210*, **13**, **57**, **61**
  plank, 191, **51**
Captain Jack, Modoc chief 202
carbon 14 dating 3–4
caribou 33, 218, 221, 234, **67**
Carson, Kit (town of) 8; defeats Navajos, 174
Catlin, George 41, 61
catlinite (pipestone) 18, 32, 41, **32**
cave shelters 6
Chicanos 242
chiefs 19, 25, 26, 27, 31, 60–1, 76, 97, 100, 167, 171, 182, 192, 198, 213, 237
childhood 24, *39*, 52, 88, 89, 169, 171, 184, 223, 231, 236
children, unwanted 24, 184, 223, 237
Chile, Pleistocene site in 4
Chimayó weaving 176
Chinook Jargon 217
Cíbola, Seven Cities of 80, 84
cigarettes 11, 75, 100
clan 27, 58, 87 *et seq.*, 171, 200, 213
Cliff-dwellers 79, **8**
clowns, sacred 90, *91*
club (weapon) 36, **22**, **32**, **62**
  See also tomahawk
Cochise, Apache leader 172
Clovis projectile points 3, 7, 7
Cody, Buffalo Bill 69, 70
Cody site, implement from 7
Collier, John, Commissioner 240

conch shells in trade 18
copper, use of 14, 18, 177–8, 220, 236, **10**, **45**
'copper' (ceremonial shield) 214, *215*, **59**
coracle ('bull-boat') 11, 64
Coronado, Francisco Vázquez de 48, 81
cotton 75, 76, *91*, 96, 100
coups 59
'Crazy Dogs' 59
Crazy Horse, Oglala chief 67, 68, 69
Crook, Gen. George 68
currency 192, 194–5, **54**
Custer, Lieut.-Col. George A. 68–9

dead, treatment of 6, 15, 17, 25, 63, 99, 169–70, 184, 192, 209, 237, **35**, **61**
Death Cult 19–20
deer 5, 10, 23, 53, 100, 171, 189, 191, 193, 195, 198, 203, **53**
Deganawida, co-founder of Iroquois League 31
dentalium shells 194, 221, **32**, **54**
descent 25, 27–8, 31, 58, 87–8, 167, 205, 213, 237
Desert Tradition 73, 74, 77, 182
dire-wolf 7
dogs 24, 48, *49*, 50, 170, 198, 211, 213, 223, 234, 238, **26**, **58**
Dorset culture 227, 228
dreams 42, 57, 59, 165, 224, 236
  See also vision quest
drills 32, *32*, *95*, **67**
Dull Knife, Cheyenne chief 69
Dutch colonists 32–3, 34, 36, 37
dwellings *16*, 19, 21, 23, 31–2, 38, *40*, 47, *47*, 57–8, 63, 75, 77–8, 84, 99, *99*, 170, *175*, 183, 190, 191, 194, *194*, 197, 206, *207*, 208, 224, 229–30, *230*

eagles 55–6, 84, 192
earth-lodge 47, 50, 63, 75, **27**, **28**

Eden points   7
Eirik the Red   227
elephant species   5
    See also mammoth, mastodon
elk (wapiti: *Cervus*)   53
emetics, ritual ˙ 28, 93, 180
English colonists   26, 28, 32, 36, 38, 44
engraving and etching of shells   19, 76, **10**
Etowah site   20

False-face Society masks   35–6, **20**
feathers as insignia   53–5
    See also war bonnet
'Finn-men'   *232*, 233
fire-making   24, *188*
fish and fishing   23, 26, 48, 100, 169, 170, 187, *188*, 189, 193, 194, 198, 200, 203, 211, 217, 235, **13**, **67**, **68**
Five Civilized Tribes   28–30
floral art style, diffusion of   34, **22**, **65**
Folsom projectile points   *2*, 3, 6, 7, **4**
foot-racing, ceremonial   92, 192
Franciscan missions   81–2, 93, 195–6
Fremont culture   79
French colonists   21, 26, 28, 34, 35, 38, 44, 51, 225
fur trade   36–8, 44, 51, 200, 217, 225–6, 238

G-string (breech-cloth)   22, 52, 85, 168, 183, 198
gambling   24, 61, 75, 184, 193, **31**
Gerónimo, Chiricahua chief   *172*, 173
Ghost Dance
    (*1870*) 195
    (*1890*) 69, *70*, *71*, 72, 186
glacial kame burials   15
glacial periods   1, 4–5, **1**
grass-house   47, *47*
grease-trails   211, 220

Great Sun (Natchez ruler)   25
Greenland, Norsemen in   227
ground sloths   6, 9, **2**
guardian spirits   42, 56–7, 192, 199, 215, 220
    See also vision quest
guns in trade   36, 49, 225

Handsome Lake, Iroquois prophet   35
Háwikuh, pueblo of   81
head deformation   22, 197, 206, *216*
head trophies   214
healing practices   42–3, *43*, 73, *94*, 165, *179*, 179–81, *180*, 215, **44**, **62**, **69**
    See also Midéwiwin, shaman
Hiawatha   31
hoes   19, 23
Hohokam culture   75–7, 78, 79, 98, 100, **7**
Hopewell culture   17, 17–18, 47, **10**
horse
    Pleistocene, 5, 6, 9, **2**
    modern, 48 *et seq.*, 59, 169, 172, 184, *199*, 200
Hrdlička, Dr Aleš   2
Hudson's Bay Company   200, 225–6, 238
    See also fur trade
human sacrifice   17, 25, 64
Husk-face Society masks   35–6, **20**

igloo   229, *230*
Indian Claims Commission   224
Indian Reorganization Act   240
Indian Territory   28–30, 239
insects as food   183, 191
intoxicants (native)   100/165
iron tools, pre-contact   191, 209, 236
irrigation   76, 94, 98, **7**
Ishi, last Stone Age Indian   187, *188*, 189

Jenízaros   82

Jesuit missions   35, 166–7
joking relationship   171
Joseph, Nez Percé chief   69, *201*

kachinas   89–90, **39**, **41**
kayak   232–3, *232*, **66**, **67**
kinikinik   41
kiva   77–8, *78*, 84, *88*, 89, 91–2, *94*, 95
komatik (sledge)   234
   See also toboggan
Koryak kayaks   232
'Ksan Historic Indian Village   217

labrets   205, 231
lacrosse   28
lamps   211, 228, 230
language   11, 21, 26, 41, 47, 64, 82/84, 98, 170, 182, 190, 197, 204, 217, 218, 229
League of the Iroquois   31
Lindenmeier site   3
liquor in trade   51, 225
   See also intoxicants (native)
Little Bighorn River, battle on   67–8
Llano culture   7
London, Indian delegations to   38, **21**

macaws   76
maize ('corn')   12, 19, 23, 27–8, *29*, *30*, 37, 38, 40, 47–8, 74, 77, 94–5, 100, 167, 174, 182, **6**, **12**
mammoth   3, 6, 9, 12, 73, **2**
   ivory   236, **67**
maple sugar   38, 41
Marcos de Niza, Friar   80–1
marriage and divorce   24, 27, 31, 58, 87–8, 167, 171, 184, 195, 213, 223, 237
   See also clan, descent
Martin, Mungo, Kwakiutl carver   209
Martínez, María, Pueblo potter   96
mastodon   6, 9, **2**

medicine-bags   42, 43–4, *43*
medicine-man   *see* shaman
Meeker massacre   184–5
Mesa Verde   78
mescal (as food)   100, 170
   See also peyote
mesquite 'beans'   100, 169, 171
metate   10, 84–5, 100, 183, **47**
meteoric iron   236
Métis   242, **22**
   See also mixed-bloods
Mexican influences   12–13, 16, 18, 19, 64, 74, 76, **9**, **10**
Mexico, early man in   4, 11–12
mica   16, 19, **10**
   cosmetic   205–6
Midéwiwin   *43*, 43–4
Mississippian culture   19, *20*, 21, **9**, **10**, **17**
mixed-bloods   28, 29, 39, 82, 226, 240, 242
   See also Métis, Jenízaros
moccasins   22, 33, 52–3, 86–7, 98, 171, 205, 221, 222, **22**, **32**, **65**
Mogollón culture   74–5, 77, 78, 79
monarchy   25, 26
moose-hair embroidery   33–4, 222, **22**, **65**
Mormon belief   1, *70* (*caption*)
Morning Star sacrifice   64, *65*, 66
mother-in-law taboo   31, 171, 178
mounds and 'Mound-Builders'   15, 16, *17*, 18, *20*, 41, 76, **9**, **10**
Moundville site   20
mountain goat   211
mountain sheep (bighorn)   10, 168, 211, 235
music   *see* singing
musk ox   5, 9, 218, 235

names, personal   52
Nampeyó, Pueblo potter   96
narcotics   28, 72, 192
   See also tobacco
Native American Church   72

Native Brotherhood   217, 241–3
Negro slaves   28, 44, 240
Norsemen   227
North-West Company   225
North West Mounted Police   69, 226, 242

obsidian   18, 193, 195, **53**
Okipa ceremony   63, 64
Old Bering Sea culture   229
Old Crow Flats site   4
Old Copper culture   15
Olmecs   12, 16, 18
Olsen-Chubbuck site (bison hunt at)   8
Oñate, Juan de   81
orenda   35
origin legends   1, 73, 174, 183
Osceola, Seminole chief   29
Ozette site   203–4

painting, body-   22, 42, 61, 64, *91*, 92, 99, 168, 183, *185*, 190, 192, 205, 224, **30**, **37**, **40**
palaeo-Indians   5–6, **1**, **3**, **4**
Pascola festival (Yaqui)   167
Patayan culture   79
pearls   23
pemmican   57, 200
Petalésharo (Pita-rísaru), Pawnee chief   64, *65*, 66
peyote   72
Pilgrim Fathers   38
piñón nuts   183
pipes (tobacco)   11, 16, 18, 41–2, 59, 100, **10**, **22**, **32**
Plano culture   7–8
Pleistocene Man   1–9, **3**, **4**
Pleistocene fauna   3–9, **2**
  extinctions   8–9
Pocahontas   25, 26
pochteca (Mexican traders)   19, 64
polygamy   39
  See also marriage
Pontiac, Ottawa chief   44

population   8, 19, 21, 22, 48, 79, 82, 181, 189, 196, 228, 238, 239–40
potlatch   200, 210, 214–15, 217, **59**, **62**
pottery   16, 18, 20, 23, 36, 38, 52, 74–5, 77, 96, 165, 169, 171, 183, 192, 210, **10**, **41**
poultry   24
Poverty Point site   16
Powhatan, 'King of Virginia'   26, 34, **15**
prayer-stick (*paho*)   94–5, 180
priesthoods   28, 35, 89, 91–3, 97, 171, 180, **40**
puberty and initiation   56–7, 169, 171, 184, 190, 192, 193, 199, 214, 215, 220
Pueblo Bonito   *78*, 78–9
Pueblo Revolt   81, 173
pueblos   77–9, *78*, *83* (map), 84, *85*, **8** (*for inhabitants see* Tribal Index)
purification rites   28, *56*, 63, 165, 180
pyramids   11
  See also mounds

quillwork   33–4, 53, 222, **22**, **32**, **65**

rabbits and hares   182, 183, 191, 198, 218, **49**
rattles   43, *43*, *86*
Red Cloud, Oglala chief   66–7, *67*
'Red Indians'   224
Red Paint culture   15
religion   12, 14, 19, 25, 35–6, 42–4, 60, 69–70, 72, 81–2, 89–93, 167, 171, 179–81, 192, 215
  See also guardian spirits, priesthoods, shamans, vision quest
Removal (Five Civilized Tribes)   28
reservations   44, 66, 69, 72, 166, 174, 181, 184–5, 196, 239–44
Roman Nose, Cheyenne chief   55
rubber balls   76

Russians   196, 231, 234, 238

sabre-toothed cats   7, 9
Salado culture   79
sand-paintings   89, 180–1, 192, **44**
sandals   75, 168, 191
scalping   24, 28, 39, 51, 59, 97, 165,
    169, 173, 193, 199
seals   227, 230, 234–5, **67**
seeds as food   10, 12, 100, 183, 187,
    191, **55**
Sequoyah and the Cherokee
    alphabet   29–30
Serpent Mound   *17*, 18
Shálako ceremony   90, **39**
shamans   35, 42, 52, 165, 171, 179,
    182–3, 215, 224, 236, **62**
    See also healing practices
sheep, domestic   80, 174, 179
shells and shellfish   10, **15**
    See also beads, dentalium
sign language   49
silver   18, 86, 96, 177–8, 217, **45**
Sinagua culture   79
singing and musical instruments   42,
    43, 52, 58, 60, 61, 64, 72, *80*, 89,
    100, 167, 171, 179–81, 192, 195,
    215, 236, **69**
Sitting Bull, Arapaho   72
Sitting Bull, Hunkpapa (Sioux)
    leader   67, *68*, 69, 70–1
skin-dressing, technique of   57
slaves   24, 28, 37, 44, 51, 82, 173,
    200, 213, 217
    See also Negro slaves
smallpox   63–4, 225
Smoki Indians   84 *footnote*
Snake Dance, Hopi   91–3, **40**
Snaketown site   78
snowshoes   183, 223, **64**
social classes   25, 195, 200, 203, 213
societies   35–6, 60, 61, 97, 215, *216*,
    29
Soto, Hernando de   25, 26
Spanish influence   29, 48, 80 *et seq.*,

172, 173, 195–6
spear-thrower (atlatl)   6, 75, 233, **3**
squash and pumpkins   12, 40, 47,
    100, 167, **6, 12**
stone-boiling   10, 183
subsistence areas (map)   **5**
Sun Dance   61, *62*, 63, 184
sunflowers   16, 167, **6**
sweat bath   *56*, 63, 191, 193
symbolism   15, 19, 27, 32, 44, 60, 61,
    63, 87, 89, 90, 192, 205

taboos   42, 55, 100, 171, 178, 184,
    198, 213
tapir   6, 9
tattooing   22, *45*, 99, 168, 183, 191,
    192, 205, 221, 231, **14, 49**
Tävibo, Paiute prophet   69
Tecumseh, Shawnee leader   44
temples   19, 25, **9**
Tenskwátawa, Shawnee prophet   44
Tepexpán Man   11–12
textiles
    native American   *see* weaving
    European/American   34, 53, 86–7,
    171, 176–7, 206, **19, 59**
Thule Eskimo culture   227, 228
Thunderbird   42, **60**
tipi   *49*, *50*, 51–2, 57–8, 197, 200, **31,
    35**
Tippecanoe, battle of   44
tobacco   11, 16, 25, 41, 48, 89, 100,
    169, 191, 192, 236, **6, 12**
    See also pipes
toboggan   223, 234
tomahawk   36, *36*, **22**
torture   24–5, 27, 32, 36, 59
totem, defined   27
totem poles   *208*, 208–9, **57, 60, 62**
towns   19, 27
    See also pueblos
trade   15, 18, 41, 49, 51, 167, 190,
    192, 194, 200, 217, 227, 237
    See also fur trade
'Trail of Tears'   28

travois   *49*, 50, *50*, **26**
treaties   66, 226
toys, Eskimo   236
Tularosa Cave site   74
turkeys   22, 24
turquoise   *95*, 174, 178, 180, **45**

umiak   *233*, 233–4
Ursuline nuns   34

vaccination by Hudson's Bay Co.
    225
Vargas, Diego de   81
Vérendrie, Sieur de la   51
vision quest   42, 56–7, 192, 199

wakanda   35
wampum   32, *32*, 37, **22**
war bonnet   55–6, 200, **32**, **36**, **70**
warfare (intertribal)   24, 28, 36,
    37–8, 48, 59, 97, 165, 169, 172,
    193, 194, 199, 213–14, 237–8
war paint   22
    See also painting, body-
wars and conflicts with white men
    26, 28–9, 38, 39, 44, 66–72, 81,
        167, 172–3, 174, 184–5, 189,
        200–2, 225, 227
wealth   51, 194–5, 200, 213–14
weaving and textiles   23, 33, 75, 76,
    95–6, 168, 176–7, 198, 211, **38**,
        41, **42**, **43**, **49**, **54**, **58**, **59**
'Welsh' Indians   63–4
whaling   211, *212*, 228, 235
White, John   26
    Pictures by, **12**, **13**, **14**, **17**, **(66)**
White Deer Dance   195, **53**
Whitman massacre   200
wigwam   221, **23**
wikiup   170
wild rice   40–1, 48, **6**, **24**
Windigo   224
Winnemucca, Sarah, and father   185
Wisconsin glaciation   5
witchcraft   97, 171, 181, 184, 198,
    224
wood-carving   35, 209–10, **57**, **60**, **62**
Wounded Knee   71, 186, 242
Wóvoka, Paiute prophet   69, 186

Yeibichai spirits   177